MW01534926

The Catholic University of America
Center for the Study of Culture and Values
Columbus of School of Law
and
The International Society for Iranian Culture

Islam and the Political Order

Edited by
George F. McLean
Ahmad Iravani

ISBN: 1-59267-058-X

Cover Design
Marina Zalesski

Distributed by
Global Scholarly Publications
220 Madison Avenue, Suite 11G
New York, NY 10016
www.gsp-online.org
books@gsp-online.org
Phone: (212) 679-6410 Fax: (212) 679-6424

Table of Contents

PART III
IMPLICATION OF THE RELIGIOUS FOUNDATION OF THE PERSON

PART IV
DISTINCTION, RELATION, SEPARATION? THE PROPER INTERFACE OF RELIGION AND THE POLITICAL ORDER

Introduction

As the process of globalization forces the great civilizations inexorably to interact with each other, it becomes newly urgent to understand their foundations and their mutual compatibility. It is now generally recognized that each civilization is founded in a great religion and conversely that each great religion generates its own civilization. Nowhere is this more consciously and devotedly the case than for Islam.

In contrast, political liberalism begins by removing religious and other cosmic or integrating visions behind "a veil of ignorance" as a condition for the development of the political order. Some even consider the aspirations of the freedom and autonomy of the human person to be challenged by the recognition of any transcendent order.

Today the seeming collision of these two visions—religious and secular—generates tremors which shake the world. It is most urgent therefore to examine both in depth and in detail the proper relation of religion to the political order, both within the Islamic world and in the broader pattern of global interchange.

This urgency has deep roots. In the past both thought and political life have moved especially from the top downward. For Plato, at the apex were the ideas of either 'The Good' or 'The One' from which all else descended as image and participation. This served both Christianity and Islam in appreciating and interpreting their revelations and applying them to political life. In Christianity once this meant that the Pope not only blessed, but endowed the Emperor with power and could also retract it. In Buddhism and Christianity the life of the founder of the faith is archetypical and this has been true as well for the public community in Islam.

It is then the greatest moment when the entire horizon revolves and governments come to be seen to be -- in Lincoln's words -- as "of the people, by the people and for the people," when for its sources theology adds to scripture and tradition the life of the people, and when interrelations in terms of cultures and civilizations become the major determinants of peace in these newly global times.

The work begins with a prologue by S.H. Nasr entitled "Diverse Currents of Islamic Political Thought and the Significance of Islamic Political Philosophy Today" which brings to the endeavor the sure hand of one of the most experienced and insightful of Iranian Islamic scholars. His guidance sets all on a proper course.

In this delicate yet crucial investigation it is best to begin by listening to those most involved as they begin to chart out the field as only they can see it. Thus Part I "The Islamic Context" has three chapters: "Ethical and Political Challenges for Religions in Building a Healthy Society" by Ayatollah Mahmoud Mohammadi Araghi; "History of Politics in the World of Islam" by Reza Davari Ardahani; and "The Islamic Revolution and International Law" by Medhi Sanaie.

Part II focuses on the crucial question: "If God is Lord of All, Is There Room for Man?" The greatest of all challenges is how the one God who is Lord of all can create not only a physical world, but free creatures: persons and societies. This problem is stated in three ways in the three chapters: "Political Legitimacy and Human Freedom in Islam" by Ayatollah Amid Zanjani; "The Qu'ran as Negative Theological Texts: The Evidence of Sara II" by Aryeh Botwinic; and "Divine Will and Human Needs" by Hossein Nur Mohammad Sadeghi.

Part III "Implications of the Religious Foundation of the Person" begins a positive response to this question by understanding human freedom not as opportunity to rebel against God, but as the creative capacities of a humankind made by God to be his vice gerents in ruling the world. This is investigated in four chapters: "The Person in a Religious Horizon" by Kenneth L. Schmitz; "Ethics and Politics within the Context of Religion" by Ghalam Reza Aavani; "Western Democracy from the Viewpoint of Islamic Studies" by S.M. Mohaghegh Damad; and "Islam and Human Rights" by Ali Asganyazdi.

Part IV "Distinction, Relation, Separation? The Proper Interface of Religion and the Political Order" comes to the heart of our issues. How can these vice gerents of God not only live together in a passive coexistence but work together in that very gerency which is the political order. Above, some spoke of the religious and the political order as being simply separate, others have seen religion as inseparable from politics. If they are inseparable but distinct how indeed can they relate? What is the proper interface between religion and the political order?

Here two leading political theoreticians grapple with this issue in the following papers: "The Idea of

Political Pluralism," "Religious Violence or Religious Pluralism," and "Religion and Political Authority" by William A. Galston, and "Religion, Ethics and Liberal Democracy: A Possible Symbiosis" and "Religious Democracy: Some Proposals" by Fred R. Dallmayr.

The Epilogue looks to the task ahead. If we are really entering upon a new post modern age then the past pattern of political theory and practice can be expected to be inadequate. Yet the proper road ahead is not yet visible. In this circumstance we can conclude the work by identifying some of the crucial elements that can enable us to move ahead in faith, namely, that religions and cultures were originally one, that the thrust toward objective or scientific clarity may have excessively separated them, and that the new awareness of human subjectivity may be opening new and deeper ways of relating the religions and the political order both between themselves and across cultures and civilizations for global times.

George F. McLean

Prologue

Diverse Currents of Islamic Political Thought and the Significance of Islamic Political Philosophy Today

S. H. Nasr

Islam has always been concerned with the whole of life which must of necessity include the domain of politics. The teachings of the Quran and *Hadith* as well as the experience of the early Islamic community served as a basis for the development of classical Islamic political thought, which displayed diversity based on both the methodological approach to the subject and different schools of Islamic thought within which such diversity was to be manifested. In classical Islamic thought we see specifically political thought developed in several schools: (1) the juridical (*fiqhi*) both Sunni and Sunni with figures ranging from Abu Hanifah and al-Mawardi to Ibn Taymiyyah in the Sunni world and Naraqi and Na'ini in the Shi'ite world; (2) the theological (*kalami*), again both Sunni and Shi'ite as seen in the works of Abu Hamid Muhammad Ghazzali and 'Allamah al-Hilli; (3) philosophical including a distinguished tradition stretching fro! m Farabi, Abu'l-Hassan Amiri, Ibn Sina and Ibn Rushd to Nasir al-Din Tusi and Ibn Khaldun; and (4) certain Sufi works such as some treatises of Ibn Qasiy, Ibn 'Arabi, Ahmad ibn Idris and others along with the practical political directives of the Safavids, the Idrisids, and other Sufi based political moments. It is important to note that in his later political theory, Ayatollah Khomeini tried to draw from all these sources.

It is of interest to note that when the revival of Islamic political thought began in the 19th century in the Islamic world among so-called reformers there was not a continuity within this long tradition especially with its intellectual and philosophical dimensions. Even such men as Jamal al-Din Asadbadi (al-Afghani) and Mawlana Mawdudi who were well acquainted with Islamic political philosophy, wrote about Islamic political thought more as general religious thinkers and jurists than as philosophers. And this happened at a time when there was a deep need for an Islamic political philosophy presented from the point of view of Islamic philosophy, rather than of *kalam* or *fiqh* because there were basic philosophical questions which Muslims were forced and are still forced to confront as a result of the challenges of modernism: who is authorized and qualified to pass judgment on political theory and action? Who is to rule over society, God or the people? From where does the government derive its legitimacy and authority? What is the relation between Divine Law and human law, Divine Rights and human rights, human reason and revelation? What makes Islamic political thought , institutions and practices Islamic? Are such qualities as being just sufficient to make a government Islamic? These and many other basic questions could have been answered from within the walls of the citadel of faith, that is from the point of view of Islamic Law and theology and faith in the revelation as long as the whole citadel of Islam was not being challenged by the powerful forces of modernism and secularism. But once this challenge became a reality, the responses had to come from Islamic political philosophy and philosophical theology.

Paradoxically enough, this aspect of Islamic philosophy has become dormant for some centuries. In the Sunni world the last political thinker with a philosophical perspective was Ibn Khaldun, if we exclude Shah Waliullah of Delhi whose political writings were anyway more *Kalamic* than philosophical, although he was also a philosopher. In the Shi'ite world where philosophy itself has survived up to our own days, the last major philosophers to write on political philosophy were Afdal al-Din Kashani, Nasir al-Din Tusi and to some extent Jalal al-Din Dawani and Ghiyath al-Din Mansur Dashtaki. Why such major later philosophers as Ibn Turkah, Mir Damad, Mulla Sadra, Aqa 'Ali Mudarris, and Sabziwari did not deal with Islamic political philosophers is a subject of great interest that needs to be investigated separately.

What is important to realize today is that the basic questions mentioned above and similar ones not noted in this summary continue to persist and to pose a major challenge for the whole of the Islamic world. What is therefore needed is a revival of the authentic tradition of Islamical political philosophy and philosophical theology which alone can provide an Islamically and at the same time rationally satisfactory answer to those similar questions. During the past few decades such figures as Muhmamad Baqir al-Sadr, Mirza Mahdi Ha'iri Yazdi, Husayn 'Ali Muntaziri and Mustafa Muhaqqiq-i Damad have sought to deal in an explicitly philosophical manner with some of these issues and a step has been taken in the direction of creating a new chapter in the long history of Islamic political philosophy and philosophical theology. But there is still a long way to go. Moreover, the future of political institutions in the Islamic world and their viability and stability will depend on the revival of a political philosophy which will be authentically Islamic and at the same time be able to provide meaningful responses to the challenges that a dominant secularized worldview poses for the Islamic and, in fact, for all views of man and society based on the centrality and ubiquitous nature of the Sacred.

George Washington University

PART I

THE ISLAMIC CONTEXT

Chapter I

Ethical and Political Challenges for Religions in Building a Healthy Society

Ayatollah Mahmoud Mohammadi Araqi

Here I would address first the general ethical question for this time of great change, namely, "What should we do?" and then apply this to the political order.

THE ETHICAL ISSUE

Religious leaders today are duty-bound to build a world in which there is peaceful coexistence among different religions and communities. The first step towards the creation of such a world is the establishment of mutual understanding between various religions and communities. How can this be accomplished?

All Abrahamic religions have the same root, come from a single source and have a single God, goal and objective. Unfortunately, due to purposeful or ignorant misinterpretation on the part of some, a great gap and estrangement has been created between the religions. Some have a wrong understanding not only of these religions, but of their history as well. For instance in the current literature we come across a series of books starting with the following phrase: "the end of..."; "The

End of History," "The End of Religion," etc. Others write of a "clash of civilizations".

The result is estrangement and phobias. Such mentalities unnecessarily foster animosity and hostility among the followers of the Abrahamic religions, all of whom have the same root and are virtually brothers and sisters. Their objective is to establish justice and the realization of human welfare in this world, as well as salvation in the hereafter.

Let us look at the situation of the world in which we are living today in order to realize where we are living, what we are doing, and what we can and should do for each other. But first let me recount a brief historical event during the rule of our first infallible Imam, Ali (AS), the forth Muslim caliph ruling the Islamic world after the demise of the holy Prophet (PBUH) of Islam. When a non-Muslim army arrived in one of the newly conquered territories, a soldier removed a silver chain from the legs of a Jewish woman. When the Imam learnt about it, the agonized Imam said: "If one passes away out of the agony of this tragedy, he has every right to do so!"

Sa'di Shirazi, one of our renowned poets, inspired by a Prophetic tradition, composed a couplet, which has been written on the entrance of UNESCO: "People are like a single body in their friendship and humanity. When one part of the body laments, other parts will accompany it by remaining awake."

In another tradition, the holy Prophet of Islam states: "people are equal just like the ribs of a comb."

The couplet states:

> Children of Adam are members of the same body
> They've have been created from the same gem
> Illness of one member
> Will render other members restless
> Thou art not agonized about others' hardship
> Hence, you may not be called human being

With this in mind, let us look at the world in which we are living today:

- a large number of people live below the poverty line;
- a large number of people do not have access to drinking water;
- a large number of people suffer from malnutrition;
- a large number of people cannot even read or write their own names;
- a large number of people who are victims of AIDS count their moments before death;
- a large number of people are sexually abused by the members of their family, even by their fathers;
- a large number of homeless people are victims of war and state-sponsored-terrorism and live in other countries as refugees;
- a large number of addicts in the world live a subhuman life; and
- a large number of girls and boys are victims of child abuse or flesh trafficking.

Now let us have a look at the figures regarding war in the world today:

- The military budget of a great number of under-developed countries is billions of dollars annually, though this is where most of the above-mentioned people live. The sum is higher than their health, education and development budgets.
- The third world has now become a fertile ground for civil wars and wars between countries. Ironically, the weapons they use to kill their brothers in these fratricidal wars come from the West.
- The US military budget has almost doubled over the past two years.

What is wrong with our world? How can we as religious figures join hands to put an end to this nasty picture, or at least to reduce the agony of the people if we cannot eliminate it?

One of the main problems the international community faces today is an absence or lack of ethics in the arena of politics, as well be noted more extensively below. For now we would note only that most of the world's politicians now maintain that the end justifies the means; but I do not agree. Probably most remember that during the war Iraq imposed on Iran, we held fast to the ethical values even during the harshest of times. We did not attack civilians, even when our border cities were chemically bombarded. Now, more than a decade later, the wise people of the world admire us for remaining committed to moral values.

Religion is the surest source of ethical values and criteria. By religion we mean all Abrahamic religions, which are Islamic as well: "Verily, true religion before God is Islam" (The holy Qu'ran). Islam means surrendering to God – all followers of the divine religions in essence and truth should surrender to God.

Addressing all human beings irrespective of their religious affiliation, race, ethnicity, color, etc., the holy Qu'ran states:

> O you men! Surely We have created you of a male and a female, and made you into tribes and families that you may know each other; surely the most honorable of you with Allah is the one among you most careful (of his/her duties); Surely Allah is Knowing, Aware (49: 13).

This indicates that Islam is essentially a religion of equality among all human beings, regardless of gender, race, ethnicity, or other affiliations: the only distinguishing factor is the degree of piety. The holy Qu'ran states:

> We have given a law and a way of life to each of you. Had God wanted, He could have made you into one nation, but he wanted to see who are the more pious ones among you. Compete with each other in righteousness. All of you will return to

> God who will tell you the truth in the matter of your differences. (5: 48)

In brief, my answer to the question, "what we should do?" is: religious leaders should educate the followers of their respective religions that all respect the followers and beliefs of other religions; should teach them tolerance and peaceful coexistence with the followers of other religions; and should teach them to build a world suitable for development, prosperity, spirituality and ethics. This is a world in which soul and body go hand in hand, a world which is a suitable ground for welfare here and salvation in the hereafter.

POLITICAL ISLAM

Here I would turn to one of the bases of the political order in Islam. In order to understand the Islamic political order one has to understand one of the fundamental principles of Islam and for that matter of Shiism, namely, the inseparability of religion and politics.

What happened in the West on the heels of the Middle Ages was the advancement of the theory of separation of religion from politics. The West had every right to advance such a thesis, for the domination of the Church during Medieval times projected a negative image of intermingling ethics with politics.

But Islam and Shiism do not believe in the separation of state and religion or of religion and politics. On the contrary in Shiism religion is inseparable from politics for the following reasons:

First of all, politics in Shiism is the best way to conduct and educate society. In other words, politics itself is a means for educating the people, but is not unbridled. There are conditions and preconditions for politics and politicians to conduct and educate people in the society.

Politics will become a means for conducting life and educating the people only when it is conducted by an Imam. That is, the Imamate is the best method of governance.

In history we come across diversion from the right path for two reasons:

- Ignorance on the part of governors and rulers. The reason for their ignorance is their limited knowledge of human beings and human society. Therefore they commit many mistakes.
- Since the rulers have limited knowledge, they commit treachery knowingly or unknowingly, and therefore trample upon the rights of others.

In the Imamate system, the Prophet is basically a vicegerent of God. The Prophet is infallible; he receives his knowledge from God through revelation. Hence he is free from the two above-mentioned weak points. After the demise of the Prophet, we believe that the infallible Imams succeeded him. They did not receive any revelation, but were infallible and inherited their knowledge from the Prophet and Imam Ali, the son-in-law of the Prophet and the fourth Caliph succeeding him.

Such a political order is an ideal system for all human beings regardless of their religious affiliation. This is why almost all major religions of the world maintain that one day a messiah will come to establish such a just political order. In Christianity, too, it is maintained that Jesus Christ will return to the earth for this Muslims too believe that Jesus Christ will return and join our messiah, Imam Mahdi, to establish such a political order.

When there is no immediate access to the infallible Imams, Islam proposes an alternative that is closest to the ideal system. During the absence of an infallible Imam, a just governor, with the specific characteristics mentioned in our religious texts, is able to establish a political order to pave the way for the return of our messiah. The outstanding feature of such a ruler should be justice and, of course, popularity among the people; such a leader must be elected by the people.

Our contemporary world is suffering from a number of ailments, which have their roots in the two weak points just mentioned. For instance, a major portion of our world is suffering from poverty, mal-nutrition, illiteracy, inadequate healthcare, AIDS, addiction, wars and civil wars, interfaith conflict, corruption, abortion, undermining of the institution of family, and so on.

An example in our history of the ideal political order is the first infallible Imam, Imam Ali, the fourth Caliph who ruled the vast territory of Islam for about five years. A famous letter addressed to one of his governors, Malik Ashtar, appointed ruler over Egypt, stated that those who are governed by you are either your brothers-in-faith or similar to you in creation.

If Jesus Christ had the opportunity to rule, he would have introduced a similar political order, that is, one based on justice. Justice is a universal goal: all wise human beings are eager to establish and realize justice and to be treated justly. This is the most fundamental term common to all Abrahamic religions. All advocate the establishment and realization of justice, for peace without justice is neither complete nor sustainable.

Secondly, ethics too is universally advocated by all Abrahamic religions.

Thirdly, all support the freedom of man. Though been born free, in fact persons everywhere are in chains. Imam Ali said: Do not be a slave of anyone, for God has created you free.

At the same time the Abrahamic religions do not support an unbridled freedom of man, for this will undermine ethics and morality. A perfect man – like Jesus Christ, Prophet Muhammad or Imam Ali - would willingly limit his own freedom in order to remain committed to ethical principles. Freedom is good, but its misuse is bad. We should not sacrifice all sublime ideas and ideals at the altar of freedom. All divine religions believe unbridled liberty to be detrimental to the health of the society.

Unfortunately, like freedom, religion too has been misused in the course of history. Priests and kings both have misused religion to advance their own goals. We find misuses of religion in the Christian Middle Ages and in Islam in the rule of the Umayyad and Abbasid dynasties. Hence we should go back to the roots of the Abrahamic religions to find a common platform to introduce an ideal political order so that humanity will be able to live in peace and harmony.

Our contemporary world lacks morality, spirituality and justice. Fortunately the divine religions have envisaged rational and practical ways to deal with these problems.

Here my answer to the questions: "What can we do or what should we do," is to go back to the roots of the Abrahamic religions. Let us search out the common grounds and a common platform to deal with the major problems our world faces. Some of these problems were mentioned above, yet other problems which loom large for the fate of man today are: terrorism, breaches of human rights, drug trafficking, the gap between the rich and the poor, lack of freedom, etc.

A single prescription imposed by a single power on the rest of the world not only will not solve these problems, but will sow the seeds of animosity and estrangement among the nations and civilizations.

If then mutual understanding is better than misunderstanding then how can we reach this? The first step towards the realization of this goal is mutual respect. We must give up hostile attitudes, and stop pointing fingers at the followers of other religions. In the aftermath of September 11, some major political figures pointed fingers at the followers of one religion accusing them of being terrorists and called for a crusade against them. This will only foster animosity and hostility; it will not help to solve the problem.

If the common enemy of the followers of the Abrahamic and other major religions of the world are ignorance, poverty, uni-lateralism, disrespect and mutual affronts, then our common goals must be: peace, peaceful coexistence, justice, development, prosperity, morality, ethics and spirituality.

We must seek a mutual understanding that will lay the foundations of a world in which all human beings, regardless of their race, color, faith, and other affiliations, can live in peaceful coexistence and strive for a prosperous, healthy and just society whose atmosphere is permeated by spirituality.

President,
Organization of Culture and Islamic Relations
Tehran, Iran

Chapter II

History of Politics in the World of Islam

Reza Davari

1. Molavi, known as Roomi in the West, tells the story in Mathnavi about the Caliphate of Omar Ibn Al-Khatab, the second caliph of Islam, during which a messenger from the Roman Empire came to Medina (Dar-Al Caliphe) and asked someone where the palace of Caliph was. He was told that the Caliph had no palace, and that he lived like other people, and that one could see him in the downtown. The messenger was surprised and wondered how was it that the man that ruled the whole world of Islam, and whose territories extended as far as Africa and East Europe, being the neighbor of the Roman Empire, yet he had no palace, court and formalities. Thus, he too dismissed his attendants and ignored formalities, and began looking for the Caliph in the downtown until he reached a palm-plantation where he asked a woman if she knew where the Caliph was. The woman pointed to a man who was sleeping in the palm-plantation, and said that the man was the Caliph. At first, the messenger could not believe his eyes, yet he approached the Caliph, looked at his face, and was scared. He had seen a great number of kings, rulers and commanders, and had fought in many battles; however he had never been so frightened and nervous. The Caliph awoke and soothed the frightened man, and began talking

to him. The subject of their dialog is not significant for us; and story telling is not our aim either. Instead the purpose is nearly to elaborate one of the conclusions that Molavi has drawn from this story: In the teaching and beliefs of Islam, it is God that is omnipotent; people are the manifestation of the power of God, and anyone who represents His power and charisma he is respected by the people.

The explicit conclusion that Molavi draws from this story is that anyone who respects God is respected by all. God's precedence which was said to be one of the characteristics of the Iranian kings, and which has been mentioned in Sohrevardi's philosophy in the part related to politics in his philosophy, may be the concrete dimension of the power and charisma that Molavi has attributed to Caliph.

The Islamic government began in the way just mentioned, and continued in the same manner until the era of Bani Omyaeh, who changed the caliphate into monarchy. As stated by Ibn Khaldon and many other historians, the Omavi and Abbassi caliphs studied the government system of Iran and Rome, and established their own government system on these bases. A government that was apparently religious, yet different from the traditional government of the Islam prophet and the Rashedin caliphs.

2. Differences of opinion harden over the question of whether Islam has a politics or not. Some have maintained that Islam did not have politics in the past and that it had become political in recent decades. It is true

that Islam was not political at the outset, but has become so in recent epoch. However one cannot claim that Islam has been devoid of politics. We must remember that the origin of the history of Islam is the year that the prophet emigrated from Mecca to Medina, where he established his government.

The difference of opinion existing between the Shiites and Sunnitees was a political one. This was due to the different interpretations of two groups about the meaning of imamat (leadership) adl (justice). It goes without saying that adl relates to politics. The Shiites and Sunnites do not differ significantly in their worship and religious actions. Their difference is in their understanding of the principles. This has affected all other dimensions of life, including politics. In addition to the three principles of to hid (unity), nabovat (prophecy), and maad (resurrection), the Shiites believe in two other principles, which apparently they have added to the principles of religion. However, this is not the case: the principle of adl has been derived from the interpretation of the Shiites of the divine essence, attributes, names and actions, and the existence of the good and bad in the self. The principle of imamat in turn is essential to the belief in the end of prophecy. This has a place in the Islamic philosophy. Since the era of Sohrevardi, philosophers have included the interpretation of prophecy in their philosophy. Sunnites and Shiites both believe in the God's justice. The Shiites believe that God has created the universe on the basis of justice, and that all his actions conform to justice. The Sunnites too believe in the justice of God, but state that whatever He does is justice, and that one cannot set a criterion for His justice. Regarding imam and imamat, the difference between the two is that the Shiites consider the imam as the one who continues the prophet's way, and who is bestowed with chastity. But Sunnites hold that chastity is exclusively bestowed on prophets. This difference of opinion too has had paramount impact and outcome in the works and the history of philosophy, culture and politics of the Muslim people. As a result of these differences, the Sunnites and Shiites have different political views, works and books.

In the world of Islam, there are four types or forms of political texts: 1. The works written by philosophers: these are more famous than others. The most prominent of these books are the views of the residents of Medina and Farabi's Fazeleh. 2. Political books containing reports on the political practices, methods and measures. Nezam Almolk's political Letters is one such example. 3. Collection of received wisdoms and pieces of advice of the Scholars and wise, whose addressees are the statesmen, and rulers in some cases. Abo Ali Moskoyeh's Javidan Kherad (Eternal Wisdom) is one of the most important works of this category. 4. The books that can be termed political jurisprudence. These are about the religious rules of the government and administration of religious government. Maverdi's Ahkam Alsotanieh (Monarch's Decrees) may be the most prominent work of this category. Philosophers, who have been either Shiite or have had an affinity of view with the Shiites, have mostly written the books of the first and third types. The books belonging to the second or fourth group have been mostly written by Sunnite political figures of scholars.

3. Sunnites' and Shiites' differences are rooted in politics; yet, numerous views on political instructions are held in common. There are cases where both have referred to the same sources, one of which is the speeches and lectures and statements of Imam Ali Ibn Taleb. The first lesson is that the ruler must not be the captive of, or subdued to, political power; he should not buy it at any cost. In his first speech after the caliphate, Imam Ali stated that if the people had not asked me, and if God had not committed the wise to take the rights of the persecuted from the persecutors, I would hand over the reins of power. In this speech, the political and social politics are summarized into four principles:

(1) Ruling is not desirable on its own. (2) The wise and those familiar with the way of God must not ignore aggression and tyranny; they must not let the aggressors and tyrants do whatever they wish, or let the needy people be hungry. (3) Under appropriate conditions, the qualified people are obliged to accept the responsibility of administering affairs. (4) People's satisfaction of government and their assistance and support are prerequisites for establishing the government and ensuring its maintenance and stability.

When Malek Ashtar was assigned to rule Egypt, Imam Ali wrote him a letter in which he enumerated the duties of a ruler:

1/ Taking, maintaining, and spending the taxes and incomes in the right way.

2/ Defending against the attacks of enemy and establishing security.

3/ Striving to improve people's affairs and well-being.

4/ Developing the cities.

When these instructions are compared with the manner of ruling of the Omavi and Abbasi caliphs, one notices that they had the vast domain and territory of authority, since those governments were mostly engaged in taking taxes or fighting against enemies. A few of them, however, cared about the development of their territories. Nevertheless, the welfare of people had no place in their ruling mandate. Nezam Almolk for instance, established School of Nezamieh, simply because he intended to compete with Ismaeelian teachings and propaganda, who had founded the School of Al Zahra in Egypt.

Obviously, we do not want to under value Nezam Almolk's great task, yet we should keep in mind that for the first time in the world of Islam and Iran Ismaeelian and Nezam Almolk joined science and politics in a way that politics would be at the service of science (Unless we take the attention of Maamoon, the Abbassi caliph, to science and philosophy, and his discussion on beliefs as political measures. In this case, Maamoon would have used science for advancement of political purposes before Nezam Almolk). It is noteworthy that in the Alavi politics plan, the primary aim has been the education and training of people. Nevertheless in Imam Ali's view, the interference of government in people's affairs has not been very much when it is compared with the governments duties in the modern era, or when the views of those who support the minimum interference of government. That government was neither despotic nor totalitarian.

4. Muslim philosophers who had become acquainted with the Greek philosophy, interpreted Plato and Aristotle's views from a religious standpoint. The views of these philosophers may be summarized as follows:

4-1. Philosophy and prophecy are not against each other. Rather, philosophy and religion are two manifestations of a single matter. Thus, Farabi holds that the master of Medina Fazeleh (Utopia) is a prophet. He calls this master the king philosopher and king of devising the principles of nature.

4.2. The ideal of politics is happiness, and happiness is achieved by wisdom. Thus there exists an ethical politics or even ethics itself is set in the political truth advanced by Islamic philosophers.

4.3. In the philosophical plan of politics, more attention has been paid to the master of Utopia and the ideal life, since the authentic laws in the world of Islam are the religious laws and regulations. The philosopher had to clarify the relationship between prophet and philosophy, and when he arrived at the conclusion that the prophet and philosopher both learn from a single teacher, then it would not have been necessary for the philosopher to devise the codes and rules for politics.

4.4. In the works of the Islamic philosophers, there have always been relations between politics and prophecy. Gradually, however, the tie has become firmer and stronger. For instance, when we take a look at Farabi's and Ekhvan Alsafa's works, we may find philosophy to be the dominant element. Nevertheless, Abolhassan Ameri, Avecina and Sohrevardi attempted to make a balance between the two and at the end of the road, and in Mola Sadra's political views politics became more religious.

5. There seems to have been no relation between philosophers' political plans and the policies and the dominant despotic traditions of the time. Particularly because of the emerging weakness in the caliphate, wars have determined the destiny of governance in Islamic lands. Yet, there are some points that should be considered in order to understand the history of Islam in its true sense. Firstly, every movement, which was set up to oppose the caliphate, was the one associated with the wisdom and gnosis domains or was supported by the Shiites and Sunnites. Ghaznavian and Saljughian were Sunnite and were supported by the jurisprudents and preachers; they tried to invite the scholars to the court. The other important point is that in the world of Islam, judgeship, education, science and school have been separated from and independent of matters pertaining to political and military power. Yet such despotism is not the same as monarchy and individual despotism because the despotic rulers of the Islamic nations had to observe and consider people's beliefs and religious laws.

6. When the Islamic countries became familiar with the West and modernity, the historical and cultural geography of the world of Islam began to change. At the initial stage, Muslims acquainted themselves with the military and political aspects of the West, and still associate the West with its military power (This imperfect familiarity still dominates the minds of people and has complicated many affairs.). The contact with the West shook the old societies in Islamic countries, and resulted in reactions which were not wise. The lay people were not aware of what was happening in the West, and those who were aware, reacted on the basis of their perception, talent, and the degree of their beliefs in their own traditions and religious and racial background. They accepted, rejected, proved, or opposed something. A few people asked what modernity was and where it had come from, and what relationships they had or should have with it. The acceptance and rejection were not equally effective, and on the whole neither had a profound and determining effect on the state of the affairs.

The most vivid and principal encounter was the one that originated from the people that belonged to the mystic community, and believed in the truth and essence of religion. They even fought against the colonist military forces, and lost their personal belongings for the sake of their belief and country. Obviously, they were unable to win a formal war. Among them, Abdolghader Aljazayeri was one of the greatest combatants. The anti-colonism nationalists following the above group, fought to achieve the Western values. They were similar to the former group in some respects, yet they did not continue their way. The important chapter of the political history of the whole developing world is devoted to the national movements. What was just mentioned suffices to illustrate the point.

Another group adopted whatever they have absorbed from the modernity literature; they held that its the unconditional adoption was in line with expediency and wisdom. To pave the way they began looking for the flaws and shortcomings in the religious, cultural and mental traditions of the past. This was by no means criticism in its true sense. They were socialists, or social democrats or supporters of democracy. They wrote books and articles against the heritage of the past and in favor of the need to approach modernity and to adopt its traditions. These works did not have many readers, and the succeeding generations were not usually aware of their existence. Yet, one cannot deny their effects altogether. Another reason for familiarization with the West was that it was felt that the time was ripe for the advent of the promised Mahdi, the savior. Hence, claims on Mahdaviat appeared in India, Iran and Africa in different forms almost concurrently, and its fever covered the whole world of Islam, from India to Sudan. This had some political outcomes as well, but it failed to have any direct influence on expressing political views. As a result, one cannot save a place for it in the history of political thinking.

There was also a circle of people who concluded that the Muslims had gone away from the original Islam and the practices of the pious successor, and that committing sins was widespread. This circle advised the Muslims to avoid unnecessary deeds, and to follow the Islamic regulations properly. These people were heterogeneous and were mostly superficially religious; those who were the most superficially religious gave way to fundamentalism. On the other hand, as the acquaintance of Muslims about the West increased, their concerns about the future of the religion decreased. This concern had both a good and useful dimension and a bad and undesirable dimension. It was good because the outcome was awareness, and it was bad because the concern would result in a lack of motivation for the little research that was being conducted about the West or that the relations would become merely economic and military. About 100 years ago the subject of modernity that had been set forth ambiguously had negative allocation. That is, the principle of secularism influenced affairs in an obscure and ambiguous way. In the view of the inhabitants of the non-western world, the West had two opposite faces: one was the face of democracy and welfare, and the other, the face of colonialism and the colonist. The first had to be welcomed and the second to be avoided. Consequently, the encounter with the West took the form of national and anti-colonist movements. A great number of religious figures joined this movement, while being silent about its secularism.

In the last 50 years, national movements have faced difficulties and disillusionment, while religious movements have soared. In Iran, such movement resulted in the Islamic Revolution in 1979. Ever since, there have been issues about the policy of the Islamic government and religious policy against socialism, democracy and other ideologies. The constitution of the Islamic Republic of Iran, with its anti-despotic nature, was sanctioned. The people's right to choose and political freedoms are emphasized in the constitution. How to plan an Islamic democracy should be a topic for experts in politics to deal with and research. What can be said now is that, in this system, fundamentalism, terrorism and nihilism has no place.

President, Academy of Sciences of the Islamic Republic of Iran
Professor of philosophy, University of Tehran
Tehran, Iran

Chapter III

The Islamic Revolution and International Law

Mahdi Sanaee

The Islamic Revolution of Iran, which happened in a country with several thousands years of history, is considered among the greatest events of the twentieth century. The Islamic Revolution, after the advent of Islam, led to great developments inside the country. It is almost impossible to study the current developments of Iran, its domestic policies and its stances towards the international community without proper attention to the various periods of the historical development of Iran.

A study of the behavior of the Islamic Revolution and its stances towards the international community and norms of international law is possible only in the light of paying due attention to the constituent elements of the social behavior of the Iranian nation, which is influenced by its history and culture. Hence, in order to accomplish this task, one should study the historical developments of Iran and the existing government system as well as the decision-making processes in this country.

It goes without saying that in any study of the existing realities of the Iranian society, two factors of Iranianism and Islam should be taken into consideration. The Iranian nation enjoys an ancient history and a millenniums-old civilization. Overlooking the pre-Islamic era of Iranian history in any academic study will render the study incomplete, for it will leave out many crucial aspects of the Iranian history. At the same time Islam was warmly welcomed by the people in Iran and the Iranian nation generously applied their culture and civilization to spread and develop Islam and the Islamic sciences.

A large number of renowned Muslim scholars of the Islamic period came from the Iranian territory. Nevertheless there are tendencies among some scholars to lay emphasis on one of the said two aspects -- Iranianism and Islamism -- and in some cases the advocates of these two aspects confront each other. As a matter of fact most writers have maintained that the interaction between Islam and Iranian culture and civilization must be taken into consideration when the developments of the post-Islamic era, particularly those of the last century, are studied. However, a serious question has come to the fore, which calls for due consideration: are the Iranian people Iranian Muslims, or are they Muslim Iranians? The main concern of such questions is to set the priority of the two elements in relation each other in determining individual, social and official behaviors in Iran.

A proper understanding of the present government of Iran is possible only through sufficient knowledge of Islam, the intellectual currents in the early Islamic period, the historical developments of state in Muslim societies, and the developments in the contemporary trends of political thought in Islam. The government of the Islamic Republic of Iran is a religious government whose pillars are based on religion in accordance to the Sharia of the holy Prophet (S) of Islam. No other explanation would be as useful in understanding the outstanding role of religion in politics and government in the Islamic Republic of Iran as the inextricability of religion and politics in Islam. The followers of Islam, like those of other divine religions, differ on their interpretations, explanations and analyses of some parts of the principles and secondary principles of the religion.Yet any scholarly research would conclude that Islam through its comprehensive plans and programs for the individual and society has established deep ties with politics and power as its tools for the implementation of those plans and programs. Through paying due attention to these points, one may conclude that there is a specific inclination among the Muslims towards politics, which stems directly from the Islamic teachings.

If the essence of politics is the expression of the way of life of the players and of deliberations of the affairs of the society, a quick look at some principles of Islam such as alms tax, hajj, jihad (holy war) and the "commandment of good and prohibition of evil", would reveal how these principles are meant to create a collective spirit and social solidarity among the Muslims.

Some other thinkers opine that if the essence of politics is an attempt to grasp political power, without any doubt Islam has a political worldview. Recognizing the human nature on the basis of his physical and mental needs, Islam never confines itself to the expression of its ideals, rather it constantly endeavors to procure the tools required for the fulfillment of those ideals.

This was why as soon as the Prophet of Islam had to migrate from Mecca under the pressure of the Quraysh, he established an Islamic government in Medina. After the departure of the Prophet, history bears testimony to the fact that the four caliphs and other dynasties established Islamic governments in the Islamic society.

Also in order to have a better understanding of the government of the Islamic Republic of Iran, one should study Shia Islam and the history of Shiism thoroughly, for its teachings constitute the base of present government system in Iran within the framework of a government notion called Wilayat-e Faqih (Guardianship of Jurisconsult).

Shiaism throughout history has been making endeavors to establish a righteous government under the leadership of a just leader and on the basis of this argument it did not deem necessary to follow the vote of the majority of Muslims. On the basis of Shia theory, it is only the infallible Imams -- and in their absence, their successors, that is, just jurisprudents -- who are entitled to establish the Islamic government. Due to this outlook, the Shias throughout the history, except for short periods, remained as Muslim minorities in Islamic societies. At some stages of history they were under vigorous pressures, but at the same time they followed their own ideas, advocating the establishment of a just government and spread of Islamic teachings. What really grants historical legitimacy to the Shias to hope for the final victory over oppression is the expectation of the reappearance of the disappeared Imam [savior]. The above argument does not mean that the Shias have never compromised with the established governments, rather, the Shia jurisprudents at certain stages of history deemed it expedient to adjust themselves to the established governments in order to guarantee the survival of their followers. A combination of the aforesaid features, that is, disobedience to the majority, belief in historical legitimacy, and utopianism constitute the historical identity of Shiism.

According to the notion of Wilayat-e Faqih (guardianship of jurisconsult), which is based on the Quranic verses and traditions, the only group entitled to rule over the Muslims are the clerics (religious scholars). The three fundamental prerequisites for a Muslim ruler are: enough command of Islamic teachings (individual inference); justice and virtue; and awareness of, and acquaintance with, the requirements of time. Individual inference is one of the main features of Shiism, which has its roots in the early years of the formation of Islam and Shiism. In fact, relying on this very principle, Shiism opposed the Akhbaris (Traditionists), who maintained that Muslims could perform all their duties through direct reference to the Quran and traditions.

The notion of Wilayat-e Faqih (guardianship of jurisconsult), which had already been put forth by the Shia jurisprudents but introduced in a comprehensive manner by Imam Khomeini, stems from the features of Shiism that allude to the comprehensive programs of Islam for the management of the society and the necessity of grasping the political power to implement the Islamic principles.

The notion of Wilayat-e Faqih (guardianship of jurisconsult) is based on three principles:

- Complete subservience and commitment of social-governmental structures to the Islamic laws
- Supremacy of a jurisprudent at the apex of the three branches of government
- The duty of every Muslim to endeavor for the establishment of the Islamic government

Although the notion of Wilayat-e Faqih (guardianship of jurisconsult) stems from the teachings that were introduced in the past, it is quite a popular government. The role of the people in the election of the leader is not at all negligible. Although the leader or Wali-e Faqih must enjoy the characteristics necessary for a leader of the Islamic society, the people's role in his appointment or election either directly or through their representatives is vital and crucial. An article of the Constitution of the Islamic Republic of Iran envisages the role of the people in the election of the ruler.

In 1979, at the time of the designation of the new government in Iran, Imam Khomeini insisted on the concept of “Islamic Republic” and opposed the conservatives who advocated the designation of a “just Islamic government”. Imam Khomeini insisted that the two features of "Islamic" and "Republic" would go hand in hand in the Islamic government of Iran.

The Islamic Revolution of Iran can also be studied within the framework of contemporary reformist movements in the Islamic world. The Islamic civilization, which spread across the world for about eight years, led to considerable developments in the Arabian Peninsula, Iran, Asia and some parts of Europe and Africa, but began to decline from the 14th century onward. Since then the Muslims were entangled in stagnation, deterioration, cultural retrogression and backwardness. Thus the renaissance and spread and development of industries in the West happened simultaneous with the decline of Muslim countries some of which were finally colonized by the Western colonial powers.

Since the late 19th and early 20th centuries, a number of great thinkers emerged in the Islamic world, who followed two important goals. First, severing the hands of the aliens from the resources and wealth of the Muslim countries and as a result, achieving political and economic independence; and second, creating of a kind of reconciliation between Islam and modernism.

Thus, reformism and self-awareness spread among the Muslim scholars, that is, awareness of the domineering presence of the Western countries in the Muslim societies and the detrimental impacts of the colonial era led the Muslims towards seeking independence.

Meanwhile crisis in the last chain of Islamic caliphate and the spread of modernism and modernization led to the emergence of the idea of establishment of an Islamic government among the Muslim scholars, both Sunnis and Shias. The domineering presence of the colonial powers in the Muslim societies had an inevitable consequence, that is, the growth of the idea of "unity" and solidarity among the Muslims. The Muslim scholars over the past two centuries have followed Islamic unity as a major goal.

With regard to reformism in the world of Islam, Seyed Jamal ud Din Assadabadi, Mohammad Abdu, Rashid Reza (d. 1935), Mohammad Iqbal Lahori, Ali

Shariati (d. 1977), Morteza Motahhari (d. 1980) and last, but most important of all, Imam Khomeini (d. 1989) are on the frontline of this movement.

All these thinkers who were scattered from the east to the west of Islamic territories considered the establishment of an Islamic government and unity among the Muslims as the only solution for the redemption of the Muslims.

The Islamic Revolution of Iran was a protest against the domination of the West over the House of Islam (Dar ul Islam). It was an attempt to establish a government in which all the Islamic values and teachings were employed with new techniques and methods.

The approach of the Islamic Republic of Iran to the Islamic values has not led to neglecting reality. This issue can be studied within the framework of the dynamism of "individual inference" (ijtihad) as well as by taking into account the ideas and viewpoints of the Muslim scholars. This interaction and coordination between the values and realities is also reflected in the foreign policy of the Islamic Republic of Iran.

The foreign policy of the Islamic Republic of Iran is a result of continuous interaction between religious ideology reflected in the ideas of Imam Khomeini and the practical realities of the International society. While Iran was pursuing the revival of Islam and consolidation of Islamic unity in the world, it never replaced this objective with its national interests as a guideline for its foreign policy in order to create a sphere of influence for itself in the region.

While the preference of Islamic unity over nationalism, emphasis on the export of the Islamic Revolution during the first decade of the revolution, the doctrine of strong action in the Third World, gradation and classification of the governments, and questioning some international norms all stem from the law of "siar" -- Islamic International law-- other aspects of the foreign policy of the Islamic Republic of Iran and the method of persuasion of these objectives indicate that the Islamic Republic of Iran has always tried to achieve its goals in the light of the existing international realities and through the application of the very existing norms.

This is why the main impetuses of Iran's foreign policy in many areas were the geopolitical, historical and economic factors of the pre-revolutionary era, while taking distance from that period and the establishment of the Islamic government aimed to provide the people with welfare and better standards of life.

Since the Muslim societies remain deeply divided within the framework of nationalist divisions, Islam is used as a uniting factor in Iran's foreign policy, which is compatible with the national interests of Iran. In a number of cases the announced goal (Islamic unity) is used for the mobilization of the masses as well. In understanding the formation of the foreign policy of the Islamic Republic of Iran, attention should be paid to another factor as well: Given that the Islamic Republic of Iran is a result of a long-term non-governmental function of the Sharia, while the international community and international law are effective in the formation of the foreign policy of the Islamic Republic of Iran, they are at the same time effective on the kind of formation of output of the Islamic government to the international community.

Unfortunately a number of studies undertaken thus far about Islamic revivalism and the Islamic Revolution of Iran lack realism. In other words, these works have studied Islamic ideology within the framework of traditional, and in some cases discarded, backgrounds. Also these studies overlook the existence of different values and interests in international society.

These studies have some times superficially concluded that the Islamic Revolution aims to revive Islam and Islamic unity by nullifying the notion of nation-state on whose foundations lies the international law. Such an approach overlooks the complicated interaction between the political ideology of Islam and the international law.

The behavior of the Islamic Republic of Iran both in domestic and foreign policies, bears testimony to its intertwining with the international order. A study of the political ideology of the Islamic Revolution shows that the political behavior of Iran stems from the interactions between the traditional principles of the Sharia and the factors that emerge due to the requirements of government in the contemporary era. The foreign policy of the Islamic Republic of Iran simultaneously reflects the two sides of this phenomenon, that is, on the one hand, Iran invites other nations to Islamic unity and, on the other, it is committed to its national interests.

In studying the relations of the Islamic Revolution and international law, it should be mentioned that international law just like an item composed of many parts does not lend itself to a clear definition. This chaos to some extent is due to the absence of an independent, centralized executive mechanism in the realm of international law. This lack of integration prepares the grounds for a precise study of the Islamic Revolution in international law.

The Islamic Revolution of Iran is inclined towards applying the norms and applications of the international law. On the one hand, this orientation reflects the widespread demand of the international community for revision of the processes of international law and negation and abolition of the impacts and remnants of the domination of the interests and exigencies of certain parties to international law (great powers); and on the other, this orientation specifically reflects Islamic values.

With the continuous growth of Europe and the decline of Asia in the 19th century, the universalization of the international law increasingly concentrated in Europe and did not take Asia into account in its new definition and concept. All of sudden the Asian states found themselves in a juridical vacuum; and while they had no role in the establishment of this new law they became the subjects of this law. The first serious challenges to the universalization and generalization of Western values and European system of international law came to the fore with the establishment of the Soviet Union after the 1917 Bolshevik Revolution. Inspired by Marxism, the Soviet Union rejected the general principles of international law as the embodiment of demands of the ruling classes of the capitalist states.

Anyway what still persists as a reality is negligence of the popular values of the oriental nations in the compilation of international law. Today a greater number of elected actors in the international community have found a position in the system of international law, who represent a spectrum of values and diverse interests. However the recognition by international community of these values -- and the interests they have at the level of nation-states -- remains a dream and a great aspiration to be fulfilled in the future.

In studying the relations of political ideology of Imam Khomeini and international law, a few points are to be taken into consideration:

First, in studying the behavior of a divergent political system, the pressures exerted on this system by the political, economic and legal international systems for its conformity and coordination cannot be neglected. In pursuing its goals, the Islamic Revolution of Iran has been under pressure in many cases, but has been able naturally to take advantage of the existing tensions in the powerful international system. Therefore, a distinction should be made between some of the ideals of the Islamic Revolution which cannot be materialized under the prevailing circumstances in the international relations - in fact the Iranian government now years after the victory of the Islamic Revolution is not interested in remembering them (like the establishment of a global Islamic government) - and some other objectives inside Iran within the framework of law which have been institutionalized and can be pursued at the international level through the existing norms (like giving priority to the Islamic world).

Secondly, the impact of revolutionary fervor and domestic power struggle on the performance of the Islamic Revolution during the early years and during various stages of the revolution should be taken into consideration. Naturally, the post-revolution fervor and excitement is confined to the immediate post-revolutionary era and emerges in all the revolutions. After this period, we have witnessed, especially during the second decade of the revolution, that the objectives of the revolution were pursued mainly by observing the realities of the international society and pragmatism; and also we witnessed that the national interests received their due attention and found their weight in policymaking. During this period the Islamic laws and objectives of the Islamic Revolution became more institutionalized.

Thirdly, although the Islamic Revolution, and more broadly speaking, the Islamic revivalism, has demonstrated some features which stem from specific characteristics of the Islamic values and ideals, this reevaluation of the norms, doctrines and functions of international law, to a great extent, reflect a greater arena which indeed encompasses the developing world.

These interests and interconnected Islamic values exert a distinct pressure on the present models of structures, agreements and arrangements of international system. As the experience of the French and Russian revolutions has demonstrated, some new structures will find a new permanent place in the arena of international relations. Hence, one should wait and watch to see if they will leave any impact on the sands of the coast of the post-revolutionary storm. The Islamic Revolution of Iran may be considered an example of the demand of the Islamic world, or more broadly speaking that of the Third World countries, for revision of the rules, norms and values of international law. The demand of the Islamic Revolution for a better understanding of various values in international relations will also help a better understanding of the notion of "Dialogue among Civilizations."

The Dialogue of Civilizations does not accept an international society with one-sided values, rather, it acknowledges an international society by considering diverse values, principles and cultures. Among those cultures, Islam as a dominant culture of more than one billion population of the world should receive due attention as the founder of a great civilization.

On the other hand, the notion of Dialogue among Civilizations rejects Samuel Huntington's theory of a "Clash of Civilizations" which was put forth few years ago and analyzes the international developments within the framework of clash among various civilizations, particularly between the Islamic and Western civilizations.

The notion of Dialogue among Civilizations maintains that the common principles and general foundations of the world civilizations are so intertwined and intermingled that their clash will never happen. If there are some confrontations or incompatibilities, they stem from the existing prevailing order and attempts for domination of the world by some powers. Otherwise, if the diverse values and the existing poles of powers be recognized, there will be no need for a clash of civilizations.

The notion of Dialogue among Civilizations humaintains that if the mankind is liberated from the bondage of groupings, if knowledge of various historical and cultural backgrounds of other nations is increased, and if there is mutual understanding the grounds for many clashes will evaporate. The best way to accomplish this task is dialogue and only dialogue.

Deputy for research,
Organization of Culture and Islamic Relations
Tehran, Iran

PART II

IF GOD IS LORD OF ALL, IS THERE ROOM FOR MAN?

Chapter IV

Political Freedom in Islam

Amid Zanjani

In the life of the Muslim world the prevalent idea in the analysis of the history of modern political thought in the last two centuries has been the fact that the developments in the era of the movement and Enlightenment in Europe drew the attention of many Muslim scholars and intellectuals towards freedom and political rights and caused many similar developments in the Muslim world.

Analysts do not all agree in their conclusions. Some consider this approach to be a positive, progressive and suitable solution towards the goal of political expansion. Others deem it a blind imitation of Western thought and culture, and consider it to be a destructive force and cause of dependency [on Western powers], bringing about the loss of independence and growth in the Muslim world.

At any rate, the comparative study between the developments of political thought in the eighteenth and nineteenth centuries in the Western world, and the dominant political idea in the nineteenth and twentieth centuries in the Muslim world shall help us arrive at a conclusion on the amount of mutual influence, imitation, similarity, or transmutation of political identity between the two.

Throughout the history of Islam up to the downfall of the Ottomans, it was military power and weaponry that determined the form of government and political developments, and governments would change with whoever was victorious at the time. It was this very factor that decided the fate of governments in the West before the start of the era of freedom and enlightenment, and especially the French revolution.

With the dawn of the age of enlightenment and the realization of political rights and freedoms, it was the vote of the people, instead of military might, that became the decisive factor in government, and once again, the Muslim world, after a brief relapse, inclined towards imitating the West. Following this development, new governments surfaced with new criteria and structures and diverse political, economic, cultural, social and even military institutions Islamic countries turned to new constitutions based on Western standards when they achieved independence.

All those who analyze these developments, whether optimistically or pessimistically, agree that scientific and industrial progress in the West has been the most influential factor in this approach, be it rational or copied.

In reality, history repeated itself once again and just as the West had a wake-up call in its approach towards Islamic civilization and enriched its material life by profiting from the science and technology of the Muslims, the Muslims, faced with the outstanding developments in the West in the areas of science and technology in the 19th and 20th centuries, also rose to overcome their own backwardness through political development. It must be said that, in the era of enlightenment [in the West] neither was the West completely geared towards democracy and novel political ideas, nor was the Muslim world totally immersed in tyranny and corruption. On the one hand, during the enlightenment movement, the West would commit the most heinous acts akin to those perpetrated in the Dark Ages on the path of colonialism, expansion of political hegemony and economic domination. On the other, the Muslim world, under the dominance of the Ottomans, India and Iran, would advocate the most "Oriental" political ideas on equality and social justice. In terms of conflicts and opposition, the West and the Muslim world moved side by side and the problem of ambiguity, divergence and crisis of identity can be observed on both sides. The similarities stand out to the extent that to some Islamic intellectuals the movement of enlightenment in the West is a type of inclination towards Islam in its earliest ages and purest form. Muhammad Abduh's saying that there is Islam without Muslims in the West and Muslims without Islam in the Muslim world attests to this viewpoint.

Thus, some come to doubt the intellectual originality of the West and to consider it only to be a chronological and historical precedent. Despite the chronological antecedence of the East, they emphasize the originality and novelty of the ideology and political thought in Islam, and added to the complexity of the analysis of the concept of awakening in the Muslim world and the study of Western thought.

FOUNDATIONS OF APPROACHES TO WESTERN THOUGHT

Many analysts and intellectuals have been overcome by doubt and are inclined to be ambiguous in their definition of this new-founded approach in the Muslim world towards the West. Some have referred to it as a revolution, some as a movement, others as reform, modernization and intellectual phenomenon, similarly Western scholars have referred to the events of the French Revolution and the ideological and political developments following it as movement, reform, modernization, and the era of enlightenment.

On the issue of following Western models, Scholars such as Seyed Jamal Assad Abadi, Sheikh Muhammad Abduh, Kawakibi and Seyed Ahmad Khan came to the conclusion that human beings have a common historical identity and following generations must take up their path from where those preceding them left off. They believed that starting from "square one" for the Muslim world would be to try what has already been tested, and considered the essence of the path and its fundamentals to be one and the same despite ethnic, religious and cultural differences. Many intellectuals and theorists, with Shiite scholars during the constitutional movement [in Iran] and afterwards, in their lead, were considering the revitalization of Islamic identity and turning back to their roots. To begin the new movement, and move in sync with the modern era and the developed Western world, they emphasized starting from square one. Apart from their initial skepticism towards the West, they considered the Western model an unsuitable one for the Muslim world, and considered the total hegemony of Western capitalism, which was the crowning achievement of the Western movement, to be clear proof of this claim. In this vein, the ideas of Iqbal Lahury and Sheikh Fazlollah Nouri may be studied side by side despite their differences. It should be noted that the principle of "starting from square one" is one of the main pillars of the political thought of Imam Khomeini in the Islamic revolution.

Doubtless in the analysis of the approach towards the West, we witness the conflict of two entities, each with its own particular historical, cultural, ideological and social path, and these diverse beginnings have formed two different identities. Even if we dismiss the diversities, and outline the common elements of East and West, they will still have their own separate identities and peculiar characteristics, which shall ultimately create fundamental problems in our effort to view them uniformly and create similar patterns.

The proponents of the idea of eclecticism with regard to advanced civilizations in the context of the historical interaction between cultures believe that the glorious Islamic civilization, similar to the West, also has its basis in ancient Greek civilization, and that, today, the interconnected chain of Western civilization receives its vitality from Hellenic civilization.

These scholars have overlooked the fact that neither European civilization arises from Western civilization, nor does Islamic civilization arise from the Greek. Greek civilization is only one of many factors that have paved the way for the formation of the historical path of Islamic or Western civilization. It is in this close analysis and comparison that ascribing one civilization to the other becomes seriously problematic. The familiarization of Western culture with Greek culture through encountering Islamic culture (with the help of the likes of Avicenna, Farabi, and Ibn Roshd) is an example of that factor. The reason one must investigate the other factors is that neither the West nor Islamic civilization hold all the characteristics of ancient Greek civilization, and therefore no conclusion as to the sameness of the two can be drawn.

Absorbing the positive and progressive elements of other civilizations is not so simple as to be done with one's eyes closed, so to speak. In this grouping, there is the possibility of the stains, dust, and the sunken residues created by the conflict of the shaping elements of that, and also the viruses and pollutants of the culture of "another" being absorbed into "our own".

The historical evolution of modern Western thought has led to liberalism on the political scale, and to capitalism on the economic one; ultimately, individual freedom has come under the yoke of "capital", which in turn has become a tool for exploitation. These elements are neither compatible with Greek civilization, nor are they absorbable by our own Islamic civilization.

The Muslim world is faced with an entirely different situation than that of the past. Past approaches, whatever they may have been, belong to history. To find a solution to today's issues, one must re-evaluate the past. Special attention must be given to the issue of whether we would have chosen the same path had we been in the same situation or would there have been another way? This revision not only sheds light on the past, but clears the path for the future. We must keep in mind that future generations shall revise their ideology and approaches as well. The French revolution spoke of the equality of all citizens by negating the elite status of the clergy and priesthood, rejecting the hierarchy of human beings and the classification of the leaders of the church as superior class citizens, without rejecting religion.

Expressing hatred of religion and its distancing from social platforms entered the ideology of the era of Enlightenment only because it was perceived as a form of resistance against the social movement. Eventually it led to the inevitable retreat of the Church. Thus, from the social arena, Christianity returned into its Churches.

A conflict between the Church and the movement of enlightenment and freedom in the West, and its consequences in the Muslim world, has been expressed by the proponents and adherents of the Western Enlightenment. A conflict between religion and freedom, without the previous setting and its applicability to Islam, was set forth as the main idea of secularism. This whole issue is in truth a misinterpretation and "miscomparison" of the diverse roles of religion in the West, and of Islam in the Muslim world, and of the dissimilar stances of the Christian clergy and Muslim clergy towards freedom.

Secular scholars in the Muslim world did not endeavor to research and acquire knowledge of the West as much as Westerners undertook the task of coming to know the East. Therefore secularism [in the Muslim world] took the form of an unsubstantiated idea without historical precedent and rational motives, to the extent that it could not even be considered an imitation [of the West]. Following the progress of the enlightenment era in the West, scientists and experts each followed their own chosen path and, disregarding the will of the Church and its controllers, utilized secularism in it positive form. In the Muslim world, secularism was spoken of in its negative aspects, and [the proponents of Western secularism] began to challenge the presence of religion in the social scene, and attempted to distance it from politics and society and to isolate Islam as much as possible.

Naturally, this unusual animosity towards Islam led its adherents to resistance and the effort to protect the sacred elements of religion, and thus a one-sided war brought about bilateral attacks and confrontations.

THE GROUNDS FOR IDEOLOGICAL CRISES

This ideological crisis in the Muslim world reached its climax when in fact the very nature of Islam was opposed to the actions of both warring groups. Islam was against neither rationalism, scientific progress, freedom or rights, nor was it incapable of having an active role in social scenes.

If the ideological, enlightening and scientific movement had progressed in the Muslim world the way it did in the West, it would not have come into conflict with Islam. It would have found richer ground for progress within Islam and would have found it a suitable bedrock for growth and advancement. There would then have been no need for Islam's isolation, and Islamic supporters would not have opposed rationalism and growth.

Muslim intellectuals could have started re-examining and reassessing the history of Islam and its culture which Muslim nations have come to know as "Islam" instead of turning to secularism in its negative aspect (distancing Islam from the social scene and attempting to isolate it). They could have begun cleansing it of superfluities and unoriginal elements, and to bring a pure Islam out of the impurities, similar to the efforts of such scholars as Seyed Jamal and Abduh. The height of this kind of approach manifested itself in the political thought of Imam Khomeini. This ideology which emphasized the uniqueness of pure Islam created the most constructive and vigorous intellectual current in the Muslim world. It protected the originality of Islam against the emerging Western thought and culture, and revitalized the mosque and the ancient glory of Islamic civilization. From the heart of this principle emerged the concept of challenging the history of Western thought. Muslim scholars began to assess and evaluate Western culture and ideology, revealing the weaknesses hidden beneath the veil of the West's advanced science and industry, and indirectly responding to the West's critique of Islam, its ideology and civilization.

The least outcome of this evaluation and study was that Muslim nations would no longer be intimidated by the advanced Western technology or its culture. By learning to distinguish between its strengths and weaknesses, they would employ rationalism in selecting the superlative aspects of [Western culture]. Then they would not have plunged into the abyss of colonialism, degeneration and imperialism in the hopes of profiting from the dazzling lights of science and industry.

In truth, the era of the "Movement" in the East and the awakening of Muslims did not begin with an inclination towards negative secularism. It began when Muslim scholars began to expose all the aspects of the West and revealed the positive and negative sides of Western culture and civilization. Thus they acquitted Islam of the accusations heaped upon it by the secular sympathizers of the West.

The era of the expansion of negative secularism in the East was indeed a dark age. Not only did it not awaken Muslims from the deep sleep into which Colonialists had induced them, but plunged them further into it, and paved the way for the advancement of colonialism within the Muslim world.

Some believe that going to extremes in the attempt to evaluate the West can also be catastrophic for the Muslim world, deprive Muslims of growth, and cause the West to retaliate by imposing sanctions on them. They consider this kind of approach to be just as destructive as total assimilation of the West.

If they refer to the works of such scholars as Seyed Qutb in Egypt, Iqbal in India and Imam Khomeini in Iran, those with the aforementioned concerns will find that challenging the ideas of the West has never been done blindly and ignorantly. At the basis of this critical approach exists a close and accurate study of the limitations of Western civilization. The observers are implicitly called to an accurate understanding of Western culture and civilization.

A comprehensive knowledge of the West and an awareness of its various aspects and past and present developments shall prevent the critique of the West from turning into a zealous hatred and blind rejection of its principles. That is exactly the terrible quagmire that secularism in the East sank into in its approach towards Islam.

The blind current of secularism [in the Muslim world] proved that any ideological movement lacking close observation and accurate understanding of the facts can lead to catastrophic results.

RETURN TO ORIGINAL ISLAM

At present, many Muslim scholars in Egypt, Morocco, Algeria and Lebanon, in accordance with the ideas of Imam Khomeini, are emphasizing the coexistence of these two approaches. They believe that the most effective way of releasing Islam from its colonial past and taking it towards growth, renovation and progress is to revitalize it and assess the disruptive elements hidden in it, accompanied by an educated analysis of the West.

Today the blossoming of this ideology and outlook in the Muslim world is such that it promises the end of the era of negative secularism, and comes as a disappointment to those who harbor hopes of returning thereto.

The new approach emerging in the Muslim world is one of progress, construction, development, and revitalization based on what pure Islam can generate. It distinguishes between the dark and bright points of Western culture and benefits from the positive without falling prey to the negative. It cleanses the science, industry and contaminated culture of the West, while avoiding eclecticism and blind prejudice. It moves towards advanced science as quickly as it distances itself from Western hegemony.

This rejuvenating idea in the Muslim world neither neutralizes Islam within the lawful bedrock of Western science, industry, and culture, nor does it create a leftist or rightist Islam. Rather, it arrives at a pure, original Islam by analyzing Islamic history. It achieves liberation from the swamp of blind imitation, and stable growth through the educated critique of Western lines of thought. Thus it returns to its roots through the analysis of ideologies, self-improvement instead of opposing its own heritage, and finally, progress and renovation through the comparison between "us" and "others".

The dominant ideology in the future of Islamic nations will be based on this approach. The new civilization will be built by devoted Muslim scholars and especially the young generation, repeating once more the glorious past of Islam.

In the present age, ideologies in the Muslim world have always cut across each other. Negative secularism [in the East] was not the only idea to come into the greatest prominence with the aid of Western propaganda. In the past two hundred years, sporadic ideologies emerged in the Muslim world and vanished without a trace, because the nature of these Western-dependent ideologies called for such a fate. For example, one can name the concept of "benevolent dictatorship", which was a decisive factor in political developments in the many parts of the Muslim world. Foreign agents paved the way for this through fueling an atmosphere of fear, feudalism and internal war, and bringing foreign lackeys as saviors and national heroes into power.

In many Muslim nations, this concept was adopted by many scholars and political figures, causing them to support these types of "national heroes". We have witnessed this in our own country in the form of Reza Shah, and the way many observant political figures and scholars rose to support this colonial agent as the savior of Iran. Activists like Modarress were unable to warn them against the dire consequences of the rule of such a tyrant despite their clarion calls.

The [supporters of benevolent dictatorship] did not believe dictatorship resulted in tyranny and corruption per se. Therefore they explored the possibilities of freedom and justice in such concepts as security, not knowing that dictatorship and the eradication of freedoms is in nature inseparable from tyranny, corruption and insecurity. Imam Ali's said, "I see no greater catastrophe than that of Bani Ummayah", in answer to those who suggested that it would be necessary for Muawiyah to remain in power in order to prevent insecurity, chaos and further catastrophe. This bears witness to the fact that one catastrophe cannot be utilized to alleviate another, nor one form of oppression to remove another.

THE GENERAL CHARACTERISTICS OF POLITICAL THOUGHT IN ISLAM

Islamic political thought, or any meaning ascribing any form of political thought to Islam, must incorporate two main elements aside form the aforementioned ones within itself:

1-Islamic political thought is ideological in nature and based on monotheism; in Islam no idea can be separated from the monotheistic outlook in any way. Islamic ideas are based on the monotheistic worldview in all aspects and secular political thought has no place in the Islamic thought on the grand scale.

2-A political idea may be construed as Islamic when derived from texts pertaining to Islamic prophethood and divine revelation, i.e., the Book and Tradition. However, this does not mean that political thought based on a rational and philosophical viewpoint is rejected by Islam. Rather, when divine revelation is known to have a particular approach on a certain matter as stated in the Quran and Tradition, [guidelines] must be taken from those sources.

It must be added that if a certain issue is inevitable due to religious or rational expediency, and there exists no clarification on it in the context of divine revelation, then from a religious stance, one must act in accordance with the requirements of philosophical or scientific rationalism. Such action will be in line with Islamic principles.

Now, let us assume that there exist no guidelines on political concepts and theories in the Quran and Tradition, and that establishing a political system is inevitable from a rational point of view. We can therefore consider a political ideology based on a philosophical or scientific viewpoint as a guideline for creating a political system within an Islamic system, on the condition that the philosophical and scientific foundation does not transgress the boundaries of Islamic ideology and does not violate religious principles and laws. Lack of a political system can never be used as an excuse to label any political idea as a political ideology without first observing the main characteristics of an Islamic political thought system.

Among Muslim intellectuals there are prominent figures who have outstanding ideas on one or more political subject, but who do not have a political ideology. Yet from their whose ideas others have benefited in defining political concepts.

At any rate, we observe an inclination to both extremes in the political theories of Muslim scholars which is noteworthy, and there are those who absolutely reject the existence of a consistent political ideology in the viewpoints of Muslim scholars and thinkers.

IMPEDIMENTS ON THE PATH TO THE IMPLEMENTATION OF POLITICAL FREEDOM

Aside from the problems inherent in democracy, the supporters of democracy and political freedoms must also face impediments to its implementation in the Muslim World. Even if we assume that these problems do not exist in the West, they will doubtless arise in religious societies and most Muslim countries.

These obstacles do not emerge from within the nature of the freedoms themselves. Yet, when our aim is to apply them in the Muslim world, inevitably their impracticality, due to the problems extant therein, will bring the principle of protecting political rights and freedoms under question, resulting in their rejection. These obstacles can be divided in to two groups: Conventional, and Religious.

Conventional Obstacles

The culture, traditions, conventions and situation of each Muslim country is such that it renders the implementation of democratic methods impossible. A simple example may be used to clarify this point.

In most traditional environments in Muslim countries respect for the elderly and seniors is an inseparable element of the process of decision-making and the execution of power. How then can democratic elections be held while preserving this old tradition? We know that if these traditions are not provided for in the law, the people themselves shall demonstrate their commitment to such conventions. For example, elections will be held under the supervision of elders, while denying youth the right to supervise is in contradiction to democratic methods. What will occur, then, when a group of young people demand the right to supervise elections? Sacrificing traditions and customs rooted in the people's culture may be beneficial to democracy in the short run, but will ultimately be dangerous for it.

A large part of the Muslim world, as all third-world countries, struggles with poverty, illiteracy, lack of material and spiritual benefits. Even the political expertise necessary for democratic elections, and the operation of democratic instruments such as political parties and factions, and separation of political powers, call for certain practical conditions that cannot be democratic. It is not a matter of legalization of freedoms; many Muslim countries have the most superlative and modern constitutions. But in practice they are faced with problems stemming from lack of favorable conditions for implementation of freedoms.

To pave the way for the implementation of democracy, the West has somehow solved problems such as terrorism, discrimination and propaganda for itself, but has utilized all of these in its cultural invasion of the Muslim world. It has created and encouraged terrorism, spread various forms of discrimination, and has used propaganda and deception of public opinion.

The norms of freedom and democracy, as weapons and medicines, are fashioned by the West. Just as it possesses the defenses against its own weapons and the antidotes to its own medicines, it also possesses the antidote and counter-offensive to democracy. At a time when the West's expediency has brought it into opposition with the Muslim world, and the awakening of Muslims has created an anti-Western movement, how can one hold any hopes for actual democracy?

Religious Obstacles

Parts of the Muslim world may be indifferent towards Islam, and therefore cannot be considered as religious societies. But we must assume that the debate on democracy is brought forth by those who are believers in Islam and who do not want to sacrifice it to the advantages of democracy.

With such an assumption, there arise numerous obstacles in the way of implementing freedoms, which are either born of the circumstances in Muslim societies or from the fact that the proponents of democracy are themselves Muslims who do not want Islam to be the price they pay for democracy.

It cannot be doubted that, based on all classic political hypotheses, ideas of governance and religious jurisprudence, the rulers of Muslim countries must possess certain characteristics. Although these characteristics differ according to different points of view, on the whole, those who lack these qualities are not permitted to be candidates for the governance of Islamic societies. For example in most denominations of the Sunni sect, the ruler must be from the Quraishi tribe. Thus, as there is no way to determine one's own race in Arab countries, let alone non-Arab ones, most people are unsuitable as rulers of the Islamic state.

Based on the verdict of most Shiite jurisprudents, the ruler of a Muslim nation must be a jurisprudent. With a look at the proportion of those possessing this prerequisite to those lacking it, we can guess the number of people who will be disqualified as rulers.

In the religious society, based on religious belief, law-making is not a free process, and must be done in the framework of Islamic principles. We might consider Islamic principles to be so flexible as to include all religious jurisprudence, and assume that concordance with one religious fatwa is the only requisite. Yet there would still be many instances when members of parliament and the representatives of the people would not have the right to pass laws that are in violation of Islamic principles (in their broad sense).

If a Muslim nation is not bound by Sharia, or chooses not to implement it in practice, the Muslim proponents of freedom and democracy must at least find a solution to these religious impediments. Islam and democracy must be applied side by side and in harmony, without any part of Islam being omitted or overlooked, or political freedoms impaired.

In practice, democracy demands leniency and tolerance towards adversaries, equality between Muslims, Hypocrites, and atheists, and also the governing [of Muslims] by foreign infidels who are probably invading enemies as well. Harmonizing these methods with Quranic verses at least in their literal form is a daunting task. But freedom necessitates that all people benefit equally from civil rights and social justice. This poses religious problems as regards such matters as the division of inheritance among male and female heirs, the Qisas of men and women, family rights and, in legal matters, standing witness and passing judgment. Resolving these issues unilaterally in favor of democracy, at least with the existing jurisprudential licenses, is not possible.

Constructing a democratic government where the laws of Sharia are balanced with the principles of democracy and organized in a homogenous combination demands a novel Islamic exegesis that Sheikh Ansari labels “new jurisprudence”.

Democracy may require such prerequisites as freedom, equality, justice and the participation of all people in government, entail the control of the governing body’s power, rationalization of politics, the unbiased dismissal of inefficient officials, restoration of rights and securing the best interests of the people, and implementation by such instruments as elections, parliament, parties, separation of powers, expansion, and free press. The religion of Islam has a viewpoint, be it negative or positive, on each of these issues. If we do not judge matters prematurely and do not impose any foreign element upon the Sharia, we shall observe that the pairing of Islamic Jurisprudence with these concepts poses certain problems, which cannot be overlooked so as to provide more freedoms while religious principles are preserved and upheld. The only solution is that pursued by the leader of the Islamic revolution. It prepared the majority of the nation for the acceptance of the rule of Islam, and made religious democracy possible through the creation of such a foundation.

Professor of Islamic law, Tehran University
Institute for the Study and Research of Islamic Sciences
Tehran, Iran

Chapter V

The Qu'ran as a Negative Theological Text: The Evidence of Sura II

Aryeh Botwinick

INTRODUCTION

For the past ten years, my family and I have resided in a racially, ethnically, and religiously mixed neighborhood in the western part of Philadelphia called Overbrook Farms. The neighborhood consists largely of an African-American population who are mostly Christian, a Muslim population, and a minority of Jews. The Muslims in the community (including their imam) are for the most part American converts to Islam, who were inspired by their personal relationships to a Sufi sheikh known as the Bawa who emigrated from Sri Lanka and lived in the neighborhood during the Sixties and Seventies to convert to Islam after his death. As I walk the streets of my neighborhood going to and from the synagogue (or on various other errands) wearing my kippah (skull cap) or a hat, I am often greeted by my Sufi neighbors going to and from their mosque with the traditional Muslim greeting (which is also a blessing) of "Salaam Aleikum" ("Peace be upon You") to which I respond with the Jewish version of the traditional Muslim retort of "Aleikhem Shalom" ("Upon you, peace, as well.") I was so enchanted by the serenity and sense of inner contentment exuded by my

Sufi neighbors that I was eager for further contact with them. Over the last five years, I have participated in a number of public Muslim-Jewish dialogues with the imam of the neighborhood mosque which were attended by members of the mosque as well as by Jews living in Overbrook Farms and other adjacent neighborhoods. Our topics have ranged from the personality of the patriarch Abraham from Jewish and Muslim perspectives to key prayers in the Jewish and Muslim liturgies. Some of these dialogues have borne the character of seances – they were so saturated by an overflow of warmth and good feeling.

September 11, 2001 and its aftermath have put barely a crimp in the aura that surrounds the meetings of the dialogue group. However, our meetings have set me thinking about whether it would not be possible as a sheer intellectual exercise to reconfigure the text of the Qu'ran in a way that would match Sufi sensibility and sense of priorities. Sufism, in many respects, represents an operationalized negative theology.[1] The Sufis focus so intently on nurturing the values of fraternity and community because for them God subsists at such an unbridgeable distance from ourselves. Hence, willy-nilly and almost by metaphysical default human life – including human religious life – has to focus on the here-and-now, the moment-to-moment engagements in religious transactions and activities, to make sure that they are already suffused with the values and the attitudes

---

1. The phrase is Warren Zev Harvey's, who is a professor of Jewish thought at the Hebrew University of Jerusalem.

that cultivation of a religious approach is supposed to bring about. In a negative theological setting – with God in a palpable, literal sense always situated beyond the conceptual and existential horizon – a premium is necessarily placed on the means matching the ends, on making our journey to get to where we want to go approximate as fully as possible to where we are supposed to be going – since we may never get there.

In the post 9/11 world, many commentators have pointed to the need for locating and exploring cultural continuities between Islam and the West by way of defusing Samuel Huntington's thesis of a "clash of civilizations" which seemed to have been given such explosive corroboration by the events of 9/11. One of the most promising ways of doing this may be to investigate whether – and to what extent – the Qu'ran can be interpreted as a negative theological Scripture. The phrase "negative theology" signifies that we can only say what God is not – but not what He is. Our only mode of specification of the Divine essence, character, and attributes is to unremittingly highlight the literal inapplicability of our traditional litany of descriptions to the monotheistic God.

On the surface, the Muslim Scriptures seem like a ripe candidate for this sort of investigation because unlike the Christian Scriptures they reject the triune character of God. Just like for Jews, for Muslims, as well, God is radically, unadulteratingly One. The Qu'ran attributes the character of prophet to Jesus (which Judaism rejects) – but this does not affect the radical oneness of the conception of Divinity which Muslims affirm.

In what follows, I shall be engaging in a thought experiment – testing whether it is possible to exhibit the Qu'ran as a negative theological text. I shall be focusing upon the second Sura (or chapter) of the Qu'ran called "The Cow" – which because of the numerous, characteristic themes and topics that it covers is known as "the Qu'ran in miniature." I shall follow my exegesis of the second Sura with a commentary on some key theological passages in the writings of Avicenna, the great 10th and 11th Century Muslim philosopher and theologian whose writings are steeped in references to the Qu'ran thereby constituting an implicit commentary upon them. I am attempting, in however limited and halting a way, to reconstruct for Islam a parallel to Moses Maimonides', *The Guide of the Perplexed* relationship to the Hebrew Scriptures. Just as Maimonides in outlining his negative theology in the *Guide* in the 12th Century provides us with a very ample and encompassing Midrash or exegesis of the text of the Torah, the Prophets, and the Hagiography in negative theological terms – so, too, I shall try to argue that it is possible to configure Avicenna's philosophy and theology as offering us something approximating to a negative theological hermeneutical key for making sense of the text of the Qu'ran.

SURA II AND BELATEDNESS

A central theme of the second Sura of the Qu'ran is something we might call (following the literary theorist Harold Bloom[2]) the belatedness of Qu'ranic Revelation. Here is the way the Qu'ran describes its own location in the chain of monotheistic Revelation:

Say you: "We believe in God, and in that which has been sent down on us and sent down on Abraham, Ishmael, Isaac and Jacob, and the Tribes, and that which was given to Moses and Jesus and the Prophets, of their Lord; we make no division between any of them, and to Him we surrender."[3]

The Qu'ran thus depicts one long continual chain of monotheistic Revelation that starts with Abraham and culminates with itself. What is the theological weight of the monotheism to which Islam lays claim as being its latest examplar and propounder? A central clue for addressing this question is contained in the passage just cited. Belatedness is not just an explicit theme of the Qu'ran – as the text records the failure of the previous monotheistic Revelations to transform the world and the

---

2. Harold Bloom, *The Anxiety of Influence* (New York: Oxford University Press, 1973); *A Map of Misreading* (New York: Oxford University Press, 1975); *Kabbalah and Criticism* (New York: Seabury Press, 1975); *Poetry and Repression* (New Haven: Yale University Press, 1976).

3. *The Koran Interpreted*. A Translation by A. J. Arberry. (New York: Simon and Schuster, 1996), 2:130; p. 45. All references to the Qu'ran in this paper will be to this edition.

consequent belated need for Islam to fill the breach created by these failures. The historical belatedness of Islam can be read as a metaphor for the belatedness endemic to monotheistic doctrine generally. Monotheism captures the sense in which the metaphysical condition of the human community is sealed in eternal belatedness. The rational quest that triggers the postulation of the One Supreme God is the search for the ultimate reason or cause for the phenomena that we encounter in experience. On the surface, the monotheistic God seems like the ideal candidate to bring the explanatory quest to a halt because His total dissimilarity from things human disenchants any effort to pierce beyond Him in accounting for the human world. But by the same token that God is the ultimate explanatory datum, He also ends up explaining nothing at all. His ultimacy is achieved by His Total Difference (in a way that prevents us from even making sense of what the term "Difference" signifies when applied to Him) from things human – but that very factor debars Him from explaining anything in the human scene. Once God is conceived as having His Being beyond the threshold of total difference, all of the verbs and adjectives that function in our explanatory vocabularies can only be applied to Him metaphorically. In a literal sense, He cannot figure in our explanations at all. In this crucial sense, therefore, the theological vocabulary of monotheistic religion is belated in that it can only be invoked after the fact of incoherence – after the project that it is supposed to verbally condense and represent has already failed in the breakdown of the dynamics of language that is supposed to reflect or enact it. Or – more precisely stated – our attempts to reduce our grapplings with ultimate explanation to language (as if it were possible to conceive of them as taking place outside of language) is already the occasion for our belatedness. The supreme irony is that to be a monotheist in one's search for ultimate origins is already to be belated – to be graphically dramatizing the extent to which origins elude us.

There is an interesting parallel to this phenomenon of belatedness in the text that inaugurates monotheistic Revelation – namely, the first few verses in the book of Genesis. The great medieval Rabbinic commentator on the Hebrew Scriptures known by his acronym, Rashi (Rabbi Shlomo Yitzchaki), points out (following the Midrash, Bereshit Rabbah) that the first two verses in Genesis are really sentence fragments and need to be read as subordinate clauses to verse three – so that the three verses together constitute one concerted linguistic unit of discourse which should be paraphrased as follows: "In the beginning of God's creation of heaven and earth, when the earth was without form and empty, with darkness on the face of the depths, and the Spirit of God was hovering on the face of the waters, God said, 'Let there be light,' and light came into existence."[4] From this Rabbinic perspective, therefore, monotheistic Revelation begins with a sentential fragment – as if to symbolically encode that "middleness" or belatedness is the community of

---

4. The translation I have used comes largely from Aryeh Kaplan, *The Living Torah* (New York: Maznaim Publishing, 1981), p. 3 – with some emendations.

believers' enduring condition. Rashi's discussion of the content of the first three verses in Genesis confirms this analysis. Rashi points out that in Biblical and Rabbinic cosmogony the heavens ("Shamayim" in Hebrew) are composed of fire and water - "Eish" and "Mayim".[5] Yet, in the account of Creation given at the beginning of Genesis nothing is mentioned about the fashioning of fire and water. They are simply textual givens - there to be transmuted into something else - without their original creation being disclosed. Rashi's insight into the text is corroborated by the Rabbis' striking formulation that God created numerous worlds and destroyed them before He finally opted for this one[6] - as if to suggest that Creation is an ongoing story, with no discernible beginning or end.

In the Babylonian Talmudic tractate, Sanhedrin 26b, the Amoraic sage Rav Hanin explains the Hebrew phrase "tohu wa-bhohu" (translated as "without form and empty") occurring in the second verse of Genesis as not just telling us something about the context of Creation -

---

5. Babylonian Talmud, Hagigah, 12a.

6. "R. Abbahu said: Hence we learn that the Holy One, blessed be He, went on creating worlds and destroying them until He created these [sc. heaven and earth], and then He said: 'These please Me, those did not please Me.'; R. Phineas said: The proof of R. Abbahu's statement is: And God saw everything which He had made and, behold, it was very good. [Genesis 1, 31. Rendering: And God saw all that He had made - i.e., all the worlds He had made - But behold, i.e., only what had now been made ('behold' has that significance: see now!) was very good." *Midrash Rabbah: Genesis: Volume One*. Trans. H. Freedman. (London: Soncino Press, 1983), p. 64.

but as cluing us into a central feature of Creation itself. In Rashi's gloss on part of Rav Hanin's statement: "No verbal formulation has any real feeling [i.e., materiality, intrinsic or irreversible identity], just like this tohu. Nevertheless, the world is based upon them."[7] In accordance with Rashi's exegesis of Rav Hanin's text, the world is based upon – is created – by the power of speech. The form that the world has (rather than its persisting in its original state of formlessness) is a function of speech. The primacy attached to language in the act of creation suggests that words are underdetermined by things. It is the words that are used that give shape to the world, rather than the things of the world being classifiable by one univocal appellation in each case. However, since this skeptical inversion of the common sense understanding of the relationship between words and things gives rise to a whole set of logical conundrums and aporias epitomized by the dilemma that to be consistently skeptical requires one to be skeptical of skepticism as well as of other possibilities (so that even the verbal categoriztion of skepticism is inadequate to the phenomena it seeks to reflect), then the formlessness connoted by the phrase tohu wa-bhohu is preserved as the pregnant underside or shadow of the multifarious forms imposed by words. The formlessness is sustainable as an indefinite openness which suggests that Messianism in one direction as well as a return to primal chaos in the other direction both coexist alongside all of our exercises in fragile

---

7. My translation.

worldmaking in which (in accordance with the Biblical account) words have ontological priority over things.

What emerges from our discussion, therefore, is that (very ironically, again) the theme of "belatedness" is central to the original account of monotheistic Creation in the book of Genesis – and is not just a function of the belated location of Islam in the chain of monotheistic Revelations. "Belatedness," as it were, is intrinsic to the content of monotheism – and is not just an extrinsic feature attached to Islam's historical location.

To return to our explication of "belatedness" in Sura II: A supplementary angle of vision converging upon the same point I was making earlier: When one realizes how the attempt to verbally trace the radical oneness of God burns all of the conceptual bridges to our existing vocabularies (oneness in a comparative human setting which would allow us to conserve literalism in our conception of Divinity would render God from a monotheistic perspective just another human artifact and not the Supreme Being residing above and beyond all that we can perceive and know), one begins to appreciate how this radical oneness can only be conceptually plotted through persistent and unrelenting acts of disowning. Oneness (and the other attributes that we ascribe to God) needs to be understood in metaphoric (but not in literal) terms. The only way that we can conceptually map God – that we can be sure that our focus is the monotheistic God and not some projected human substitute – is by continually divesting all of the attributes that we ascribe to Him of literal import. However, this immediately gives rise to a paradox. How can we have a grammatical subject to disown, if our only form of access to – our only mode of identification of – this grammatical subject consists of the very acts of conceptual disowning themselves? The paradox surrounding negative theology bears a close resemblance to a key paradox surrounding skepticism. The skeptic who questions everything does not question the legitimacy of his questioning. Both negative theology and skepticism stand poised to eviscerate themselves in their own critiques – so that if negative theology and skepticism were consistently applied, there would be no subject matter labeled either negative theology or skepticism that could themselves serve as the object of their critiques.

Once the problematic of conceptually delimiting the tenets of the negative theological construal of the monotheistic God is explored, we have an additional perspective from which to appreciate how monotheism is belated. To try and discursively state what monotheism is about is already after monotheism – leaves it depleted of (coherent) content.

The monotheistic conception of God enshrined in the Bible and the Qu'ran leaves us with an infinite string of metaphors to describe and refer to God – without an Ur reality that can be designated and delimited. In this crucial sense, as well, monotheism is belated.

If monotheism is acknowledged to be belated in the senses I have described, then skepticism, toleration, and liberalism in the sense of the philosophical principle of authority being grounded in consent are built into monotheistic doctrine. From the belated series of perspectives I have described, the phrase "monotheistic religion" represents an institutionalized tension. Monotheism is largely about the absence and conceptual non-negotiability of God – and religion is about a way of life whose central symbol and legitimating source is God. How does one begin to make sense of – to theoretically reconstruct – the transition between the two – monotheism and religion? I would submit that the most plausible way to do this is to invoke mechanisms of consent all the way from the Prophet and the prophets on down to communities of believers at large to interpret the relevant metaphors and to abide by their contents in ways that yield the respective monotheistic traditions of Judaism, Christianity, and Islam in all of their richness and complexity. Correlative to the centrality being assigned to consent in this theorizing of monotheism, therefore, is a recognition of a plurality of monotheistic traditions as legitimately following from the most coherent theorizing of "monotheistic religion" we can come up with.

SOME OF THE OTHER MAJOR THEMES OF SURA II

Thought

In 2:1 (p. 30), the Qu'ran refers to "the godfearing who believe in the Unseen, and perform the prayer." The swift juxtaposition of these two phrases ("believing in the Unseen" and "performing the prayer") appears to be classically negative theological. Believing in the monotheistic God renders God unseen not only in the empirical sense that we do not as a matter of fact get to see Him, but in the deeper theoretical sense that given His Radical Oneness and Uniqueness verbs of perception are not applicable to Him at all - so that as a matter of principled theological delineation no human beings ever get to see Him. The incompleteness and irresolvability of human thought in its efforts to intellectually grasp God exposes thinking itself as a species of doing since it is not able to consummate its object.

Thinking is an effort, a movement, an initiation of something - rather than something thoroughly self-sufficient and transparent as our classical images of thought tell us it should be. Incomplete thought can only have as its sequel unlimited acts of doing such as those connoted by the term "prayer." Thinking that cannot penetrate its object becomes itself a form of prayer - a kind of watchful waiting and nurturing of a hope that fulfills itself (to a large extent) in the waiting and the nurturing.

At 2:18 (p. 31) the text states, "Truly, God is powerful over everything." This sentence obliquely and cryptically announces the riddle of human freedom. If there were no countervailing category to "God's power," then, indeed, the writing of this sentence (and the whole Qu'ranic Revelation itself) would be pointless. If God, as it were, got His way all the time, then it would not make sense for the Qu'ranic Revelation (with this sentence included) to appear at all - with its obvious concern to guide human beings onto the ways of God by overcoming temptation, inertia, slothfulness and all the other propensities that periodically deflect human beings away from what their higher selves would affirm. The grammar of the term "power," therefore, is such that in this context (as in most other contexts) it needs to be construed in relational terms. God is powerful over everything only if the human beings over whom He supremely exercises this power retain a significant degree of freedom capable, as it were, of resisting Him (and also of following Him), so that His power needs to be exercised over them. The Qu'ran, in fact, embraces a doctrine of radical human freedom at 4:80: "Whatever good visits thee, it is of God; whatever evil visits thee is of thyself." In order to sustain its intelligibility and coherence, therefore, "God's power" needs to be correlated with human freedom. We need to theorize both categories, both levels of analysis – the omnipotent God and the free-willing human being – so that they do not interfere with and neutralize each other. Perhaps, the most cogent way to accomplish this is by a negative theology – to say that we do not literally know what power signifies in relation to the monotheistic God, so that as a matter of definitional postulational acknowledgement God's power is thoroughly reconcilable with human freedom. What I have said would explain why the Qu'ran at this point in its exposition makes reference only to the one category and not to the other. Since from a negative theological perspective both categories can be real and neither category interferes with the other, one can start out from either of them and traverse the same ground covered by a contrasting organizing perspective provided by the other category.

Another negative theological devolution is expressed at 2:19: "O you men, serve your Lord Who created you, and those that were before you." In this verse we seem to move from the negative theological God to the primacy of religious tradition ("serve ... those that were before you"). On negative theological grounds which debar us from having literal access to God, when we serve God we can only be serving and following those who preceded us in the chain of religious tradition.

Freedom and Covenant

The theme of human freedom and its negative theological resonances are echoed again at 2:23:

> God is not ashamed to strike a similitude even of a gnat,
> or aught above it. As for the believers, they know it is the truth from their Lord; but as for unbelievers, they say, 'What did God desire by this for a similitude?' Thereby He leads many astray, and thereby He guides many; and thereby He leads none astray save the ungodly such as break the covenant of God after its solemn binding.

This passage emphasizes how human freedom is secured by the uncertainty of God's signs which are interpreted in conflicting ways by believers and unbelievers. The monotheistic God communicates with his human followers in a necessarily ambiguous way. What He is trying to tell us is communicated through symbolic systems that do not carry their sense or reference on their sleeves. For someone whose interpretive framework is monotheistically-suffused, the appearance of a gnat within one's field of experience might be a harbinger of some secret message from God concerning the steps that the believer needs to take in order to bring his life into greater harmony with God's requirements. For the unbeliever, the gnat is a sheerly naturalistic phenomenon to be engaged on a surface level relating to its possible utilities and nuisance capacity as an insect. God can address us by inserting a gnat in our environment, but He cannot constrain the interpretive framework – whether that of the believer or the unbeliever – in which we place him. If He crushed that freedom rendering the theological reading of the gnat the only one possible – or (what converges with the same point on a more sublimated level) if God outfitted us with a transcendent perspective so that we would look at the gnat the same way that He does – then we would not be the appropriate human partners to God's Revelation that the Qu'ran envisions.

In this context, it is significant that the central theological term in this passage is the word "covenant." From the time of the Hebrew Scriptures onward, the language of covenant is the definitive idiom of negative theology. "Covenant," which belongs to the same family of terms as "compact" and "contract," highlights the pivotal role of will rather than intellect – of agreement rather than knowledge – as forming the basis for our relationship with the monotheistic God. The imagery of "covenant" places at the forefront of our consciousness the idea that we cannot know God but can only conform our will to His by entering into an agreement with Him. The catchphrase of the first monotheistic nation – the Jewish people – when they enter into their covenant with God under Moses' tutelage at Mount Sinai is "Na'aseh V'Nishmah"[8] – which literally translated means we will do and we will listen. Doing – conforming to the terms of the covenant – comes before listening and rationally grasping what these terms are about. In relation to the rationally impenetrable and inscrutable monotheistic God, this ordering of responses does not constitute a reversal of the most intelligible order but is the only way that any response altogether can take place. The listening and understanding that follow such a primary doing can only consist in grasping why the doing has to come first if any response at all is to be forthcoming.

To be properly consistent in our delineation of the vocabulary of "covenant" we would have to say that God's will, just like His intellect, is not accessible to us in literal terms. The category of "will" is invoked in relation to the monotheistic God in order to block our recourse to the term "intellect" – but is in no way itself transparent. "Covenant" is deployed in the Bible and the Qu'ran as the manifestation of what we might call a negative hermeneutics[9] – to deflect us away from a rationalistic construal to our relationship with God,

---

8. Exodus 24, 7.

9. See my discussion of a "negative hermeneutics" in *Skepticism, Belief, and the Modern: Maimonides to Nietzsche* (Ithaca: Cornell University Press, 1997), pp. 81-82.

without legitimating on a literal level an irrational construal (grounded in will) of that relationship.

Sura II then goes on to proclaim God's omniscience: "and He has knowledge of everything" (2:27). An analogous paradox to what impels us to reconfigure our conception of God's power affects our theorizing of God's knowledge. In order for the term "knowledge" to be relevant in the sentential contexts that we are familiar with, what is known has to have some degree of even problematic independence (as in the case of skeptical idealism) from the knower's ability to know it. But in the case of God one of the classic monotheistic ways for registering the overwhelming chasm that separates Him from us is to say that for Him there are no hiatuses or transitions between the Knower – the Process of Knowing – and the Objects of Knowledge[10]. For God, all of this occurs in one fell swoop – one point-instant – the temporal metaphor itself being but a human metaphoric projection. The most promising route seems to be with regard to knowledge (as it is with regard to power) to say that we do not grasp what God's knowledge is and that what is relevant for our theoretical and theological stock-taking are the human modes of knowledge that have been historically developed.

The unbridgeable ontological distance separating us from God is again emphasized at 2:99: "but God singles out for His mercy whom He will; God is of bounty

---

10. See the discussion of Avicenna – who formulates this position – later in this paper. Also, see Moses Maimonides, *Code: Book of Knowledge: Laws of Repentance,* Chapter Five, Paragraph Five.

abounding." God is not accountable to human canons of morality and goodness. He is beyond our vocabularies and canons of judgment altogether. In what sense, then, is His "bounty abounding"? How can what from our perspective must necessarily look like Divine arbitrariness be symptomatic of "bounty abounding"? I think that one persuasive way of making sense of this phrase in the Qu'ran is to say that the very detaching of Divine canons of morality and judgment from their human counterparts (their metaphysical dissociation one from the other) is the source of the "bounty." What follows from the disengagement of the two vocabularies is the indirect underwriting of unlimited human freedom which is the source of the "bounty abounding." Not being able to touch base with God by juxtaposing our thoughts and actions to His literally-stated and graspable canons of morality and judgment not only enhances our freedom (and makes us in this crucial sense more God-like, if we conceive of God as the repository of supreme freedom), but also most importantly from the perspective of this passage confers upon us the ability to behave more morally. Correlative to the notion of enhanced freedom goes the idea of expanded responsibility – so that God's "bounty abounding" is underscored for us by His making available to us through His very impenetrability and unknowability the categorial tools to fashion the most richly moral life.

In the light of the negative theological hermeneutic that I have been both applying to and teasing out of the Qu'ran, a familiar sentiment such as that expressed by the following lines can be interpreted in a new way: "Whoso exchanges belief for unbelief has surely strayed from the right way" (2:103). Aside from alluding to the repeatedly stated rewards that accrue to the believer and the often repeated punishments that await the unbeliever, the passage can be read as affirming the value of belief generally and calling attention to the disutilities attached to unbelief. The pattern engendered by the negative theological paradigm of God is not unique to God but gets duplicated in most other areas of human thought and practice. Just as the ontologically unbridgeable distance between us and God requires us to believe in Him before we can lay claim to knowing Him – our systematic knowledge of Him can only be built up on the basis of a prior belief in Him, rather than our epistemological case for Him being so strong that it invites belief – so, too, with regard to most other phenomena in the world belief precedes knowledge.[11] The infinite distance that separates words from things microcosmically encodes the infinite distance that separates God from the cosmos as a whole. Given how most things, events, states of affairs in the world are susceptible to more than one verbal description (and sometimes even conflicting descriptions can manage to make equal sense of them), unless we believed in one or another of these verbal encapsulations of events we

---

11. This is an idea which in the history of religious thought is famously associated with St. Augustine. See the discussion by James Smith, "Is Deconstruction an Augustinian Science: Augustine, Derrida, and Caputo on the Commitments of Philosophy" in James H. Olthuis, ed., *Religion with/out Religion: The Prayers and Tears of John D. Caputo* (London: Routledge, 2002), pp. 50-61.

could not set in motion the cumulative dynamic that facilitates the acquisition of knowledge.

Belief

From this monotheistically-inspired perspective on the field of knowledge generally, belief is the phenomenon that facilitates the attainment of the human good. ("Exchanging belief for unbelief" – succumbing to the temptation of trying to become a totally free spirit, if that were indeed possible – represents a straying "from the right way.") The idea of belief in a crucial sense is more important than the content of belief in order to promote the human good. The Qu'ran echoes a text at the beginning of Genesis that I referred to earlier when it says: "And when He decrees a thing, He but says to it 'Be,' and it is" (2:111). One of the most remarkable features of the story of Creation at the beginning of Genesis is that God is conceived as creating through speech. This formulation represents a further ramification of the theme of belatedness that I discussed earlier. A reversal of roles appears to have taken place between the exemplar and its example.

As I suggested in the previous paragraph, monotheistic theology appears as the exemplar of the idea of infinite ontological distance between God and the world – and the example of this idea of infinite ontological distance that seems to pervade the world that we collectively inhabit is that which prevails between words and things given the underdetermination of words by things. Yet, in the account of the monotheistic God found at the beginning of Genesis (which the Qu'ran affirms), the metaphor has switched directions. The question of what is being seen in the light of what has become muddied. God's unbridgeable distance from the world is captured in the very terminology - calling, affixing a name - which is supposed to be the hallmark of what is being construed in the light of the monotheistic conception of God, namely the not-fully-grounded and residually arbitrary character of all of the words that we use to confer being and identity upon (to individuate as discrete items) the diverse furniture of the world. The apparent conflation between the exemplar and the example in the Biblical and Qu'ranic accounts of Creation constitutes a further strand of belatedness in those accounts.

At 2:116, the text states: "Children of Israel, remember My blessing wherewith I blessed you, and that I have preferred you above all beings." The preference for the Jews seems to be a form of reiteration of pure monotheism. Islam commits itself to the pure monotheistic belief represented by Judaism, in contrast to Christianity. In further specifying what the nature of this monotheism is, the text continues a few verses later: "Who therefore shrinks from the religion of Abraham, except he be foolish-minded? Indeed, We chose him in the present world, and in the world to come he shall be among the righteous" (2:124). Islam sees itself as a continuation of the religion of Abraham. The religion of Abraham embedded in the Biblical narrative of his life and career is a rationalistic faith. Abraham is concerned to discredit and dispel the fallacies and the fantasies of the faiths of the polytheistic nations in his environment who situate divinities everywhere within their natural landscapes and strives instead to discover the one overarching, unifying principle responsible for all of the multiplicity he encounters in nature and history. The Platonic dialectic of the One and the Many[12] is not a monopoly of Greek consciousness but is very dramatically and forcefully evident in the Hebrew Bible. One of its nodal points of exemplification is the personality and career of Abraham. The rationalistic faith of Abraham lends support to a negative theological reading (which pushes religious rationalism to its logical conclusions) of monotheism generally and of the theology of the Qu'ran in particular.

In close juxtaposition to the passages I have just cited in the second Sura is the one I cited in the previous section of the paper which situates Islam along the chain of monotheistic tradition commencing with Abraham and Judaism and culminating with itself. In accordance with the Qu'ran's own description of its pedigree, Islam at its founding represents the inauguration of a new monotheistic tradition alongside several preexisting traditions. Qu'ranic Revelation is about the need to found a new monotheistic tradition to more effectively disseminate the pristine content of the old ones – not to articulate in new terms the content of monotheistic Revelation. The Qu'ran stresses the need for a purified, fully committed, and revivified monotheistic tradition – not the suspension of tradition for the sake of connecting

---

12. Plato, *The Republic*, 596a.

as many people as possible with the charismatic source of monotheism.

At 2:143 the verse states: "The truth comes from thy Lord; then be not among the doubters." Notice the distinctiveness of the formulation here. The Lord, as it were, is not the truth – but the truth *comes from Him*, is distinct and separable from Him. Even if (as negative theology advocates) the truth turns out to be a truth of limitation – highlighting what we are not able to do, the distances that we cannot traverse – it comes from the Lord. You do not need to work with a more maximalist truth than this in order to become heir to monotheistic teaching. This reading receives corroboration from two verses further down which refers to the role of the Messenger or Prophet as being "to teach you that you knew not." The teacher – the Prophet – teaches us preeminently the depth and extent of our ignorance. What the human mind is not able to accomplish through direct validation and argument even with regard to this-worldly affirmations, shows the pervasiveness of skepticism; that is of how skepticism even defeats a coherent formulation of itself negatively considered, – i.e. that those who attack God are as logically vulnerable as those who defend Him) – this creates the space for the possibility of God.

The text continues a little further on with the statement that "Surely God is with the patient" (2:148). Patience is a key virtue because endless deferral is the distinguishing feature of monotheistic religion. To believe in the monotheistic God requires you to endlessly disown the literal applicability of the terms that you use to describe Him. The monotheistic believer scrupulously and unrelentingly peels away all of the outward conceptual layers that are officially supposed to delimit God without getting to the core. He remains fully and everlastingly preoccupied with discounting the counterfeit conceptual approximations to God without arriving at God in the full-blooded positive sense. The ethical correlative to monotheistic belief is patience – sustaining an endless waiting without succumbing either to the finality of despair or the false allure of apocalyptic deliverance.

At 2:159, the Qu'ran conjures up an Argument from Design:

> Surely in the creation of the heavens and the earth and the alternation of night and day and the ship that runs in the sea with profit to men, and the water God sends down from heaven therewith reviving the earth after it is dead and His scattering abroad in it all manner of crawling thing, and the turning about of the winds and the clouds compelled between heaven and earth – surely there are signs for a people having understanding.

The Argument from Design enshrined in this passage coheres very well with the tenets of negative theology. There is an intimate conceptual bond between negative theology and the Argument from Design. We might say that having been banished by negative theology from existing in the heavens in a literal sense, "God" is reinscribed in the natural order as the beneficiary of an argument from design. In order for the nonliteral, conceptually vacuous monotheistic God to hover in the furthermost cosmological reaches – to be nowhere humanly cognizable and attainable – His actions must be engraved in nature; then we can appropriately demarcate Him from all the verbs and adjectives that we might be tempted to mobilize in describing Him. God has to be transparently inferable from the order of nature to yield the string of verbs and adjectives through which monotheistic theology theorizes Him as the hidden God. However, negative theology's draining of all literal content from God forces the Argument from Design to proceed by way of analogy with the work of a human artificer, not by way of a direct reading from nature.

Ascetic and Life Values

The strongly anti-ascetic impulse of Islam is expressed in Sura II. As a motto for this impulse, one can cite the verse – "God desires ease for you, and desires not hardship for you" (II:181). There is a parallel text to this in the Bible as Rabbinically interpreted: "Ye shall therefore keep my ordinances and my judgments; which if a man do, he shall live in them," says the verse in Leviticus.[13] The Rabbis draw an immediate inference from this saying "And he should not die in them."[14] For example, when the laws of the Torah conflict with the imperative of life, the laws are suspended in favor of the preservation of life. All of the laws of the Sabbath not

---

13. Leviticus 18, 5.
14. Babylonian Talmud, Yoma 85b.

only can be but should be transgressed in order to facilitate the rescuing of a sick Jew on the Sabbath. Apparently, within the legal horizon of Judaism, religious law is viewed as an instrumentality for promoting and enhancing life – and not as a basis for weakening it or snuffing it out altogether.

A sentiment in favor of all that the value of life connotes is expressed in the Qu'ran. During the month of Ramadan when Muslims fast the whole of each day, the Qu'ran goes out of its way to state that "Permitted to you, upon the night of the Fast, is to go in to your wives" (2:183). The asceticism connoted by the month of Ramadan in the Muslim calendar alternates with physical pleasure on a daily basis. The ethics of daily living in Judaism and Islam is drawn to the same scale as monotheistic theology. Just as we have seen that monotheism is bound up with cultivation of an everlasting middle so, too, with regard to the conduct of daily life there is no warrant for pure asceticism. One has to forge strategies for sustaining the middle – which means that at best withdrawal from pleasure has to alternate with pleasure.

With regard to regulations pertaining to relations between the sexes, there is an overall parallel structure between Jewish law and Islamic law. Both Judaism and Islam prohibit sexual relations with menstruating women. Both religions require a rite of purification through water before the sexes can be rejoined. This is the way the Qu'ran expresses it: "When they [the women] have cleansed themselves, then come unto them as God has commanded you" (2:223). The reentry into sex after the mandatory separation during the woman's period is not simply a permission in Jewish and Islamic law; it is a positive requirement. In Judaism and Islam, having sexual relations with one's wife is not just an indulgence; it constitutes fulfillment of a Divine commandment.

Unlike traditional Catholicism, both Judaism and Islam sanction divorce. Radical monotheism which is responsive to the rationalist scruples of the probing, inquiring mind feeds into a respect for persons in broader legal spheres. In their divorce laws, both Judaism and Islam allow respect for persons to trump the principle of the sanctity of marriage. If a couple are seriously not getting along and thwarting each other rather than nurturing each other's existence, then dissolving a marriage might have more religious sanction than sustaining it. In introducing or affirming disorder in people's lives, the rationalist, calculating sensibilities of Judaism and Islam warn us that we must proceed in an orderly fashion. The Rabbis had earlier decreed that there must be a three-month waiting period between a woman's marriages to allow us to decisively distinguish the paternity of her offspring.[15] If a woman were to be allowed to remarry immediately after divorce, and she gave birth in the seventh month after her remarriage, we could not tell with certainty in an age prior to genetic testing whether the woman became pregnant from her first husband and the child had been in gestation nine months – or whether she was impregnated by her second husband and the child was born after seven months. In

15. Babylonian Talmud, Yebamoth, Chapter Four, Mishnah 10.

order to remove all doubt, the Rabbis required a three-month waiting period between the marriages. In this, they are echoed by the Qu'ran: "Divorced women shall wait by themselves [i.e., in their divorced state] for three periods" (2:226).

There is also a very interesting reaffirmation in the Qu'ran of the Rabbinic law concerning the betrothal of women – known in Hebrew as Kiddushin (literally, sanctification, or setting aside). The Qu'ran states: "But do not make troth with them [i.e., women] secretly without you speak honorable words" (2:235). According to Qu'ranic law, a woman does not become betrothed to a man unless he recites to her a specific verbal formula to which she consents. One of the major precursors for this is the Rabbinic requirement that a man recite to a woman in the presence of two witnesses the formula "You are hereby betrothed ["mekudeshet" in Hebrew] unto me with this ring [or other object of monetary value] in accordance with the law of Moses and of Israel" in order for her to become legally betrothed to him. Kiddushin and its Islamic counterpart constitute performative utterances in J. L. Austin's sense.[16] They involve a saying that is also a form of doing, a type of enactment. By verbalizing a particular string of words, something is irrevocably altered in the real world – a new relationship between two human beings has come into being.

---

16. J. L. Austin, *How to Do Things with Words*. Ed. J. O. Urmson. (Oxford: Oxford University Press, 1962); J. L. Austin, "Performative Utterances," in *Philosophical Papers*. Ed. J. O. Urmson and G. J. Warnock. (Oxford: Oxford University Press, 1961), pp. 220-239.

"Kiddushin" is etymologically linked to the word "kedushah" which means holiness. Kiddushin symbolically encodes – or encapsulates – the secret of Kedushah in monotheistic religion. The holiness emanating from (or attached to) monotheistic religion – just like the sanctified status of marriage in Jewish and Islamic law – is a function of speech doubling as a deed. Since monotheism stipulates that we do not get to God in a literal sense, our whole religious vocabulary of statements that invoke and describe God and insert Him in multiple contexts in our everyday lives have the effect of also serving as the deeds that render God real for us – transforming His very unbridgeable distance into a pervasive presence in our lives.

Further examples of this phenomenon in Judaism are Kiddush, Kedushah, and Kaddish – all terms that are etymologically expressive of holiness. "Kiddush" refers to the blessings recited over – the sanctification of – the wine which must precede dinner and lunch on the sabbath in order for one to be able to eat. The recitation of these blessings is both a verbalizing of formulaic statements – and an enactment, so to speak, of the Sabbath. The holiness of the sabbath is conjured up out of a prosaic and biologically necessary occasion of eating and drinking by the saying of the blessings. Through the speech-act of Kiddush, ordinary Jews help to fashion and refashion on a weekly basis the Sabbath.

The central part of the Jewish prayer service is called the Amidah – literally, the standing, since the Jew must recite it standing up rather than sitting down. In the way that the structure of Jewish prayer is envisioned by the

Rabbis, at the Amidah the Jew stands closest to God – in the inner sanctum, so to speak, after having penetrated figuratively speaking through the recitation of more preliminary prayers the outer precincts of the Seraphim, Cherubim, other angels, etc. After the Amidah is recited silently by each member of the congregation, it is publicly-repeated by the prayer-leader, and after the second blessing the Kedushah is said. (The weekly Amidah consists of nineteen blessings – the first three affirming God's greatness and bounty – the intermediate thirteen consisting of petitionary prayers in which we beseech God's help across the board for our needs ranging from knowledge to justice to sustenance – and the final three expressing thanksgiving to God for all the good He has bestowed upon us. The Sabbath and Holiday Amidah [except for the High Holidays of Rosh Hashanah and Yom Kippur – New Year and the Day of Atonement] consists of seven blessings – the first three and the last three remaining the same as the weekday Amidah and the intervening seventh blessing extolling the Kedushat Hayom, the specialness of the day, in the Jewish calendar.[17]) The Kedushah is mainly devoted to affirming God's kingship over us – and the holiness and specialness attached to that kingship. Again, the Kedushah is most tellingly classified as a speech-act – in which we not only describe God in certain ways, but the very verbalization of these descriptions fixes Him in our consciousness as

---

17. See the essay by Rabbi Joseph B. Soloveitchik, "Prayer as Dialogue," in Abraham R. Besdin, ed., *Reflections of the Rav* (Jerusalem: Alpha Press, 1979), pp. 71-88.

harboring those characteristics that we attribute to Him. He becomes holy, as it were, through our affirmations of His holiness.

The Kaddish which is the special prayer recited by mourners for departed family members at the conclusion of the regular prayer services exhibits a similar motif. The Kaddish to a large extent is about reconciliation – reconciling the individual Jew who has just experienced a keen sense of loss to the greatness, majesty, and holiness of God. The reconciliation is achieved (if it is achieved at all) not through any particular phrases in the Kaddish which articulate this theme – but merely through the juxtaposition of the impenetrable holiness of God voiced in the Kaddish to the very earth-bound, deep, and festering suffering experienced by the individual mourner. The yawning distance between Divine greatness and human paltriness evinced by the Kaddish in its inability to generate an adequate response to the mourner's sense of grief and loss paradoxically becomes itself the source of reconciliation for the mourner. The language of the Kaddish does not and cannot engage the intensity of the mourner's despair. The overwhelming distance between the plight of the mourner and God's holiness leaves the mourner confirmed with his question(s). The refusal of any easy answers that is enshrined in the Kaddish paradoxically clues the mourner into noticing how willy-nilly the question(s) itself (themselves) must become the answer(s) – how reaching rock bottom cannot help becoming the orientating moment toward a new future. None of what I have just said is ever articulated in the Kaddish. It is rather enacted and dramatized through the recitation of the sentences celebrating God's majesty which constitute the major part of the overt content of the Kaddish.

Kedushah – holiness generally in monotheistic religion – is thus a function of a series of speech-acts – of strings of words that also constitute central aspects of a specially structured and inhabited world.

There is a very arresting passage at 2:186 (which is reiterated at 2:212) which could be read as cluing us in to the depth theological structure of the Qu'ran: "But aggress not: God loves not the aggressors.... Persecution is more grievous than slaying. Then, if they fight you, slay them." "Persecution is more heinous than slaying." What emerges from these passages is an ethic of rigorous self-defense. The defense for slaying is only saving or defending one's own life.[18] The community of the faithful is theologically debarred from aggressively hunting down others unless it is a matter of preserving or conserving one's own life. Being an aggressor automatically puts one's own life at risk and therefore the only way to be faithful to the imperative to conserve life is to fight defensively – i.e., when not to respond at all would jeopardize one's life more profoundly than responding. The supreme value in these passages seems to be assigned

---

18. The Rabbis in the Babylonian Talmudic tractates of Sanhedrin 72a and Yoma 85b famously enunciate a parallel principle: "Hence the Torah decreed, 'If he come to slay thee, forestall by slaying him.'" The Biblical verse from which this inference is drawn is found in Exodus 22, 1: "If the thief be found breaking in, and be smitten that he die, there shall no guilt of blood be incurred for him."

to life itself. What is the connection between primacy being assigned to life and the negative theological framework of argument that seems to be so prominent in this chapter of the Qu'ran?

Agnostic and Humane

As we have seen, negative theology (just like skepticism) persistently undermines itself by continually presupposing that which it relentlessly attacks. Negative theology attacks the thick, literally resplendent notion of God by discounting all of our literal descriptions of God as metaphors. God's radical oneness it proclaims is incompatible with any even tenuous insertion of God into a comparative human context. Hence, the need for a metaphoric reading of all of the attributes that we ascribe to Him. However, the theological character of negative theology is disrupted by this very move. If our only strategy of conceptual access to the monotheistic God is through a perpetual disowning of the literal import of the attributes ascribed to Him, then in what sense can negative theology claim to be theorizing the nature of God? This is analogous to the paradox confronted by the skeptic who in the course of questioning everything has somehow left out of account the questioning of the enterprise that he is embarked upon - namely, the questioning of everything. The skeptic seems to have gone so far in his critique of knowledge that he fails to realize that his critique has deconstructed even his own skepticism. By the same token, the negative theologian does not seem to realize that in his pervasive and systematic attack on a literal construal of the attributes traditionally ascribed to God, he has undermined our ability to talk about God at all.

Perhaps the most coherent move to make at this point is to say that the cash value of negative theology (just like the cash value of skepticism) is as a generalized agnosticism. Negative theology keeps the question of God continually open - without providing us with a definitive answer. The negative theological regrouping of the attributes ascribed to God as metaphors terminates in paradox and incoherence which keeps us more narrowly focused on phenomena and experiences in this world - but this does not translate into a *disproof* of God's existence. With regard to this question negative theology can consistently remain agnostic. The skeptic, analogously, in order to retain the consistency of his position does not have to discard skepticism - he just has to question it alongside all of the other doctrines that he questions. In other words, the skeptic only has to generalize the agnosticism of the negative theologian in order to emerge as consistent.

A generalized agnosticism places a special premium on life as the supreme value. From a generalized agnostic perspective, in any given human generation the returns are not yet fully in with regard to the traditional range of questions driving human inquiry - from God to the structure of the most elementary particles of matter. Each human generation is both a recipient and custodian of the inquiries and speculations of its predecessors - and a placeholder for the reflections and investigative work of its successors. In a generalized-agnostic thought-world where the most we can achieve are interim revisions of interim hypotheses, a special value attaches to life itself (the nourishing and sustaining of it) as the crucial medium that enables these protracted and endless revisions to take place.

I am arguing that given the consistency with which a negative theological framework seems to be applied in the second Sura of the Qu'ran that when in the passages cited above it affirms the primacy of life it resonates with the set of metaphysical understandings I have just charted. Life is primary and needs to be secured to the furthest extent possible because in all of our lurchings to the beyond-life we get catapulted back to the primordial rhythms and limits of life itself as the indispensable means for imagining and perhaps in the course of time attaining some degree of transcendence of these limits. So far the human record in its logical, experimental, theological, and theoretical domains seems to be that our efforts to get beyond the metaphysical middle just restores us to that middle – which is to say an affirmation and embrace of the means, of life itself.

There is a striking convergence between the Qu'ran's singling out for special vigilance the middle prayer of its daily regimen of prayers – and the Talmud stressing the importance of Mincha (the middle prayer in the daily schedule of prayers) for the religious and spiritual life of the Jew. The Qu'ranic formulation is as follows: "Be you watchful over the prayers, and the middle prayer" (2:239). In the Babylonian Talmudic tractate of Berakoth 6b, we find the following statement: "Rav Helbo further said in the name of Rav Huna: A man should always take special care about the afternoon-prayer. For even Elijah was favorably heard only while offering his afternoon prayer. For it is said: 'And it came to pass at the time of the offering of the evening offering [which is offered in the middle-to-late afternoon], that Elijah the prophet came near and said ... hear me, O Lord, hear me' (I Kings 18, 36-37). 'Hear me', that fire may descend from heaven, and 'hear me' that they may not say it is the work of sorcery."[19] Why is the middle prayer singled out for special emphasis and spiritual connection? One might say that paradoxically it is a result of its being the most negative theological of the prayers – the one least evocative of spiritual presence.

The reason for this is its timing. It is scheduled for the middle of the day when people are generally most absorbed in their daily activities centering around the need to earn a living and the minutiae of daily life. I once heard the great Talmudic sage and philosopher Rabbi Joseph B. Soloveitchik say in a public lecture that what is phenomenologically epitomized by the Mincha prayer is "interruption." To pray the middle prayer of the day requires one to interrupt his daily round of activities – to take time out from his myriad absorptions and distractions – to focus on momentary spiritual connection. In contrast to the morning prayer to which we can devote all our energies because we have just gotten up and our daily round of activities has not yet begun – and the evening prayer which is offered when we are winding down from our daily immersions in the affairs of

---

19. *The Babylonian Talmud: Berakoth*. Trans. Maurice Simon. (London: Soncino Press, 1984).

the world and therefore more easily poised to concentrate and "recollect in tranquility" – the afternoon prayer is said when we are still in the thick of our involvements, when it requires a specially strenuous effort to set aside time and energy to do it. The afternoon prayer – more than the morning and evening prayers – constitutes a symbolic correlative to the status of religious belief and the believer from the perspective of negative theology. Negative theology does not allow us to forget for one instant that no matter how hard we try to spiritually ascend, we still always remain in the metaphysical middle, overwhelmed by the logical untidiness of our spiritual preoccupations from reaching God. From a negative theological perspective, the monotheistic believer is always in the midst of the middle prayer – the world of logic and reason and this-worldly concerns generally is always too much with him. His nurturance of the middle prayer despite the pervasiveness of all of these adverse conditions is symptomatic of the authentic monotheistic faith cultivated as it were despite itself.

It can only be negatively supported in the sense that no other way of life is any more reputable and defensible than it is – rather than being positively affirmed. Therefore it is singled out for special reward.

In a passage at 2:256, the paradox of negative theological prayer is further elaborated:

> God there is no God but He, the Living, the Everlasting. Slumber seizes Him not, neither sleep; to Him belongs all that is in the heavens and earth; the

preserving of them oppresses Him not; He is the All-high, the All-glorious.

No compulsion is there in religion.

This passage projects God as being so powerful - He is "the Living, the Everlasting" - the epitome of self-sufficiency - that He does not need prayer. His power extends to such a degree that it bursts the bounds of literal language to contain it: "The preserving of them [heavens and earth] oppresses Him not." This verse is clearly alluding to modes of "preservation" and "oppression" that defy our comprehension. It has pushed the frontiers of language beyond literalism to the plane of metaphor. How then can prayer be theorized in relation to the monotheistic God? There is a typographical hiatus in the printed page of this text which matches the metaphysical hiatus which we have just noticed - and then the response to both converging hiatuses is forthcoming: "No compulsion is there in religion." It is as if the text were telling us that given the metaphysical self-sufficiency and literal unapproachability of God, there is no way to justify prayer as something necessary or essential for God. Prayer is a matter of the this-worldly regulation of the religious life of a monotheistic community. It is vital in terms of what it accomplishes for human beings as monotheistic believers. Being in a prayerful stance enables us to become more sensitive to our own and other people's vulnerabilities - to become more compassionate - more humble - more oriented toward the other. It is in this sense that monotheistic prayer can be most coherently justified. If this is the case, though, then there can be "no compulsion ... in religion." Prayer is a matter of how monotheistic tradition (the plurality of monotheistic traditions) regulate the lives of monotheistic believers - what sorts of regimens and structures they provide for prayer. It is emphatically not a question of a direct relationship with God that one monotheistic Revelation can validate above all others.

The theme of how monotheistic religious practices and requirements redound to the self-interest and self-enhancement of the monotheistic believer is emphasized again at 2:271-272:

> If you publish your freewill offerings, it is excellent; but if you conceal them, and give them to the poor, that is better for you, and will acquit you of your evil deeds; God is aware of the things you do.... And whatever good you expend is for yourselves.

The passage begins by expressing a theme that is also found in Prophetic and Rabbinic literature of how giving sustenance to the poor is a more appropriate way of expressing contrition and re-directing oneself toward the path of good than bringing animal sacrifices.[20] The first part of the passage concludes with the statement that "God is aware of the things you do." In close proximity

---

20. "R. Eleazar stated, Greater is he who performs charity than [he who offers] all the sacrifices, for it is said, 'To do charity and justice is more acceptable to the Lord than sacrifices.' (Proverbs 21, 3)." Babylonian Talmud, Sukkah. Trans. Israel W. Slotki. (London: Soncino Press, 1984), 49b.

to this sentence is the verse which says that "Whatever good you expend is for yourselves," which suggests that the second verse serves as a negative theological gloss on the first. "God's awareness" is translated into our "expending for ourselves." Since "God's awareness" is a metaphor, the cash value of this metaphor is that we "expend for ourselves." Apparently, from the Qu'ran's perspective, it is not just prayer but all the other religious commandments that we follow that need to be interpreted in the light of the metaphysically disrupted trajectory between God and ourselves – so that whatever we do in monotheistic religion we are "doing for ourselves."

One of the central themes of Sura II is the importance of engaging in acts of charity and kindness toward other human beings – and particularly toward those who are less fortunate than ourselves. Kindness supersedes charity – so that giving a loan under favorable conditions to someone in need is looked upon more graciously by God than giving him outright charity. The following is a relevant passage: "Who is he that will lend God a good loan, and He will multiply it for him manifold? God grasps, and outspreads; and unto Him you shall be returned" (2:246-247). When we give the poor person "a good loan" – one with favorable terms of repayment – it is as if we were "lending God" – and "He will multiply it for us manifold." The next verse implicitly bids us to follow in the ways of God. Just as He "grasps, and outspreads," so should we not only accumulate wealth but expend it to help meet the needs of our less fortunate brethren. The Rabbis share this sense of priority – of assigning a higher status to loans offered under favorable conditions over outright charity: "R. Eleazar further stated: Gemiluth Hasadim [the practice of kindness, such as is exemplified in the giving of a loan] is greater than charity, for it is said, 'Sow to yourselves according to your charity, but reap according to your hesed [signifying Gemiluth Hasadim] (Hosea 10, 12)'; if a man sows, it is doubtful whether he will eat [the harvest] or not, but when a man reaps, he will certainly eat."[21]

Kindness and generosity emerge as central monotheistic virtues. This can be conceptualized in relation to negative theology. For negative theology, arbitrariness emerges as the fundamental epistemological category. Given the premises of negative theology and the dilemmas to which they give rise, all descriptions of Divine attributes misfire: They are equally epistemologically arbitrary. None of them can be applied directly, literally to God. For monotheistic religion, the ethical correlative to epistemological arbitrariness is loving-kindness or benevolence or generosity. The type of ethical practice conjured-up by the passage I have cited from the Qu'ran is a form of unstinting, utterly gallant generosity. The lack of a basis for a knowledge statement signifies arbitrariness; the lack of a basis in worldly factors and considerations for behaving kindly toward others constitutes generosity. Generosity serves to render active the passivity, the helplessness engendered by epistemological arbitrariness. By converting the lack of a basis for action into itself a principle of action, one

---

21. *Ibid.*

achieves generosity. Ethics redeems epistemology; principles of action render pliable and humanly usable irrefragable principles of thought.

Sura II is very heavily action-oriented, trying to affect and transform how monotheistic believers behave. This is captured in the following verse: "Those who believe and do deeds of righteousness, and perform the prayer, and pay the alms – their wage awaits them with their Lord, and no fear shall be on them, neither shall they sorrow" (2:277). "Belief" in this verse is immediately translated into the kinds of action incumbent upon the believer – "deeds of righteousness," "praying," and "paying alms." Since in monotheistic religion belief has no direct, literal object, it immediately devolves into doing good deeds. The rational incompleteness of monotheism translates into primacy being assigned to action. Thinking that cannot consummate its trajectory itself represents a form of action.

The emphasis on continual doing of good deeds in Sura II is complemented by the text's rejection of any notion of the fixity of human nature: "God charges no soul save to its capacity" (2:286). This verse suggests that the ultimate negative theological mandate is to become ourselves – to become who we are. Since human identity and excellence cannot be fixed or measured in relation to a literal Divine model, the standards for what we need to become remain internal and immanentist in character. We have to become who we are as our unfolding through the vicissitudes and challenges of time discloses to us again and again (usually in slightly altered configurations) the possibilities and limits of our being.

Sura II concludes with a very striking vision of the relationship between monotheistic religious authority and consent:

> He will forgive whom He will, and chastise whom He will; God is powerful over everything. The Messenger believes in what was sent down to him from his Lord, and the believers; each one believes in God and His angels, and in His Books and His Messengers. (2:284-285)

The passage begins by emphasizing that God is not accountable to our canons of reason and morality. His forgiveness and chastisement can be meted out in ways that defy our comprehension. In juxtaposition to this statement of the rational inaccessibility and lack of moral accountability of God is a three-fold repetition of the word "believe" as if to suggest that relating to the utterly transcendent God depicted in the previous verse from the Messenger on down to ordinary members of the religious community is a function of who or what one chooses to believe in. This text implicitly endorses consent as the legitimating source of religious authority. The need for consent in order to be governed by religious authority follows from the rational irresolvability of God. In this passage, an inscrutable basis for authority displaces unto a reconstructed version of consent as having the authority to authorize authority. If religious authority under the constraints of monotheistic protocols cannot authorize, then consent to a literally absent religious authority becomes the authorizing moment of religious authority.

The displacement, in effect, becomes a double - and even a triple - displacement. Authority displaces unto consent - and belief (the registering of consent) displaces unto the myriad actions that signify membership and participation in the religious tradition. Since these actions displaying conformity to religious directives and requirements always need to be interpreted and contextualized, they become hostage to future actions which re-accentuate and reconfigure how we are to interpret previous actions. In this way the monotheistic unknowability of God translates into the unknowability of man - with both God and man awaiting an unknown future to be confirmed in their identities. The arrow of time moves backward as well as forward for both God and man.

AVICENNA

Avicenna seems to converge with the negative theological understandings I have made central to my reading of Sura II. He maps the dynamics of theological inquiry in such a way that negative theology appears as the most appropriate conclusion to be drawn from the argument. He says that "contingent beings end in a Necessary Being" and that "the Necessary Being does not resemble any other thing in any respect whatsoever." He goes on to reject the imputation of literally-conceived attributes to Necessay Being - i.e., to God: "If it were to be stated that His Attributes are not an augmentation of His Essence, but that they entered into the constitution of the Essence, and that the Essence cannot be conceived of as existing without these attributes, then the Essence would be compound, and the Oneness would be destroyed."[22] The God that Avicenna finds delineated in the Qu'ran is apparently the God that on the surface brings the everlasting quest for reasons and causes to a halt – who is able to confine the endless proliferation of contingency by being an embodiment of necessity. In order for God to be the One Unifying Factor responsible for all of experience – to embody necessity in a complete and not in a partial sense – nothing about Him can derogate from His oneness. His being and His essence have to coincide – and the whole notion of attributes in a literal sense has to be banished from our vision of Him. Avicenna states that "A being which is necessary has no reason for its being."[23] Distinguishable attributes present in our notion of God would embed God in rational and causal networks of explanation stretching both before Him and after Him and would thus diminish from His character as God.

The rigor with which Avicenna wants to denude God of attributes also propels him to want to close as much as possible the gap that separates God from the objects of His creation, knowledge, and surveillance – namely, the world and the human beings that inhabit it. His formulation has distinctly pantheistic overtones – which suggests that pantheism in early medieval thought is not

---

22. *Avicenna on Theology*. Ed. and trans. Arthur J. Arberry. (London: John Murray, 1951), pp. 25, 28, and 30. All my citations of Avicenna are from this translation.

23. *Ibid.*, p. 28.

an independently wrought cosmological doctrine but rather a solution to a negative theological riddle, namely, How a God without humanly identifiable and cognizable attributes (whose points of intersection with other rational and causal networks has been obliterated, who represents necessity in the most complete sense imaginable) could yet be situated in the world. The solution to the riddle is to embed God in the world – to make the world the only locus that we need to talk about God. This is the way Avicenna frames his solution: Speaking about God, he writes, "Intelligence, intelligible, and intelligent are one thing, or nearly so. That the object so apprehended is more perfect in itself is manifest at once; that the realization too is more intense is likewise immediately obvious, if the foregoing argument is kept at all in mind."[24] God's being is thus "neither without the world nor within it"[25] – Avicenna's gesturings toward pantheism having effaced the boundaries between "inner" and "outer." Speaking about human beings, Avicenna says that "intellectual ends are more ennobling to the soul than other worthless things."[26] In relation to God, however, who represents Supreme Necessity and who therefore cannot be decoded into any humanly intelligible formulation, "intellectual ends," too, need to be considered as "worthless things."

Avicenna is unflinching in his willingness to embrace the implications that follow from his theological position.

---

24. *Ibid.*, p. 68.
25. *Ibid.*, p. 44.
26. *Ibid.*, p. 69.

If God needs to be thoroughly de-literalized in order to sustain a sufficiently coherent notion of necessity, then what about morality? How is the idea of reward and punishment to be accommodated? Avicenna has a remarkably deflationary and human-centered notion of reward and punishment: "The continuance of the soul in a state of imperfection is the state of remoteness from God: that is what is meant by being under a curse, suffering punishment, encountering Divine Wrath and Anger: the pain which the soul has to endure is a consequence of that imperfection. Similarly the perfection of the soul is what is meant by saying that God is pleased with it, that it is near and nigh unto God and close to God's Presence. Such then is the meaning of reward and punishment: this and nothing else."[27] For Avicenna, action is its own reward - and punishment. "Reward and punishment" does not conjure up anything extraneous beyond what is engendered and experienced by engaging in the respective actions themselves. Avicenna's understanding of "reward and punishment" is prefigured in a famous statement of the Rabbis: "Ben Azzai said: The reward of a mitzvah [fulfillment of a Divine commandment; performance of a good deed] is a mitzvah [being given the opportunity to perform another mitzvah in the wake of the first one; and also the satisfaction enjoyed from performing the mitzvah itself], and the wages of a transgression are a transgression [to be

---

27. *Ibid.*, p. 39.

explicated comparably to the way I interpreted "mitzvah."][28]

In the light of our discussion so far, we can say that when Avicenna describes "the business of the soul" as being "to apprehend the very essence of perfection by attaining through knowledge the unknown" what he is suggesting is that the point of theoretical and theological activity is to grapple with and attempt to delineate the limits to knowledge. The attempt to achieve knowledge of the whole, so to speak, by moving beyond the realm of contingency altogether to conceive of God as Pure Necessity yields a correlative domain of ignorance that matches in scope and magnitude our claim to knowledge of God. To conceive of God as Pure Necessity, Avicenna argues, requires us to displace unto non-literal uses all of the material characteristics and linguistic formulations traditionally associated with God. God is no longer in the heavens and can no longer bear the attributes that Western theology traditionally ascribes to Him if He is viewed as constituting Pure Necessity. The most colossal and inclusive knowledge-datum that we can come up with turns out under Avicenna's analytical scrutiny to yield the most dense and impenetrable ignorance that we can imagine. We are able to sustain the knowledge-claim only if we can simultaneously accommodate (somehow find ways of fitting-in) the correlatively huge areas of ignorance that it unleashes.

The fate of the God-concept is emblematic of the precariousness of all of our theoretical ascents in the

---

28. Mishnah Avot 4:2.

course of inquiring into and investigating different sectors of reality. Avicenna makes clear that part of the reason why our postulation of God has such ambiguous explanatory results is that "God" is not just an explanans (a statement or category doing the explaining) accounting for an explanandum (a statement or category of what needs to be explained – in this case, the world at large). Rather for each one of the mediating factors and attendant circumstances linking the explanans to the explanandum (which includes all of the Divine Attributes that serve as the bridges between God and the world) we can raise on a more restrictive level the question of ultimacy. Are these (the Divine attributes as classically defined) the ultimate mediating links between human beings and the world and God – or are there others which are above them (say, special intervention by God or an angel) or can serve as an alternative to them? More than one of them is usually relevant on any given occasion – e.g., power, knowledge, and compassion are usually in play on most occasions when we invoke Divine intercession. How do we know which mix of these Divine attributes – and what particular configuration of them – are the ones that prevail (should prevail) on any given occasion? One could argue that with regard to the God-world relationship at least the list of classically-received attributes is exhaustive (even if the potential for regrouping their mix and configuration is infinite). That would impinge upon the question of arbitrariness for we would not have to worry about other than the traditional attributes serving as mediating links in the God-world relationship. But it would not respond to the issue of an infinite regress. Even with regard to the canonical attributes how do we know that we have an exhaustive account of what might precede them, succeed them or accompany them in the routes that connect human beings and the world to God?) As a result of considerations of this sort, Avicenna theorizes that the notion of God as a Necessary Being signifies the complete divestiture of attributes – so that an infinite regress between the world and God is definitionally blocked. However, with regard to acts of theorizing (intellectual ascents) that take place in more restrictive worldly settings where there are no canonical lists of mediating factors between the objects and subjects of explanation we need to be concerned not only with issues of infinite regress but also with factors pertaining to arbitrariness. We can never be sure that the features we have singled out in our mapping of relationships between explananda and explanans are the most relevant ones – or that the linguistic terms we use to refer to them are the most perspicuous and acute.

With regard to the relationship between theory and fact – words and things – we thus have the confluence of three sets of considerations bringing about a result of underdetermination. These factors are: (a) the arbitrariness of the categories and descriptions chosen in the light of theoretically available alternatives; (b) the presence of an infinite regress between a thing and a word in the sense that it remains meta-theoretically open where we begin and where we cut off the range of conceptualization to circumscribe a thing; and, finally, (c) the rational irresolvability of the proper mix and configuration of relevant factors and terms that would keep the relationship between words and things underdetermined even if the other two factors could be satisfactorily addressed.

When Avicenna speaks about "attaining through knowledge the unknown," one way of construing this is to say that just like in relation to God pushing rational analysis to its limits only helps to enlighten us concerning the limits to reason but does not enable us to transcend them. So, too, with regard to other domains of knowledge the upshot of knowing more is gaining a keener appreciation of our limits. Given the principle of underdetermination of words by things and the three levels upon which it operates, every knowledge-disclosure rests upon an ontologically insecure set of terms. We know how the world shapes up in relation to the terms we have chosen – but we don't know how it would come out in relation to the terms not mobilized (but theoretically available). In addition, the terms that elucidate a particular sector of experience are also terms that engender perplexities precisely in relation to whatever is being occluded and distorted by this particular set of terms. These factors ensure that each advance in knowledge is correlated with the emergence of new areas of ignorance.

Avicenna's description of the goal of intellectual exertion is also evocative of why a generalized agnosticism constitutes the most defensible epistemological position. A generalized agnosticism seeks to chart and codify how our knowledge breakthroughs remain susceptible to skeptical attack as a result partially of their theoretical categories being underdetermined by the facts they seek to describe and account for – and how skepticism itself remains defensible only when it includes itself within its ambit of questioning.

The role and goal of advancing knowledge from the perspectives I have outlined is to herald the pervasiveness and depth of the unknown.

Concerning God, Avicenna writes about "How that Essence achieves cognition without any consequent multiplicity or change of any kind."[29] When you juxtapose this sentence to a sentence that precedes it in an earlier paragraph on the same page – "For the elements of the faculty of knowledge were only to be acquired through the body" – you notice the ways in which the first sentence limits and resituates the import of the second. "The elements of the faculty of knowledge" being "acquired only through the body" suggests that our conceptions of what is enduring and universal – what we would like to subsume under the rubric of "knowledge" – is only mediated to us through the "body" – which represents limits, an obduracy beyond our control, what defeats the unbounded aspirations of reason. Knowledge, therefore, is always mediated, limited, deflected knowledge. If this is the case, then the "Essence" (referring to God) which "achieves cognition without any consequent multiplicity or change of any kind" has to be regarded by us as a string of undecodable words – whose surface sense renders their referential inscrutability all the more poignant.

---

29. *Ibid.*, p. 71.

The "thatness" of Avicenna's Essence needs to be distinguished from the "whatness." The "thatness" refers to the ongoing operations of human reason - which includes reason's ever-deepening implication in its own limitations (even skepticism needs to be counterbalanced by a skepticism of skepticism - a generalized agnosticism). This "thatness" needs to be seen as a placeholder for an ever-elusive and receding "whatness" attached to Avicenna's Essence, which given skepticism's calling itself into question alongside its other objects, we are not required to forfeit. Since protocols of consistency impel us to question our own questioning, it is legitimate for us to entertain the idea of an "Essence ... without multiplicity."

Applying Aristotle to theological speculation, Avicenna writes that "Always the Mean plucks the rational soul from the two extremes."[30] This is a deceptively straightforward formulation. What is the second extreme that Avicenna is referring to? The first extreme (the context of this passage makes clear) would be the one that inclines the rational soul too overwhelmingly "towards the body"[31] - which would make reason too subservient to the body. This is one extreme that Arisotle's Theory of the Mean is intended to help us avoid. But what is the other extreme? In the light of our discussion above, we could say that the other extreme consists in an overconfident investment in reason as being able to disclose to us indubitably the

---

30. *Ibid.*, p. 73.
31. *Ibid.*, p. 72.

metaphysical landscape that lies beyond the constant to-and-fro tuggings and maneuverings of reason. Reason in Avicenna's gloss on Aristotle is a capacity and vocation of the middle that keeps us focused on the critical, mediating moves that lead to a prolongation and expansion of the middle itself – without drawing us any closer to what resides at the ends.

"The bond which unites body and soul ... has its origin in the body."[32] One way of making sense of Avicenna in the light of his interpretation of Aristotle and his previous implicit calling-into-question of the notion of "essence" is that the idea of "soul" itself has its origins in the ambiguities surrounding the apparently indubitably given and there – what is symbolized by the notion of "the body." What is ostensibly brutely present in experience – our own bodies and the bodies that surround us – can only be engaged in a mediated fashion through language. Our words are underdetermined by experience. Other strings of words – resulting in alternative descriptions – can often capture the same "brutely given" entity that our first string of words was intended to designate. Since the nature of an entity is dependent upon the language used to pin down its identity, we cannot use the "brute item" in our experience itself to adjudicate between the competing claims of different descriptions without our argument becoming viciously circular. What are conventionally-regarded as the intention-laden, consciousness-driven, self-evaluationally and self-critically mindful aspects of bodily

---

32. *Ibid.*, p. 73.

behavior give rise to the notion of "soul" to help accommodate what appear as the non-material dimensions of bodily behavior. But the idea of "soul" is a posit or conjecture that can be systematically precluded by a more determinedly materially-oriented description (or set of descriptions) of what look like non-material manifestations of bodies. But there is nothing in the "facts" per se as they appear to us in experience that can preclude or validate either description or set of descriptions. As long as we remain systematically committed to sustaining either perspective on experience, we can manage to do so. Both the materialist and the anti-materialist visions of our experience go all the way down – i.e., encompass the very identity and nature of the objects or entities in question – so that these "objects" or "entities" cannot be invoked in some pristine, untainted form to resolve the conflict between the competing versions of what they are. The most telling supplementary argument available to proponents of either vision is to try and make the case that the theoretical vision that they adhere to harbors the promise of being more coherently faithful to the complexities of the actual experience of the objects or entities in question than their rival's vision. This move is clearly available to both (or all) sides of a theoretical dispute.

Based upon this reading of the relationship between the soul and the body in Avicenna – that what they have in common (insinuated by the way that the "body" vocabulary can overtake the "soul" vocabulary) is their equal dependence on a not-fully-validated givenness – it is easy to project how other metaphysical or spiritual entities such as God, the after-life, reward and punishment, etc. get projected in a similar manner – and how their ontological status remains as questionable and contestable as the notion of "soul." ("The bond which unites body and soul ... has its origin in the body.") By the same token, once the underdetermination of words by things legitimates by its very skepticism recourse to the soul, this sets in motion a dynamic that proliferates other non-material or spiritual entities such as God, the after-life, and reward and punishment, which buttress and reinforce our conception of soul. Once one member of a conceptual family is introduced as a skeptically-feasible posit, this sets the stage for including the others to engender a pattern of mutual reinforcement. The same logical and conceptual slack that allows for the postulation of the first entity allows for the postulation of all the other entities. There is no rigor attached to the order of generation of these entities. One can begin almost anywhere amongst the members of this conceptual family and then yield to a rhetorical dynamic to maximize persuasiveness by including all the others.

Avicenna's understanding of the bond between body and soul having its origin in the body affects all the other members of the conceptual family to which the category of soul belongs – and not just the idea of the "soul." God, the after-life, and reward and punishment also have their origin in the body. That is to say, these categories, too, are formulable in the light of common experiences of rootedness in the world which come encumbered with customary usages but which otherwise in a more narrowly rational sense do not come pre-packaged or prelabeled – and which in the light of the underdetermination of words by things create space for us to invoke these categorial entities as the most appropriate conceptual clothing to disclose and denote the nature of our experiences.

The Active Intellect that the mind of the philosopher communes with – which conjures up an image of free-ranging, dynamic thought and its intersections with and repercussions for reality – vouchsafes for him a whole domain of interconnected theological and moral possibility which his being grounded in the body renders for him near and familiar (ideas such as "soul" which are the most usual and customary set of metaphors with which to "group" our experience) at the same time that these ideas remain irretrievably metaphysically distant (as the overshooting of the limits of the bodily and the concrete by privileging a set of categories to organize some of its most recurring internal and external impressions.)

Temple University

Chapter VI

Divine Will Vs. Human Need: The Solution Offered by Islamic Law

Hossein Mir Mohammad Sadeghi

INTRODUCTION

It is one of the aims of every system of law to regulate human relations in a given society. Due to the lapse of time, however, human societies change and such relations are thus complicated. Peoples' needs also change constantly. It is, therefore, essential for every legal system to contain a degree of flexibility in order to meet this changing aspect of human society. The aim of this paper is to discuss whether and to what extent this flexibility exists in Islamic law, as a religious system, enabling it to create a balance between the Will of God and the need of man.

To start with, it can be said that the degree of flexibility contained in a legal system depends very much upon the nature of the law-maker in that system. In a dictatorship, a parliamentary system or a common law system, for example, where the major source of the law is, respectively, the wishes and orders of the man or party in power, the ideas of members of parliament, or the opinions of the judiciary, the views of the law-maker are subject to change. The law derived from these sources, therefore, is also capable of easy changes.

In a religious system like Islam, on the other hand, as the character of the Law Maker is unchangeable, neither is the law derived from Him subject to constant changes. In Islam, the opinion of one person or a group of people cannot change the law of God; it is only God who is fully aware of the necessities of human society; whereas human beings, "... have not been given but a little of knowledge".[33] The Qu'ran in verse 216/II addresses people by saying, "... you may dislike a thing while it is good for you, and you may like a thing while it is bad for you; God knows and you know not." Such a creature is thus expected to submit and surrender totally to the Almighty. This is in fact what the word "Islam" literally means, i.e., "complete surrender to God".[34] Needless to say, the situation will not change even if the opinion, which contradicts the laws of God, belongs not to one person or a group of people, but to the majority or even all people; the plurality of "wrongs" will still be "wrong". In fact, according to the Qu'ran, throughout history, every new phenomenon, including every new idea, at its

---

[33] The Qu'ran, Verse 85/XVII.

[34] 'Ali ibn Abitalib, the fourth caliph of Islam and the first Shi'i Imam, states in Nahjul-Balagha (Section on *hikmah,* "Wisdom"): "al-Islamu huwattaslim" (Islam is complete surrender to God). According to Imam Muhammad al-Baqir, The fifth Shi'i Imam, : "Anything resulting from confession and surrender is (The sign of) faith *(iman)*, and anything resulting from denial and obstinacy is (the sing of) infidelity *(kufr)*." M.Y.Kulaini, Usul min al-Kafi (Tehran: Dar al-Kutub al-Islamiyya, 3rd ed., A. H. 1388) Vol. II, P. 387.

inception has been rejected by the majority of people, although it might have been correct. The Qu'ran tells us, for example, that every prophet embarking on his mission was initially rejected by the majority and believed in only by a few. Phrases like "...few of my bondsmen are thankful", or "... most of mankind do not believe "[35] are frequently found in the Qu'ran.

It is interesting to observe that even the legal effect of *ijma'* (consensus of opinion among Muslim jurists, which is one of the four sources for discovering *shari'a* law)[36] is not based upon the majority principle.[37] Its legal effect is instead based upon certain statements of the prophet such as, "My community will never agree in error",[38] and verses like Verse 115/IV, which reads as follows:

> As for him who ... follows a path other than that of the believers, we shall leave him unto that he himself has chosen, and shall cause him to endure Hell: and how evil a journey's end.

---

[35] The Qu'ran, Verses 13/XXXIV and 17/XI.

[36] Shari'a is an Arabic word meaning the path to be followed. Literally, it means "the way to a watering place." As an expression, it refers to Islam or Islamic law.

[37] The consensus of Muslim Jurists is one of the *usul al-fiqh* (roots of jurisprudence). In other words, it is one way of discovering *shari'a* law. The other three sources are: the Qu'ran, the precedent of the prophet *(sunna)*, and analogy *(qiyas)*. The Shi'is, however, replace analogy by *'aql* (the human intellect).

[38] Ibn Hazm ('Abi Muhammad Ali) *al-Ihkam fi Usul al-Ahkam* (Cairo: Matbaat al - Asima, 2nd ed. n.d.), Vol.IV, P.496.

There are some writers who believe that the above-mentioned statement of the prophet is negative, not positive; in the sense that it merely assures Muslims that there will always be a minority who oppose a wrong decision.[39] This, however, is of no significance, because even in this interpretation the statement accepts the validity of *ijma'* if it occurs; but there are some Sunni[40] jurists, such as Ahmad ibn Hanbal, who reject the possibility of occurrence of an *ijma'* in practice.[41]

The fact that the legal effect of consensus is not a result of the majority principle can be seen more clearly in Shi'i law.[42]According to Shi'i jurists, the significance of

---

[39] M. Asad, *The Principles of State and Government in Islam* (Los Angeles: The University of California Press, 1961), p. 38.

[40] The Muslims are divided into two main sects: The orthobox Sunnis, who form the majority, and the Shi'is, who are in the minority throughout the Muslim world, except in Iran in which they form the majority of the population. The main difference between the two sects lies in the issue of the leadership of the Muslim community after the demise of the prophet of Islam. This difference has, however, led to other differences both in beliefs and in laws. The four most famous Schools of Sunni law are *Hanafi, Hanbali, Shafi'i* and *Maliki* schools, and the most famous Shi'i School is the *Ithna 'Ashari* or Twelver School, whose followers are to be found in Iran, Iraq, Lebanon and, in smaller numbers, in India, pakistan and other Muslim countries. This School has been adopted in Iran as the official religion of the state. The name comes from the fact that they believe in the leadership of twelve Imams after the prophet's demise in A. D. 632.

[41] See M. Abdulaleem. "The Hadd Punishments in Islamic Law" (*Ph.D. Thesis*, London: SOAS, 1955), p. 70.

[42] See Footnote 8.

this principle is that it reflects the opinion of the Twelfth Imam, who is believed to be living in disguise on the Earth.[43] Najm al-Din J'afar ibn Muhammad (called Muhaqqiq Hilli, d.A.H.674), the famous Shi'i jurist, in his book, al- Mutabar, states:

> In our (Shi'i) opinion, consensus is regarded as an evidence of God's law provided it reflects the view of the (Twelfth) Imam. Therefore, if hundreds of our jurists come to a "consensus" which does not reflect the opinion of the Imam, such consensus will have no legal effect. But if on the same question, two jurists, one of them being the Hidden Imam, give an opposite view, this opinion must be

---

[43] The Twelver *(Ithna 'Ashari)* Shi'is believe that their Twelfth Imam, al-Mahdi, disappeared in A. H. 329, and since then has been living among people in disguise. He will rise up by the order of God and create a just universal government. This will take place at a time when people are so distressed that they are fully prepared to help one who wants to save them from oppression. An important political result of such a belief is that the Imam is the only legitimate ruler of the Muslim Community. So a ruler can only be acceptable to Shi'is if he is empowered to rule as a representative of the Imam. Such a power is believed to have been given only to an upright jurist, who is recognised as such by the majority of people. Such a power is called *Wilayat al-Faqih*. A psychological result of the belief in the rising up and victory of the twelfth Imam, According to some contemporary writers, is that it prevents the despair of those involved in fighting oppression, by assuring them of the ultimate victory of good over evil.

> accepted; but, again, not merely because two jurists have come to the same conclusion, but because of the Imam, s opinion.[44]

This reflection (of the Imam's opinion) can take one of the following forms, according to different shi'i jurists:

Reflection by Way of Physical Presence (Hess). This is the view held by jurists of the past. According to this view, if all Muslim (or shi'i) jurists agree upon something, this would also mirror the opinion of the Imam, who is living among them. This view can be of value, only if there are some unknown persons among the consenting jurists; otherwise, it would be evident that the Imam has not been among them and consensus will, therefore, have no legal effect.

Reflection By Way of Mercy (Lutf). According to this view, every consensus leads us to the conclusion that its subject-matter is in accordance with Islamic principles for, otherwise, it would be the duty of the Twelfth Imam, as the guardian of Islam, and because he is merciful to Muslims, to break up such a consensus.

Reflection By Way of Conjecture (Hads). Most recent shi'i jurists believe that every consensus among jurists leads us to the conclusion that its subject matter is in accordance with Islamic principles, because our experience from the

---

[44] N. Hilli, *al-Mutabar* (Tehran: n.p., A.H. 1015), pp.6-7.

precedent of Muslim jurists shows that they never consent on something which is against *(shari'a)*.

There are, however, some recent shi'i jurists who believe that consensus *(ijma')* has no legal effect either *per se* or as reflecting the view of the Imam. They believe that the reason the previous shi'i jurists did not express their opposition to this doctrine, was that they were living in an era when their opposition could, firstly, harm the unity of Muslims and, secondly, cause conflict with caliphs whose very legitimacy was supposed to be based only upon the principle of consensus of the community. Jurists, therefore, concealed their true belief using the principle of *taqiyya* (lit. caution or disguise), which enables a Muslim to conceal his or her true belief to escape a danger either to Islam or to his or her own life.

To return to the concept of flexibility of the law, one can summarize what was said above by stating that in religious systems like Islam the faculty of determining different values and criteria, including enacting different laws, belongs to God.[45] People in these systems do not

---

[45] This statement must not be taken too far to say: "Islamic law ... represents not the good versus the evil as seen by man ... but rather the good and evil as seen by Allah ..." (M.A. Kara, *The Philosophy of Punishment in Islamic Law,* London: University Micro - Films, 1977). To say this is to deny completely the ability of the human mind to judge independently goodness, badness, justice and injustice; whereas this is not what many Muslims believe. In fact, there exist two opposite views in this regard among Sunni Muslims. According to Asha'ira, good, evil, just or unjust, have no meaning in themselves, and it is God who defines them for us. M'utazila, on the other hand, believe

create, let alone change, the law (of God);[46] their responsibility is limited to discovering what the law of God is. This is what is meant by divinity of law in such systems, and this is why it is offensive to a Muslim to use words such as Muhammadan law, however negligently they may be employed, as using this terminology is taken to reflect an attempt to deny the divine origin of Islam and Islamic law, and imply that *shari,a* originated from Muhammad and not from the Almighty.

It appears from what was said above that the divine nature of Islamic law makes it more resistant to social changes and less prepared to take into account the human will. This, however, must not be taken as meaning that social changes may not have any effect on this law because,

> No Muslim, however orthodox he may be, believes for a moment that it [Islamic law] dropped down complete from heaven in any way analogous to that in which the goddess Athene is depicted, in Greek mythology, as having sprung fully armed from the mind of Zeus. Instead the *shari'a* would be described by Muslims

---

that although whatever God does is good and just, this does not follow that mankind is incapable of judging good and evil independent of God's revelation. In other words, they say, God commands the good because it is good and forbids the evil because it is evil. The Shi'i view in this regard is similar to that of M'utazila.

46 This fact is emphasized by the oft-quoted statement: "Whatever Muhammad has forbidden will remain forbidden until the Day of Justice; and whatever he has permitted will remain lawful until the Day of Justice".

as both a divine law (as they always affirm), and also a lawyers' law (as most would readily admit), since it is regarded as firmly based on divine revelation, on the one hand, and as having been worked out by a series of great juris-consults on the other.[47]

In other words, although it is God who "proposes" the law, it is the duty of man to "dispose" it.[48] The role of *ijtihad* appears here to create a fusion between the "will of God" and the "necessities of man." This is made possible by the fact that the two main sources of Islamic law, the Qu'ran and the *sunna* (precedent of the prophet), are not, unlike what appears at first sight, so rigid. As far as the Qu'ran is concerned, some of its verses are allegorical (*mutashabihat,* as opposed to *ommahat:* fundamentals). In other words, they are open to various interpretations, according to the interpreter's personal capacities and the conditions of the time in which he lives.[49] This is meant

---

[47] J. N. D. Anderson, *Law Reforms in the Muslim World* (London: The Athlone Press, 1976), P.4.

[48] N.J. Coulson, *Conflicts and Tensions in Islamic Jurisprudenc* (The University of Chicago Press, 1969) p. 1.

[49] In Verse 7/ III, the Qu'ran describes these two kinds of verses in the following way:

> He it is who has revealed unto thee (Muhammad) the scripture wherein are clear revelations - They are the substance of the Book- and others (which are) allegorical. But those in whose heart is doubt pursue, forsooth, that which is allegorical seeking (to cause) dissension by seeking to interpret it. None knows its interpretation save God and those who are of sound instruction say: We believe therein, the whole is from our Lord, but only men of understanding really heed.

to guarantee the Qu'ran's ability to be utilised at all times for all people. The prophet refers to this aspect of the Qu'ran when he says:

> The appearance of this Book is beautiful and its interior deep and profound, so much so that [its full understanding] is out of the reach of [even] the most intellectual minds. It has many stars, each one of them has, in turn, many stars. The miracles of this Book are countless and its novelty never stales.[50]

'Ali ibn Abitalib, the first Shi'i Imam and the fourth caliph of Islam, orders one of his companions, Abdullah ibn Abbas: "Do not argue with your opponents (The kharijis) about the Qu'ran, as its verses are susceptible to different interpretations".[51] As a result of this characteristic of Qu'ranic Verses, some general rules have been derived from them to offer solutions to the changing problems of human society. The "Negation of Hardship" Rule, *(nafye 'usr wa haraj)* for example, which can, *inter alia*, accomodate the contents of the "theory of changed circumstances" in Islamic contract law, is based upon various Qu'ranic Verses. For example, Verse 6/V declares, "... God would not place a burden on you..."

---

[50] M.Y. Kulaini, *Usul Min al-Kafi,* (Tehran: Dar al - Kutub al - Islamiyya, 3rd ed., A.H. 1388) Vol. II. P. 438.
[51] *Nahjul-Balagha*, Letter No. 77.

And Verse 78/XXII provides, "He Hath chosen you and hath not laid upon you any hardship in religion..."

This rule has been reflected in the laws of Iran to allow a wife to apply to the court for divorce *(talaq)* if continuation of conjugal life causes hardship beyond forbearance to her,[52] and to allow a tenant to ask for a respite if immediate evacuation of the leasehold property causes hardship to him/her.[53]

As far as the Tradition of the prophet, as the second source of Islamic law, is concerned, many of his statements are in the form of general rules, which may be applied to various situations. The principle of "no unfair loss" which is co-related to the "negation of hardship" rule, is based upon the prophet' s statement "No one should cause or suffer an (unjustifiable) loss in Islam" *(La darara wa la dirara fil-Islam)* and can be used to justify legislations requiring payment of compensation for any unjustifiable loss caused to people, even though the act or omission causing the loss may not have been directly dealt with by *shari'a.* A clear example of this is losses caused by traffic offences. Similarly, by applying this principle, a contract may be avoided if its performance becomes extremely burdensome for the promisor. According to a famous Muslim jurist, "a contract whose performance becomes so burdensome as to involve great loss may be terminated."[54]

---

[52] See Ariticle 1130 of Civil Code of Iran (as amended in 1982).

[53] See Ariticle 4 of the Landlord and Tenants Relations Act,1983.

[54] Ibn al Hammam, *Fath al-Qadir* (n.p.,n.d) Vol VII, P. 222.

The principle of "no unfair loss" is derived from a decision of the Prophet in a famous case related from him in both sunni and shi'i laws with minor differences. The facts of the case, which happened in Medina, where the prophet had established an Islamic government in the years A.D. 622-632, are as follows:

A man called Samorat ibn Jondab had a tree in a garden, the only entrance to which was through another's house. He frequently entered into the house, during day or night, without asking for permission, with the alleged purpose of going to the garden and irrigating his tree, ignoring the objections of the owner. The man complained to prophet Muhammad. The prophet summoned Samora and recommended to him that he should ask for permission before entering into the house. Samora said objectionably: "How should I ask for permission, when I want to go to my own tree?" The prophet even suggested that he may sell the tree at a higher price or exchange it for one or more trees somewhere else. The prophet went as far as saying that if Samora was prepared to abandon the tree, he would, instead guarantee him a tree in Paradise, as a reward for his good faith. When all these suggestions were rejected by the owner of the tree, the Prophet addressed him and said "you are a man who wants to cause loss" *(innaka rajolun modarr),* whereas "there shall be no unfair loss in Islam." He then ordered for the tree to be taken out and given to Samora, so that he might put it wherever he wanted.[55]

The principle contained in this case is a corner -- stone of Islamic law.[56] It has frequently been invoked by traditional Muslim jurists to justify their views on unacceptability of causing undue losses or of abusing a right: Prohibition of Hoarding,[57] prohibition of causing a loss to another in order to avoid a loss to oneself, prohibition of building a house with a bathroom which causes such a great and unreasonable amount of smoke as to annoy the neighbours,[58] prohibition of staying in public places, such as mosques or markets, for so long as to make it difficult for other potenial users to enter, prohibition of taking ownership of pastures located around villages and used by the villagers to feed their animals,[59] prohibition of someone with a contagious disease living among the healthy,[60] prohibition of

---

[55] M.Y.Kulaini, *Usul min al-Kafi* Chapter on "loss", statement No.2; 'Ameli, *Wasail al-Shi'a ila Tahsili Masail al-Shari'a* (Beirut: Ihiaul - Tarath al - 'Arabi, A.H.1388) Chapter XII, Section on "Cultivation of Waste Land".

[56] The issue of *darar* has also been referred to in some Qu'ranic Verses. See, for example, Verses 231/II, 234/II, 284/II, 2/IV and 7/LXV.

[57] See: Ibn Nujaim, *Al-Ashbah wal-Naza'ir,* P. 96.

[58] Zailai, *Sharh Kanz al-Daqaiq,* (n.p.,n.d.) Vol. IV, p. 196: Abdurrahman Ibn al-Qasim, *al-Mudawwanat al-Kobra,* containing legal opinions of Malik ibn Anas (Cairo: Afandi publishers, A.H.1323) vol. XIV, p. 14.

[59] Mirzaye Qumi, *Jam'i al-Shatat* (Tehran: Rizwan, n.d.) Chapter on "Cultivation of Waste Land", the answer to question IV.

[60] *Fiqh us-Sunnah* (Indianapolis: American Trust Publications, 1991) Vol. IV, P. 11.

extravagent use of the water supply in a way that the right of other users is adversely affected[61] and prohibition of annoying the neighbours by placing odorous rubbish in one's property.[62] These are only a few examples reflecting the effect of the principle of "no unfair loss."

The principle has also been reflected in the laws of Iran. According to Principle (Article) 40 of the 1979 Constitution of the Islamic Republic of Iran, "no one is entitled to exercise his rights in a way injurious to others or detrimental to public interests."[63] Similarly, Article 132 of the Civil Code provides: "A person cannot make use of his property in such a way as would necessarily involve a loss to the neighbour, except such use as is reasonable and is required to satisfy his needs or to prevent his loss."[64] This article limits the operation of the principle of *taslit* (i.e. absolute legal authority of an owner to deal with his property as he/she wishes), as contained in Article 30 of the Civil Code. In one case, the Higher Civil Court of Tehran (*Dadgah-e-Shahrestan)* affirmed a judgment by the County Court (*Dadgah-e-Bakhsh*) and held that the

---

[61] This is based on the judicial opinion (*fatwa)* of the late Ayatollah Khomeini published in the Persian daily *Ettelaat* on 9 October 1982.

[62] *Majella*, the Ottoman Civil Code, Article 1200

[63] See also: Shahid al-Thani, *Masalik al -Afham,* Vol. V. p. 453. This can be contrasted with Article 91 of *Majella* which provides that no one is responsible for losses that he may cause to others while exercising his rights. The same rule is contained in the Latin Maxim: *nemo damnum facit qui sui jure utitur.*

[64] The principle of "no unfair loss" has also been reflected in some other articles of the Iranian Civil Code. See, forexample, Articles 65, 114, 122, 125, 132, 138, 139, 159, 591, 592, 594, 600, 833, 944, 945 and 1130.

appellant was required to cover his small garden, since irrigation of the garden caused damage to the adjacent wall belonging to the neighbor, and since this was not counterbalanced by a greater interest, namely, satisfaction of the appellant's needs or the prevention of his loss, as required by the latter part of Article 132.[65]

Before discussing in detail the meaning and scope of the doctrine of *ijtihad*, through which Islamic law can go hand in hand with human need and social changes, reference should be made to the useful principle of tolerance or *ibaha* in Islamic Jurisprudence. This principle can be used to justify legislation in respect of any need of human society, provided such legislation not contravene the terms of *shari'a.*

THE DEFINITION OF IJTIHAD

The word *ijtihad* literally means "exerting oneself in an attempt to attain an object."[66] This word has not been used in the Qu'ran, but its derivatives, such as the word *jahd* (attempt) have been used in the Qu'ran frequently.[67]

While defining *ijtihad* legally, some Muslim jurists have paid attention to the literal meaning of the word and have, therefore, used phrases such as *istifrag al-wus'a* or *badhl al-jahd,* meaning exerting oneself in an attempt (in this case

---

[65] Judgment 168/39. 27th Division of the Higher Civil Court of Tehran.

[66] H. Raghib al-Isfahani (d. about A.D. 1108) *al-Mufradat fi gharib al-Qu'ran* (Cairo: Maktabat al-Anjlu al-Misriyyah,1970), Vol. 1. P. 142.

[67] See, for example, Verses 53/V, 190/VI, and 79/IX.

to discover the laws of *sheri'a* from its basic sources).[68] Most western critics of Islam have also used the same definition; but many Muslim jurists (especially among shi'is) define *ijtihad* as "a power *(malaka)* that enables a man to discover the laws of God from its original sources."[69] It seems that *ijtihad* can best be defined as "the power which enables a jurist to apply fundamental unchangeable principles of *shari'a* to new situations, in order to solve new problems of the human society". This definition contains the two essential factors for any culture's ability to continue to exist. On the one hand, it indicates that there must exist fundamental unchangeable principles in any culture claiming permanence, otherwise it may be abandoned altogether. On the other hand, if these fundamental principles do not have the capacity to meet changing contemporary needs, the culture will cease to exist as a living force.

It may be said that the existence of unchangeable principles in Islam is due to its divine origin. These principles are not subject to change because, in the Islamic view, they are based upon human nature *(fitra)*,[70] which is not subject to change. On the other hand, the

---

[68] See, for example, the definition by M. Ghazzali in *al-Mustasfa min' Ilm al-Usul* (Cairo: Matba'at al-Amiriya, A.H.1324), Vol. II, P. 350.

[69] This defininition is from Mulla Muhammad Kazim Khurasani, the famous Shi'i jurist, in his book *Kifayat al-Usul* (Tehran: Elmiyye Eslamiyye, A.H. 1363), Vol. II, p. 422. The same definition is used by Muhammad ibn Hussain Baha al-Din (Shaikh Bahai, A.H.953-1030) in *Zubdat al-Usul* (Tehran: n.p., 1319 Sh.), p. 115.

[70] In the words of the Qu'ran, human nature is: "... the natural disposition which God has instillded into man ..." (Verse 30/XXX).

generality of these principles and, in other words, their capacity to be applied to changing situations, is due to Islam's supposed permanence, which requires it to be able to solve the problems of every age. Therefore, a good *mujtahid* (a person who exercises *ijtihad*) is one who strikes a balance between flexibilities and inflexibilities of Islamic law, in a way that neither of these two aspects of the law, i.e., divinity and permanence, is impaired.

HISTORICAL BACKGROUND OF IJTIHAD

In the study of historical perspective of *ijtihad,* a distinction should be made between the life time of the prophet and the time after his demise. In the case of the former, there exists divergence of opinion among jurists as to whether *ijtihad* by competent jurists existed during that time. The majority believe that this was the case and refer to cases such as that of Mu'az, in which the prophet ordered Mu'az, whom he had appointed as the judge *(qadi)* to yemen, to use his personal reasoning when the solution could not be found in the Qu'ran or the *sunna.* They also refer to a case in which the prophet is reported to have ordered 'Amr ibn As to use *ijtihad*; and in answering his question: "should I use my personal reasoning while you are present?" the prophet is believed to have said, "Yes. Then if you get to the right conclusion, you will receive two rewards, and if you are mistaken you will [still] receive one reward". In a third case, the prophet is reported to have said almost the same thing to 'Aqabat ibn' Amir.[71] Some jurists, however, do not regard these as authoritative cases and some even question their credibility.[72]

There is also a difference of opinion among jurists as to whether the prophet himself used *ijtihad,* or that he was guided by God in his conduct. The majority reject the using of *ijtihad* by the prophet, and those who accept it are in turn divided into those who accept it in both secular and religious matters and those who accept it only in the former case. Bearing in mind verses like Verse 3/LIII, which says, "He (The prophet) does not speak out of his desire; that (which he conveys to you) is but (a divine) inspiration with which he is being inspired," the majority view seems more acceptable; and as there is no clear distinction between secular and religious matters in Islam to separate the two and accept the prophet's *ijtihad* in one category while rejecting it in the other is not right either. It must be noted that even among those who accept the possibility of the exercise of *ijtihad* by the prophet, there are so me who, although accepting this in theory, believe that it never happened in practice.

All these divergencies, however, have little more than historical value today, as what is important for the Muslim world at the present is the status of *ijtihad* after the

---

[71] Ghazzali, *Op. Cit.*, p. 355.

[72] Although there are many Shi'i jurists who question the credibility of these cases, Shaikh Tusi (Muhammad ibn al- Hasan,A.H. 385-460?), the famous Shi'i jurist refers to the case of Muaz in his book *Uddat al-Usul.*

life-time of the prophet. To study this, it is more convenient to distinguish between sunni and shi'i law.

The Status of Ijtihad in Sunni Law

This, in turn, may be divided into two parts.

i. Within the First Few Centuries of Islam

It was quite clear from the outset of Islam that neither the Qu'ran nor the *sunna* were supposed to act as legal codes, and since then (or at least since the demise of the prophet) the exercise of personal reasoning for the discovery of *shari'a* law has been felt necessary. This power of going back to the original sources to discover *shari'a* law was freely used by competent sunni jurists within the first few centuries of Islam. They, however, had different views on how wide this power was. Some believed that it only covered analogy *(qiyas)*. Shafi'i, for example, in his famous book *al-Risala,* mentions that *ijtihad* and *qiyas* are "two terms with the same meaning."[73] But others believed that it also included other methods of discovering Islamic law, such as *istihsan* (juristic preference) and *istislah* (public interest).[74]

---

[73] M. Shafi'i (A.H. 150-204), *al- Risala* (Cairo: Matbaah Mustafa al-Babi, A.D.1940), P. 477.

[74] The word *istihsan* comes from the word *hasan* (good) and means to consider something good. The word *istislah* comes from the word *salih* (in the general interest). These two principles were used to justify departures from strict analogy where it could be shown that doing so would be in the general interest of society.

As far as the leaders of the four Sunni schools are concerned, they have not been equal in using *ijtihad*, either in its limited from of analogy, or in its more extended from to cover also some other principles of discovering *shari'a* law. Among them, Abu Hanifa (d.A.D.767) uses it more, and Ahmad ibn Hanbal (d.A.D.855) less, while shafi'i (d.A.D.820) and Malik (d.A.D.796) stand in between. From these last two, shafi'i was nearer to Abu Hanifa and Malik nearer to Ahmad.[75]

One can, no doubt, find social and other reasons for this difference in approach among founders of the four Sunni Schools. As for Abu Hanifa, while origianlly from Iran, he was living in Iraq far From the Arabian Peninsula (Hijaz), which was the main land for the prophet's traditions *(ahadith)*. He, therefore, needed to use *ijtihad* mor frequently. Moreover, he was a businessman and needed to adapt law to changing needs in the field of commerce.

Abu Hanifa's liberal view of *ijtihad al-r'ay* found expression in his political thinking, leading him to believe in individual freedom and voicing his opposition towards dictatorship. This eventually brought him into conflict with different caliphs and rulers of the time. For example, he was once beaten for refusing an offer by Abu Hubeira (the ruler of Iraq during the last years of Umaiyad period)[76] to becom a judge. He refused a similar offer by Abu J'afar,Abdullah ibn al-Mansur, the second Abbasid

---

[75] Needless to say Zahiris, because of their strict approach to *shari'a* sources, used the principle of *ijtihad* even less that Hanbalis.

[76] 44. The Umaiyads were ruling Islamic territory between A.H. 41-132.

Caliph, and this resulted in his imprisonment until his death in A.H. 150. The political views of Abu Hanifa might also have been affected by the views of his teacher, Imam J'afar al-Sadiq, the sixth Shi'i Imam, who was an opponent of the Umaiyad and Abbasid dynasties.

Contrary to Abu Hanifa, Ahmad ibn Hanbal was totally against *ijtihad-al r'ay* and relied solely on the Qu'ran and the *sunna*. The reasons for this approach were twofold: Firstly, Ahmad was facing such sects as *Mutazila* (who, like shi'is, denied the eternity of the Qu'ran and believed that is was created by God), *Murji'a* (who believed that a Muslim did not lose his/her faith through sin because, they said, what mattered was to be a good Muslim at heart and not necessarily in practice), and *Kharijis* (who were the extreme opponents of *murji'a* and believed that a Muslim could become an infidel *kafar* by committing a sin). Ahmad totally rejected these views, which he regarded to be the result of an unlimited use of *ijtihad*, and came to the conclusion that to fight these "derivations", the doctrine of *ijtihad* itself ought to be fought.

Secondly, more than being a jurist *(faqih)*, Ahmad was a *muhaddith*, studying the traditions of the prophet. In his famous book, *al-Mosnad*[77] he collected about 30,000 traditions of the prophet. Naturally, such a person would prefer to rely on traditions, rather than *ijtihad al-r'ay*.

Politically, as a result of his opposition to *mutazila*, who were supported by M'amun and M'utasim (the

---

[77] Published in six volumes (Cairo: Matba'at al- Meymaniyya, A.H.1313).

Abbasid caliphs), he was very much in conflict with these two and was imprisoned for several months during their caliphate. He did not, however, have liberal political views similar to those of Abu Hanifa.

Malik also had beliefs like Ahmad, but the former was not as extremist as the latter. Malik was an Arab and was living in Medina. He, therefore, had easy access to the prophet's traditions and many of his relatives were also involved in studying the traditions.

As far as Malik's political views were concerned, he disliked rebellion and was in favour of stability. He did not allow for rebellion even against an unjust ruler, because he believed that the disadvantages of such an act would be more than its probable advantages.

Shafi'i can be described as a moderate. The reason for this was that he was first living in the Arabian peninsula and could, therefore, have easy access to *hadith*. Later on, however, he went to Iraq and Egypt. During this period, he had the opportunity of attending lectures delivered by scholars of different schools of thought, which were in the process of development at that time. Being impressed by opposite views about *ijtihad*, he came to the conclusion that in order to get the best result, one should gather together the Qu'ran and the *Sunna*, on the one hand, and *ijtihad* (which in his opinion is no more than analogy), on the other.

Shafi'i's political thinking was similar to that of Malik. He regarded the caliphate as the sole right of the Quraish Tribe. In his famous book, *al-Umm*, he mentions different statements (attributed to the prophet) regarding the superiority of Quraish. According to him, if a man from this tribe gains the caliphate by force and people accept him, he ought to be obeyed.

ii. At Later Stages. The free exercise of *ijtihad,* which existed during the first centuries of Islam in Sunni law, ceased to exist at a later stage, and the so-called "door" of *ijtihad* was closed. This is usually believed to have happened in the 3rd-4th centuries of *hijra* (Migration of the Prophet) after the death of Ahmad ibn Hanbal, but there are some who believe that this happened in the 6th-7th centuries, after the attack by Mongols on Muslim territory. However, the fact is that whichever of these two dates we accept as the date of actual closure (and in fact it is not going to make any difference to us, apart from clarifying an historical point), the attempts made by early Abbasid caliphs to make a unique law, shows that the idea of closure existed much earlier than the time of the Mongols' attack. One example of such an attempt is the suggestion made to the Caliph by Ibn al-Muqaffa' (the Iranian minister of Mansur, the second Abbasid caliph) to order that a unique law be made and applied to all people. A similar suggestion was made by Harun al-Rashid (who became a caliph in A,H, 170) to Malik.

With the existing belief among Sunni Muslims that the door of *ijihad* was closed, the task of future jurists was limited to work within the boundary of one of the established Sunni schools of Hanafi, Maliki, Shafi'i and Hanbali. Sunni jurists during this period of imitation *(taqlid)* were usually involved in explaining and interpreting books written by their predecessors. Reforms during this period could only take place in the form of *siyasa shar'iyya* (government in accordance with the revealed law), which enabled the ruler to make supplementary administrative regulations *(qanun)* for the courts. This could either be in respect of the procedure of the court, or in respect of substantive law. As far as procedural law was concerned, the ruler could, for instance, forbid the court from hearing certain cases, such as those not supported by documentary evidence. For example, he could forbid the court from hearing a case regarding an unregistered marriage or land claim. As far as substantive law was concerned, reforms were made through the doctrine of *takhayyor* (lit. choosing). According to this doctrine, a judge (usually guided by the ruler) could either choose one of the different opinions given by jurists of different schools (normal choosing), or a mixture of two or more opinions given by various jurists (*talfiq,* lit. to piece together). By choosing the opinion (or mixture of opinions) which was most in harmony with the new conditions of the time, an attempt was made to solve new problems of the society.

With the passing of time, however, these methods of reform proved insufficient. In the late 19th and early 20th centuries, Muslim jurists started to attack the doctrine of imitation itself, no longer being interested in working on discovery of new methods for reforms. One thing which facilitated this task of the reforming jurists, was the changing nature of the Muslim society at that time. Therefore, according to some, an attempt was made to unlock the door of *ijtihad* in 1946, when the Egyptian *Law of Testamentary Dispositions* was passed, and to swing it fully open by the Tunisian *Law of Personal Status* in 1957.

Reasons for the Closure of the Door of Ijtihad in Sunni Law. It is difficult to imagine legal reasons for the closure of the door of *ijtihad*, especially if we bear in mind the objections made to the doctrine of imitation by great Sunni jurists. Examples of these objections are the following:

The Hanbalis believe that no period of time can be imagined without a person exercising *ijtihad*. Abu Hanifa has made it clear that what he has said is based on his own opinion *(r'ay)* and those coming to a different conclusion need not obey him. Imam Fakhr Razi, in his interpretation of the Qu'ran *(tafsir)*, casts doubt as to whether it is possible to imitate a late *mujtahid* who, naturally, cannot be aware of the new conditions. Jurists like Zurgani (the Maliki jurist) and Ibn Taimiya (the Hanbali jurist) have rejected the doctrine of imitation. Shahrastani (d.A.D.548), in his famous book on Religions and Sects, *(Kitab al-Milal Wal-Nihal)* mentions that *ijtihad* is essential because," the texts are limited while events have no limit. That which is unlimited can never be covered by that which is limited" *(al-nusus tantahi wal waqaia la tantahi wa ma la yatanahi la yadbetahu ma yatanahi)*. Ibn Qayyim Jawziah (A.H.691-751) believes in constant development of the law. Suyuti (Jalal al-Din Abdurrahman ibn Abu Bakr, d. A.D.1445) has a small book called "Rejecting Those Who Corrupted the Earth and did not Realize that personal Reasoning is Essential at Every Age": *(Arradu ala man afsadal- ard wa jahala annal- ijtihad fikulli' asrin fard)*.

Ibn Abidin Mentions that Harun al-Rashid, the Abbasid caliph, once asked Malik to make a unique law from his religious decrees, so that he could order all people within his territory to act upon them. Malik rejected this and told the caliph that as differences of opinion among jurists were useful, he should let anyone follow the opinion of any jurist whom he thought to be right. Muzani the author of the earliest handbook on Shafi'i law, declares at the beginning of his work *(al-Mukhtasar),* "I made this book an extract from the doctrine of Shafi'i and his opinions for those who may desire it, although Shafi'i forbade anyone to follow him or anyone else".[78]

This widespread opposition to the doctrine of imitation shows that no legal reason could exist for the closure of the door of *ijtihad.* Therefore, one may need to look for reasons in the social conditions of the Muslim society at the time when the doctrine of imitation gained public acceptance. Different writers have given various reasons. Some believe that the closure was the result of an attempt made by Muslim jurists to protect Islamic law, the very survival of which was endangered by the Mongol's attack on Muslim territory. Some others have

---

[78] For these objections, the reader is referred to the following: Ibn Taimiya (Taqi al - Din), *Rafa al-Malam anil-Aimmat al-A'alam* (Beirut: al Maktab al Islami, 3rd ed., A.H. 1390), pp. 175-184. M, Shahrastani, *Al-Milal Wal-Nihal* (Cairo: Muassisat al Halabi, A.D. 1968) Vol. II, p. 4, M. Ibn Abidin, *Radd al- Mukhtar Aladdur al-Mukhtar* (Cairo: Matba'ah Bulaq, 3rd., A.H. 1286), Vol. I, p. 63. Muzani, *al- Muktasar* published with shafi'i's book: *al-umm* (Cairo: Dar al- Shib A.D. 1968), Vol. I, p. 2.

The following secondary source is also worth referring to: M. Muslehuddin, *Philosophy of Islamic Law and the Orientalists* (Lahore: Islamic Publications, n.d.), p. 143.

mentioned the same reason, but believe that the existence of Islamic law was endangered not because of the Mongol's attack, but as a result of the vastness of the Islamic Empire. In such an extensive Empire, where no single judicial organ existed, the caliphs and the judges could easily change Islamic law under the pretext of *ijtihad*.

According to some others, the reason for closure was the existence of the belief among Muslims that no one after the founders of the four Sunni Schools could be as competent as they in discovering *shari'a* law, as it was believed that whoever was nearer to the time of the prophet, would be more competent to carry out this duty. Some other reasons may be added to the above-mentioned, but the truth is that if a society is in the process of constant changes (which would in turn bring about new problems) none of these reasons, in itself, would be sufficient to convince people to accept the doctrine of imitation. The very fact that when changes started to take place in the Muslim world this doctrine was challenged, can be taken to prove that the main reason for the closure was the inactive nature of the society, which in turn created a belief among Muslims that the whole *shari'a* was already discovered and nothing was left to be said by future jurists.[79]

The Status of Ijtihad in Shi'i Law

It is interesting to note that the word *ijtihad* has had a changing history. From the beginning of Islam (especially

---

[79] For a similar view see : Coulson, *Conflicts and Tensions* ..., p.44.

since the demise of the prophet) until about the 6th century A.D., it was a Sunni word and since then it has become a Shi'i word.

The word *ijtihad* became a Shi'i word when a change was made in its meaning. During the first few centuries of Islam, the Sunni Muslims regarded *ijtihad* as the fourth source for the discovery of *shari'a* law in addition to the Qu'ran, the precedent of the prophet (the *sunna*) and the consensus of the jurists *(ijm'a)*. During this period, shi'i jurists discussed *ijtihad* in their books only in order to reject it as, they said, it was based on conjecture *(zann)* and was therefore capable of error in discovering *shari'a* law.[80] After the time of the leaders of the four Sunni schools, however, some Sunni jurists, like Ghazzali (A.H.450-505) and Ibn al Hajib (A.H. 570-646),[81] began to use *ijtihad* in its general meaning of exerting oneself in an attempt to discover *shari'a* law. Athough the door of *ijtihad* was never closed in Shi'i law, it was from this time that Shi'i jurists started to discuss *ijtihad* in their books as an accepted concept. It is generally believed that the first Shi'i jurist who used and discussed *ijtihad* in its new meaning was jamal al-Din al-Hasan ibn al-Mutahhar (called 'Allama Hilli, d.A.H.726). In his book *Tahdhib al-Usul.* He has a chapter on *ijtihad,* and here by *ijtihad* he means to the new meaning of the word acceptable to Shi'is.

---

80 See, for example, Shaikh Tusi, *Uddat al-Usul,* p.3.

81 See: Ghazzail. *Op.Cit.*, p. 350; Ibn al-Hajib (Uthman ibn Umar), *Mukhtasar al-Muntahal Usuli* (Cairo: Matba'a Kurdistan al - Ilmiya, A. H. 1326), p.221.

As for the time when *ijtihad* began to be exercised in Shi'i law, it must be noted that the period of *nass* (lit. text: the period during which there is access to someone like the prophet whose conduct is believed to be approved by God as authoritative) in Ithna 'Ashari shi'i School continues until the disappearance of their Twelfth Imam in A.H. 329, whereas this period, according to the Sunni Schools, continues only until the demise of the prophet. This has led some writers to the wrong conclusion that the period of *ijtihad* in Shi'i law started from the 4th century after the disappearance of the 12th Imam, i.e. approximately at the same time when the door of *ijtihad* was closed in Sunni law.[82] Such a conclusion is wrong, because the Shi'i Imams were usually living in Medina far from the Shi'i lands. Furthermore, because of their conflict with caliphs, many of the Imams were put either in prison or under house-arrest for considerable periods of time. Therefore, the competent Shi'i jurists did not have easy access to them[83] and needed to exercise *ijtihad* even during their life-time.

In fact the Imams themselves encouraged such an exercise of *ijtihad* by competent jurists. Imam J'afar al-Sadig, the sixth Shi'i Imam, for example, is related to have

---

[82] See, for example, C.J. Adams. "Naghshe Shaikh Tusi" (trans. M.H. Saket) in *Hezareye Shaikh Tusi* (ed. A. Davani) (Qum: Dar al-Tabligh Eslami, 1349Sh.), Vol. II, pp. 22-28. at, pp. 27-28.

[83] The story of one of the companions of Imam J'afar al - Sadiq, the sixth Shi'i Imam, for example, who had to prentend to be a pedlar selling cucumbers, before being able to see the Imam, is very well-known. See: M. Mutahhari "Elhami az Shaikhe Taife" in *Hezareye Shaikh Tusi,* Vol. II, pp. 29-48 at p. 42.

said to one of his companions (Aban), "Sit in the mosque of Medina and give your opinion [in disputes] among people, as I like to see [competent] persons like you among my followers".[84]

Before ending this section, one last thing should be mentioned briefly. About four centuries ago a movement was started among Shi'is by Mulla Amin Astarabadi (d.A.H.1026) which was called the Akhbari movement. The Akhbaris rejected *ijtihad* altogether and relied solely on the *sunna* of the prophet and the Imams. As an example of their unjustifiable reliance on *sunna,* Wahid Behbahani, who was a strong opponent of them, says that if it can be found that a sick man was ordered by one of the Imams to drink cold water, the Akbaris give the same order to any patient, whatever his illness may be. Due to the strong opposition by famous Shi'i jurists to this movement, it could not survive as a school and it can hardly have a supporter among Shi'is today.[85]

In spite of the appearance of this movement among Shi'is, they are usually known as *Ahl al-Ijtihad* (supporters of personal legal reasoning),[86] since the dominant view in this school has always been that the door of *ijtihad* may never be closed, as the human society is in the process of constant changes.

---

[84] *Ibid.*, p.42.

[85] See M. Mutahhari, "Asle Ijtihad dar Eslam" in *Dah Goftar* (Tehran: Sadra, 1361 Sh.) pp. 76-107 at p. 89.

[86] Muhaqqiq Hilli, *Ma'arij al-Usul* (Najaf: Maktabat al- Imam al-Hakim, n.d.), p.117.

ISLAMIC CRIMINAL LAW AND THE CHALLENGE OF CHANGE

In the field of criminal law, the object of updating Islamic law is achieved by providing for "discretionary" punishments or *t'azirat*. While retaliation or *qisas* has been prescribed for intentional homicide and bodily harm (*jinaya*) and prescribed punishments or *hudud*[87] have been expressly mentioned in the Qu'ran or the *Sunna* of the prophet for a handful of predefined offences, all other offences may be punished using the concept of *t'azir*.

In answering the question why punishments of a limited number of crimes have been prescribed by God, but the duty of determining punishments for other crimes has been left to the discretion of judges, it may be suggested that the Law-Maker of Islam (*Shar'i*) determined his basic and fundamental values. He also prescribed the most fundamental offences which might be committed against one of these values, together with their respective punishments. It was certain, however, that, with the passing of time, new crimes would be created which were

---

[87] There is no consensus among jurists on the crimes punishable by *hadd*. The number or these crimes range from four to seven according to different jurists. All jurists agree that adultery (*zina*), theft (*sirqah*), resorting to arms in order to frighten people (*muharaba* or *hiraba*) and false accusation of unchastity (*qadhf*) are punishable by *hadd*. The reason for such a consensus is that these crimes and their respective punishments have been prescribed in the Qu'ran. Most jurists regard apostasy (*irtidad*), armed rebellion (*baghy*) and wine - drinking (*shurb al - khamr*) also as crimes punishable by *hadd*. No punishment has been prescribed for apostasy in the laws of Iran.

committed against one of these values (and could not possibly be mentioned in express terms some fourteen centuries ago). In order to guarantee the Islamic law's perpetual application, therefore, judges and jurists needed to be given a discretionary power to determine a proper punishment for these new crimes committed against the accepted values of *Shari'a.*

The very fact that the number of offences punishable by discretionary punishments far exceeds that of offences punishable by retaliation or prescribed punishments, signifies the former's important role in updating Islamic criminal law. To achieve this, all the offences punishable by *t'azir,* together with their respective punishments, should be codified. In other words, this duty has to be taken away from judges, who were traditionally vested with this power, and instead be given to an organ with powers similar to those of parliaments in parliamentary systems. The judges can then be limited to applying the laws enacted by the legislator. To present a juristic basis for this suggestion, one can say that at the early stage of Islam a judge had two different functions: he first had to find out what the law of God was, and then had to apply it to the particular case before him. However, as the separation of these two functions is not forbidden in *shari'a*, the principle of tolerance *(ibaha)* enables us to give each one of them to a separate organ.[88] It is certain that when a competent human being (like a judge) is permitted under *shari'a* to decide about *t'azirat,* there is no reason to

[88] Separation of the three powers of the legislative, the judiciary and the executive is accepted by Article 57 of the Iranian Constitution.

forbid another competent human being (like a jurist or a member of parliament) from doing the same. This reasoning is strengthened by the fact that when traditional books of Islamic law, speakof the person who can decide about *t'azirat,* different words have been used, such as: the Imam, the judge, and the ruler *(hakim)*. This proves that the power was not meant to be given particularly to judges, but to the sovereign authority as a whole.[89] There can, therefore, be no objection to giving it to any other officially delegated competent person.[90]

If this is done, one can hope that Muslim society can take the most advantage of the law of *t'azirat*, which is the main area for the operation of the principle of *ijtihad* in criminal law.

---

[89] N.J. Coulson, in *A History of Islamic Law* (Edinburgh University Press, 1964), at p. 132 says, "As for substantive law, the sovereign is completely free, outside the *hadd* offences, to determine what behaviour constitutes an offence and what punishment is to be applied in each case". Using the word 'soverign' (instead of judge) is noticeable.

[90] In fact, throughout Islamic history, various unsuccessful attempts were made to limit judges to applying a premade code of law. 'Umar ibn 'Abd al-'Aziz, for example, once tried to make a uniqe law from various religious decrees *(fatawi)* of different jurists of Medina. This was intended to be followed by all judges in cases brought before them, but he died before being able to finish this work. See: M. Abu Zahrah, *Falsafat al-'Uqubah fil Figh al-Islami* (Cairo: M'ahad al - Dirasat al-'Arabiyat al-'Aliya, 1963),p.85. Such an interference by caliphs, however, was, as seen before, always objected to by judges and jurists themselves. In Iran and Saudi Arabia, legal codes have been enacted which mention the main offences punishable by *t'azir* together with their respective punishments.

CONCLUSION

A religious system of law like Islam, which claims to have been originated from God and also claims perpetual validity for its application, needs to provide a certain degree of flexibility in applying the cardinal rules to actual cases in different ages. This is so because, with the passing of time, the society faces new problems which could not even be contemplated by the people living in the past. Without a provision being made to permit mankind to enact proper laws or to interpret existing laws within the general framework of *shari'a,* to deal with these new problems and to find solutions to them, Islamic law would certainly have been inadequate after the first Islamic era.

An attempt was made in this paper to show the capabilities of Islamic law, through the mechanisms provided in it, to strike a balance between the unchangeable Will of God and the changing human need and desire. This is made possible by the general nature of some of the provisions of Islamic law, embodied in its main sources, together with the acceptance of the doctrine of *ijtihad* (personal legal reasoning) in Islamic, and particularly Shi'i, law. There is no doubt that if Islamic law is to remain a living and developing system capable of meeting and solving the new problems of Muslim societies, an attempt must be made to use the principle of *ijtihad*, within the accepted limits imposed by divine command. This can be done by those who recognize the fundamental, unchangeable principles of *shari'a* and have also the ability of applying these principles to the changing situation of our present age. This practice is a true reflection of the soul of the present Muslim society, which "is reflected neither in any from of outright secularism nor in the doctrine of the mediaeval text books."[91]

Professor of Faculty of Law
Shahid Beheshti University
Dean of Faculty of Judicial Sciences
Tehran, Iran

---

[91] N.J. Coulson, *A History of Islamic Law*, p. 225.

PART III

IMPLICATION OF THE RELIGIOUS FOUNDATION OF THE PERSON

Chapter VII

Reflections on the Meaning of Person

Kenneth Schmitz

I have been asked to reflect particularly on the religious sources of the notion of the person in light of its current understanding in the so-called West. The modern prevalent understanding of the term and its reality takes its origin within a religious context that pre-dates both Christianity and Islam. From its beginnings in ancient Mediterranean culture, it has taken shape as a distinctive understanding of the human being, and travelled through a number of cultures: ancient Greek and Roman, Mediaeval Eastern and Western European, Syriac, Arabic and Persian; and currently, a secularized form of humanism.[92]

---

[92]For a fuller account, see Schmitz, "The Geography of the Human Person," with references to Grillmeier, Nédoncelle, de Vogel, J.N.D. Kelly, Pelikan and others, in: *Communio*, XIII/no.1 (Spring), 1986, pp. 27-48.--I must confess my ignorance as to an adequate knowledge of developments that have fallen outside of the linguistic cultures of Greece, Rome and the modern European languages, and I welcome additional comment.--Among studies of the Latin translations of Ibn Sina (Avicenna) and others in respect to their important contribution to St. Thomas Aquinas, see esp. Louis Gardet, "Saint Thomas et ses Prédécesseurs Arabes," and Georges Anawati, OP., "Saint Thomas d'Aquin et la Métaphysique d'Avicenne," in: *St. Thomas Aquinas 1274-1974. Commemorative Studies* (2 vols. ed. A. Maurer, CSB, Toronto:

Most recently, the secularized culture in the West has elevated the term to prominence, although it tends to confuse the term and the reality with that of the individual. Before touching upon its career, it may be well to sketch the features associated with the current usage of the term "person," at least as it has been formulated in modern political and legal documents and is currently in common use in the West.

While the two notions (individual and person) are often confused in current discussions, it is important to distinguish them. Often conflated, as though identical, their etymology and their historical origins speak against such confusion. The context in which the human being is considered an individual is implicitly a physical one, since it designates the human being as an undivided unity, related to others in and through material individuation. For the individual is related to others by way of external relations in place or space. In modern culture, other properties have come to be attached to the individual, most of them associated with the alleged impregnability of the unit, heralded usually as privacy rights.

The designation of a human being as a person, on the other hand, tends to stress a certain interiority and relatedness, reminiscent of its religious origins, and carrying with it the guarantee of a certain inalienability. Whereas an individual as a material substance may lose its unity through division (or decomposition), a person cannot be separated from his or her innate dignity; for

---

Pontifical Institute of Mediaeval Studies, 1974; respectively, vol. I, pp. 419-448 & 449-465.

that connection is a formal rather than a material or quantitative one. Moreover, whereas an individual may be taken to be exchangeable with another, as one unit for another, a person is taken to be unique, and as traditional language expresses it: *incommunicabilis.*[93]

In the topography of modern political usage, today's vocabulary ("to the left, right, or centre") assumes that the social and political polarities are between individual and collective, expressed as the opposition between liberalism and collectivism; the former favoring rights to the individual, the latter ceding them to the state; or more moderately, often seeking a somewhat shifting compromise between these extremes.

A better way of structuring this tension is to reflect upon the relation as between the person and the community rather than between the individual and the collective. Whereas the relation understood as between the individual and the collective stresses an external relation in which the two must adjust their respective claims with regard to one another, the relation understood as between person and community already incorporates an internal set of relations that affects the joint identity of each. The two terms and their realities are understood to be in an intrinsic reciprocity with one another: indeed, are co-constitutive of one another. This acknowledgement alters the atmosphere in which claims on behalf of one or the other are made and allows the common good to emerge. For the relation is then seen as

---

[93]Paradoxically, this very incommunicability is the ground for the possibility of communicability.

complementary, rather than as adversarial. No doubt, the defensive attitude put forward on behalf of the individual's claims ("I have my rights!") has arisen in part at least (and on its negative side) in reaction to the enormous power which the modern state has acquired--the power to encroach upon dimensions of life hitherto untouched and considered sacrosanct.

There is a further fall-out from the tension between society and its members when they are construed as individual and collective. For, as already mentioned, if we take the individual as the primary unit of society, we conceive both the individual and society in terms of external relations, each standing over against the other. In so doing, we disregard the interior life of the person: his or her ethical, intellectual and spiritual life, and along with it, his religious values, motivation and conduct. This misconstrues the nature of the person's membership in society. It is too easy, then, to reduce the individual, defined in terms of some limited common aspect--consumer, worker, voter, statistic--to the mass of individuals and to transfer the individual's primary and total well-being over to the state and society. This modern phenomenon of the absorption of the individual into the Giant Individual, i.e., the State, becomes, in its extreme form, totalitarian. Modern totalitarianism differs from older forms of tyranny in that it professes to carry with it a justification in terms of an ethical or metaphysical ideology. No longer does the person suffer from the arbitrary brutality of a tyrant, but from the systematic oppression by a regime that dresses itself up in some form of humanism, justifying itself in the name of race or nation or some other specific property.

The political history of the Western cultures during the first half of the past century is marked by the rise of totalitarian regimes of several varieties, most prominently the ideology of racism promoted by the Nazi tyranny and by the collectivist ideology of the Communist regimes. Each of these in its own way submerged the person in the State almost without residue. Lest we in the Western democracies congratulate ourselves too easily, however, we need to be aware that we have too often confused the person with the individual, thus isolating our shared humanity behind bastions of enclosed self-interest, armed with individual or corporate rights that take priority over the good of the community. There is a common logic at work in this polarization of individual and collective. While, at the surface level, individualism and collectivism appear to be polar opposites, at a deeper level they participate in a common ground that easily shifts the weight of power to the political center. The late Pope John Paul II signalled this commonality when he observed that whenever God is excluded from public discourse--by separating religion from society and Church from State, rather than by distinguishing their different competencies--the State inevitably usurps the place of God, determining issues of life and death and of the common good.[94]

---

[94] *Memory and Identity. Conversations at the Dawn of a Millennium*, New York: Rizzoli, 2005: While sincerely acknowledging that the Enlightenment "has yielded many positive fruits," (p. 3; and c. 18: pp.

CURRENT POPULAR USAGE

The word "person" is obviously value-loaded in much of present modern discourse. A few moments reflection upon the way we use the term illustrates its curious power and, at the same time, its ambiguity. Advertisers have caught on to the electricity in the word and have attempted to use it to their profit, using one's first name, if possible in shortened and familiar form, to entice you to purchase a product. And in the media culture, one says of a celebrity that he or she is a charming person, "has a fine personality," meaning that the celebrity makes a pleasing self-presentation. Indeed, it is common to speak of such a celebrity as a "personality," meaning that he or she projects a public image that may

---

107-114, citing the positive values of "liberty, equality and fraternity"), he remarks upon the unfortunate re-direction of thought by which Enlightenment consciousness (cf. the Cartesian turn to self-consciousness) absorbed existence (*esse*) into itself (p. 8f.): "The entire drama of salvation history had disappeared as far as the Enlightenment was concerned. Man remained alone: alone as creator of his own history and his own civilization; alone as one who decides what is good and what is bad, as one who would exist and operate *etsi Deus non daretur*, even if there were no God" (p. 10). And, recalling recent European history: "Over the years I have become more and more convinced that the ideologies of evil are profoundly rooted in the history of European philosophical thought" (p. 7). In particular, he remarks upon the enactments of "democratically elected parliaments" in matters of sexual morality and family law. And in chilling words, he observes that "it is legitimate and even necessary to ask whether this is not the work of another ideology of evil, more subtle and hidden, perhaps, intent upon exploiting human rights themselves against man and against the family" (p. 11).

or may not correspond to the reality of which it is a façade. Caught up in the flurry of the passing moment, they warn that "we don't have a second chance to make a first impression." The cheap tabloids, on the other hand, make their profit by shamelessly exploiting any suspected discrepancy between surface and depth.

But herein lies the significance of these phenomena: the word "personality," used in this way, indicates a surface impression. In contrast, however, the adjective "personal" and the noun "person" usually denote depth. I may resist a "nosey-parker" by responding to his unwarranted questions with the warning: "That's personal;" meaning that he has encroached upon matters that are not open to casual scrutiny. More deeply still, after a fruitful interview, I am liable to say: "I was treated as a person." And here we touch upon the value held within the ambience of the term.

In sum, then, at least in Western parlance, there is an ambivalence in the way we use the term "person" and its variant forms: on the one hand, they suggest something manifest, open and public; on the other, something hidden and private. It is a paradoxical term, suggesting something superficial, and concurrently something precious and all but hidden in its dignity and true worth.

ANCIENT SOURCES OF THE TERM

These present-day traits are found in the ancient sources of the term as well; and even a brief history of the term sheds light on its meaning, and on the reality for which it stands. It is noteworthy that the term has retained a remarkable consistency among the European languages. Moreover, unlike most words--such as the English "tree," the German "Baum," or the Latin/French "arbor/arbre"--it is a term whose origins are not lost in the mists of time. For its career can be traced from its origins to its present use. This indicates that it is an historically conscious term that calls each human being towards a realization of a dignity, in which the values of being human are embodied in a basic and exemplary way.

It will help, then, to locate the origins of the term and to trace the capital developments in its career, at least within the ambit of Indo-European languages. The story begins in the Mediterranean cultures, locally among the Etruscans, that little known people who inhabited the area just north of Rome. From its beginning, the term has been associated rather closely with religious sensibilities, and indeed, it takes its origin from the cult of the goddess Persephone. It is significant that she spent part of the year above the ground and part below, in the underworld; thus playing out in her mythical figure the tension between the visible surface and the hidden depth, a tension still associated with the modern sense of the term "person".

The word used for the mask in her cult was Phersu. It manifested the goddess in the daylight of her fecund power and hid her in the obscurity of her destiny. As the Romans absorbed the elements of Etruscan culture, the term underwent a rapid expansion. In the Roman theatre it was used more generally to designate the mask through which the actor spoke the character being represented. Indeed, it is still common to preface plays with the list of *dramatis personae.* The mask was that by which the actor visibly represented the character to the audience, while at the same time it was the device through which the actor sounded the character's spoken words; hence the Latin: *per-sonare*, "to sound through." In a further development, this close association with the spoken word recommended the term to the Latin grammarians who divided the speech-forms into first, second and third speakers, now termed persons: I, thou, it; we, you, they.

So far, then, the term exhibits a close association with the manifest and the hidden, and with representation and communication. But the element of dignity is present as well, derived no doubt from its mythical divine source. For in the transference of the term from the deity to humanity, Roman jurisprudence did not initially confer the term upon each and every human being, but reserved it for those who possessed full civic status. Neither children, nor slaves, nor women, nor usually foreigners, were held to be persons recognized by the law. Only adult male citizens were entitled to bring a case before the court and have it heard as a personal right. Finally, with Cicero, the term took on a metaphysical meaning and denoted what is distinctive in each individual as contrasted with the humanity shared in common by all. In the short period of three centuries or less, the Latin term had acquired an exceptionally rich contextual meaning, driven by an intuition regarding the special character of the human being in close association with divinity.

Meanwhile in Greece a term (*prosopon*) with a somewhat different etymology began a career that would eventually merge with that of the Latin *persona* in naming this distinctive reality. The Greek term *prosopon* placed the emphasis upon a direct face-to-face visual encounter (*pro* [before, in front of]-, *ops* [the eye, face]-, *on*)[95], so that the highly charged aspect of intimacy came to the fore (in the I-thou relation). For this reason, the term was associated with the human face, which, as Aristotle tells us, is proper to the human, remarking that oxen and other beasts do not have faces, only frontages. For the human face is more than a physiological structure just because it is the bearer of a distinctive inner meaning, expressive of the person.

In an affiliated development of the term, the Biblical scriptures played a role as a third source. In the interplay of late Judaic and Hellenic cultures, appeal was made to the notion of personification in order to interpret certain passages in the Bible, especially those referring to Sophia.[96] The hermeneutic is known as prosographic exegesis. Even more closely, the Septuagint translators of the Hebrew Bible into the Greek used the term *prosopon*, to designate the sounding mask through

---

[95]"To look one in the face": *eis ôpa idésthai* from *'oraô*: "to see, look, behold"; by intension: "to take heed"; and in the passive: "to be seen," also "to appear".

[96]The Book of Wisdom (in the Alexandrian canon), esp. 6:22-8:21..

which the Lord spoke: "out of "the mouth of the Lord."[97] The Latin translators naturally enough rendered that word as *persona*, so that both the Greek and Latin usages converged to introduce the term respectively into the Eastern and Western European languages.

DEVELOPMENTS AMONG THE CHRISTIAN FATHERS

And here we enter a sensitive area in our dialogue with one another, ripe with misunderstandings, so that I will preface this next section with a cautionary. For, as I move on to the next development, I move into an important difference between the faith of Christianity and the faith of Islam. It is well then to clarify the nature of inter-religious dialogue. It can occur fruitfully only if a profound respect exists for both partners in the dialogue. Moreover, it must be borne in mind that the immediate purpose of the conversation is not the conversion of one party to the other's faith. Nor is it a debate, in which one wins over the other. Rather it aims at a growth in mutual understanding; even to the point that each party may come into a better appreciation of their own faith. This is not to minimize the importance of the faith commitment of each party. Indeed, it is a requirement of dialogue that

---

[97]The Hebrew word (translated as mouth) is a dynamic one: *peh* from *pâ'âh* ("to breathe forth;" *Deut.* 8:3, *Jer.* 15:1. Cf. the more visual Greek *stómatos,* said of God speaking through the mouth of His Prophets (*Lk* 1:70, *Acts* 3:18). The connection with the expressive part of the face, and with the interior meaning carried by the voice, suggests the deeply personal communication expressed by the Word of God.

each party speak honestly, seriously and sincerely; so that both surrender to the truth as it discloses itself in the shared conviction that God, the very Source of truth itself, oversees all. It is in this spirit of dialogue that Pope Paul VI and the late Pope John Paul II have many, many times invited Christians and Moslems to enter into such dialogue for their mutual benefit.[98]

The next marked development occurred in the context of Church doctrine. For the great Church Councils of the fourth and fifth centuries wrestled with the wondrous fact of the revelation they saw disclosed in Jesus: that Jesus Christ is Lord (*Christos Kyrios*!) This

---

[98]See, in the publication by the Pontifical Council for Interreligious Dialogue: *Interreligious Dialogue. The Official Teaching of the Catholic Church (1963-1995)*, (ed. F. Gioia, Boston: Pauline Books & Media, 1997), among many such invitations and addresses to Moslem communities and representatives: [by Paul VI] to Uganda (p.164), Pakistan (168), Morocco (169), Iran (177), Egypt (204); [by John Paul II] to Kenya (226, 293)), Ghana (229), France (233), Pakistan (234), Philippines (235), Nigeria (250, 391), Belgium (284), Cameroon (290), Morocco (297), Argentina (372), Lebanon (416), Malta (434), Iran (456), Senegal (474-75), Guinea (480), Benin (506) and to the European Islamic Community (504). In addition, John Paul has held a symposium: "Holiness in Christianity and in Islam" (283), a colloquium between Christians and Muslims (424), spoken to the World Islamic Call Society (428), and sent a message at the end of Ramadan (451), among other initiatives.--Cardinal Ratzinger (now Pope Benedict XVI) spoke to the issue in a *Lectio magistralis* at the Monastery of Santa Maria sopra Minerva, Rome, May 13, 2004: "The rebirth of Islam is due in part to the new material richness acquired by Muslim countries, but mainly to the knowledge that it is able to offer a valid spiritual foundation for the life of its people." (*In the Vineyard of the Lord. The Life, Faith and Teachings of Joseph Ratzinger/Pope Benedict XVI*, Marco Bardazzi, New York: Rizzoli, 2004, p. 119f.)

demanded a new vocabulary towards which the Fathers groped, giving to the term person a central role in understanding the revelation of Who Jesus is. Once embraced, the term person received a new and deeper meaning, as do all terms said of God: for the Christian believes that Christ is "fully God and fully man"--possessed fully of both divine and human natures--yet that He is also singularly unique. The formula arrived at is confessed by Christians: Christ is the Son of the Father, a divine person (hypostatically, i.e., personally) uniting two natures (divine and human) in the Second Person of the Trinity.

Now this naming of Christ is by no means a dry linguistic event. For in uniting humanity with divinity in such an intimate way, that is, by drawing human nature into the closest possible union with the very being of the Divine, the whole of humanity is called to an unprecedented dignity.

Nor was the term person said of Jesus alone; but also of the Father and the Holy Spirit within the Trinitarian Godhead. The Christian faithful confessed the three Persons in the one God, but did not diminish the supreme and transcendent unity of God, as though Christians were polytheists believing in three gods. It was not the transcendent and supreme unity of God that was diminished or diluted by this affirmation of faith; but rather it was the very nature of unity itself that was seen to be mysteriously transformed. So transcendent and unique was the divine Oneness that theology speaks of three persons within the one divine nature.[99] This was not understood to be a reconstruction undertaken by human intelligence, but rather was confessed as a revelation grounded in the life of Christ and the Scriptures. By contrast: With each human, it is one person in one individuated nature; not so with God. The term person is for the Christian a precious and mysterious term. This revelation from God, far transcending unaided human capability or even capacity, and received by the Christian in faith, opened up a vision into the interior life of the Godhead Itself: the Father eternally begetting His only begotten Son in a love that overflows into the very person of the Holy Spirit. This mutual feast of love is sustained by the eternal "traffic" among the divine persons.

Following upon the Trinitarian love, as a model to be imitated and a reality to be participated in through grace and sacrament, a new sense of intimacy shaped the bonds between human persons. Its first expression was that of the assembly or church (*ecclesia*). A new kind of friendship, a new fellowship, emerged with the call to an unprecedented intimacy with each other and with the Persons of the Godhead. Here love itself received a new name: not *eros* or even *philia* but *agape* (*caritas* in a transformed sense). Human beings were thereby called to a new dignity, that is, to be nothing less than the adopted

---

[99]A classical theological exposition is that of St. Thomas Aquinas, *Summa theologiae* I, q. 29ff. Thomas distinguished between the substantial unity of God (the Divine Nature) and the differing relations that constitute the Persons.

children of God (*kata charin*). And so, when in the High Middle Ages Thomas Aquinas defined the human person as intelligent and free and having dominion over his own acts, he placed that definition of the human person in the context of the divine commands to Love God and neighbour.

MODERN DEVELOPMENTS: THE CONTRACTION TO HUMAN SUBJECTIVITY

The third major development of the term can be signalled by the founding declarations of modernity. In the seventeenth century the term underwent simultaneously both a new intensity and a reduction. For, in the main,[100] the center of thought shifted to an all but exclusive confidence in the human subject. The medieval theological context gave way to an intense concentration upon the possibilities of human agency, both in coming to exact knowledge and in the exercise of autonomous freedom. Now, such a contraction narrowed the horizon of possibility and expectant hope. Open transcendence had hitherto been ingredient in the religious sense of the term. Now, however, transcendence came to be seen as not part of this world, but as putatively belonging to some other world inaccessible to reason and given over to

---

[100]I say "in the main," since as in any culture, the detailed context is much more complex, containing traditional orthodox Christian believers as well as agnostics and atheists. I do not pretend here to give a history of thought, but rather select what I take to be a dominant trend in modern Western thought.

faith understood as merely subjective private opinion, no longer to be appealed to in public discourse.

It seemed as though one were slicing an orange and had left a questionable part of it aside. So it appeared; but transcendence, as a fact of human experience, is not so easily suppressed. Instead, the modern contraction is rather like squeezing an orange, so that all the elements or aspects remain but take on a new shape.

So, too, with the notion of person: all of the elements or aspects remain in the modern concept: the manifest and the hidden, the communicability, the distinctiveness, the special dignity, and the intimacy; but they take on a new configuration. Some (such as autonomous power) assume an overwhelming importance; some (such as transcendence) are so transformed as to have lost their original sublimity and exaltation, and in some quarters receive a negative, allegedly escapist value. One or another element comes to the fore, others recede. As in the instance of the fruit, the condensation and compactedness is increased, but the fibres are crushed and the perceptible features are rearranged. So, too, with the modern notion of person; it retains the essential features of the older, religiously inspired and grounded notion, but in a new arrangement, highlighting some features (such as freedom and autonomy), all but suppressing others (such as mysterious depth and transcendent openness).

We may illustrate this contraction by contrasting modern psychological introspection with religious interiority, Modern introspection is typified by Descartes' inward journey which comes to rest in the self-assurance of a finite mind. Both the religious and the psychological movements pass within from the outer world to the human subject; but introspection stops there, only to issue forth again as from a newly established starting-point--either in order to control nature (e.g., Francis Bacon and modern technology) or in order to explore intersubjective relations (e.g., in the 18th century novel).

Religious interiority possesses a quite different dynamic, for it passes beyond the human subject to acknowledge the transcendent power of a loving God. The subject becomes a footstool from which the sinner repents in prayer in order to place himself or herself in humility before the vast uplands of the sacred. In modern introspection the human subject becomes the first principle, both theoretically and practically: the *Individuum* rules, psychologically as an individual, politically as the secular state. All things, then, are referred to the human subject as to the final court of appeal.

There can be no doubt that this has engendered the enormous interest and creative energy associated with modern novels, art, autobiography, and psychology. There can be no doubt, too, about the rich yield of this intense interest in the human adventure, a richness that emerged from the Middle Ages to achieve an unprecedented appreciation of selected features of the human person. But persons of faith lament a great loss, while those without faith unknowingly suffer it.[101]

---

[101]Conscious of this loss in contemporary Europe, Pope Benedict XVI (then Cardinal Ratzinger) deplores "a foundation that seems to have

TOWARDS A CONTEMPORARY RECONFIGURATION OF THE PERSON

It is important to notice that all of the elements or aspects associated with the term are present in the contemporary understanding: the play of appearance and ground, the demand for communication, the appreciation of distinctiveness, the insistence upon dignity and value, the expectation of intimacy. At first it seems that transcendence--in the sense of a trans-human dimension--is wholly absent from this modern list of features constitutive of the person; but the hunger for intimacy so characteristic of the present culture is the form that transcendence takes in the modern milieu. Nor is the survival of a reduced sense of transcendence surprising, given that these features are essential to personhood, and that human beings have always been--and still are--persons.

If we ask how these features are related, however, it is important to determine whether they are to be understood as elements, conjoined by external relations; therefore treating the person as an individual. Or whether they are to be understood as aspects of a singular unity, integrated by internal relations, and therefore sealed within a unique integrity. We must ask eventually whether it is as elements or as aspects that these features

---

escaped from the hands of old Europe, which has thus, despite its lasting political and economic power, come to be seen increasingly as condemned to decline and fall" (*op. cit.*, p. 120).

best realize the full potential intimated by the reality of the person. And this returns us to the initial question put at the beginning of our present reflection: whether the relation is best understood as between individual and collectivity, or as between person and community.

Now, if these original features are all present in the contemporary conception of the person, the attempt to formulate a suitable contemporary understanding of the human person ought not to draw upon considerations lying outside the ambience of the concept and its reality, but ought to seek the best configuration of these features that are already-- and have always been--in play. We pose, then, a series of questions concerning the features deemed essential to the person:[102]

Does the classical modern contraction and its resultant configuration adequately realize the openness to which the person is called? Or does establishing the finite subject as primary not predispose the referral inevitably to the self as final arbiter--either to the individual self (as in classical liberalism) or to the public self (as in the political alternative of state collectivism)? And does this not introduce a certain closure, either to other selves (as secular humanism finds it ultimate value in a brotherhood and sisterhood without a fatherhood that joins them), or at least to a finite horizon of possibility?[103]

---

[102]For an initial version of these questions (here somewhat developed and nuanced), see "Reconstructing the Person. A Meditation on the Meaning of Personality," in: Crisis (April 1999, pp. 135-138).

[103]The tendency to enclose the infinite within the finite is already underway in much of modern thought, e.g., in Heidegger's defence of the finitude of *Dasein*.

Second, can there be intimacy in its deepest, nearest form without an openness that invites further communion and an inexhaustible depth? There can be no doubt that there is in our present culture a prevalent hunger for intimacy far beyond sexual intimacy.[104] Here we encounter the paradox again. For the very word itself (*intimius*: innermost) associates this hunger with relations possessing meaningful interior depth. Yet on the other hand, today's public speech forecloses all references to a dimension that surpasses functional and relatively external human achievements, as though such interiority is not worthy of consideration in the "serious" discussions within the public realm.

Third, can there be adequate depth of communication? There is today a pronounced interest in language and communication, but much of it rides on the surface--a superficiality surely increased by the proliferation of electronic modes of communication. Is language best conceived as a closed digital [0/1] system or as the dynamism that casts itself beyond expression towards an ultimately ineffable reality that cannot be exhausted by words?

Fourth can there be a dignity that is not rooted in the functional status of each person (in productivity, and tangible success), but simply in being there, in the absolute presence of another person. Thomas Aquinas gave to this actual presence the name *esse*, the very existing

---

[104]At least in some of its manifestation, the cult of celebrity, insofar as it is an attempt to identify one's own life with that of the cult-object, seems driven by a misplaced desire for intimacy.

actuality of the person. Here is the root of the existential depth in each person insofar as that depth is open to philosophy. This unique and ultimately inexpressible dignity proper to each person qua person is rooted in the sheer act of that person's act of be-ing (*esse*) as originating from the Creator.[105] Devoid of insight into the radical value of each person, will this culture move more and more towards personality in the superficial sense, with a certain emptiness as the result, in which openness will mean the barren absence of intimacy? It is a paradox that an unlimited openness also preserves the deeper sense of intimacy, a "thickness" that cannot adequately be brought to verbal expression, since it possesses a kind of secret, that suggests the mystery of the unique and that presages the adventure awaiting each genuinely personal encounter.

These questions are meant to point towards the inescapable need to liberate transcendence from total absorption confined to specific human concerns--to point towards the need to integrate the trans-human exigence at play within the contemporary configuration of the person. Among others, the Swiss psycho-therapist and philosopher, Karl Jaspers, has pointed the way by his emphasis upon transcendence. What is needed is a trans-human dimension, not that of the goddess Persephone or the pantheon of the Immortals, but more radically still, the transcendence of God, understood in not entirely different ways by the Jew as the Lordship of Jahweh, by

---

[105]Thomas received from Ibn Sina the insight that the existential principle could not be absorbed into the province of the quiddity or essence.

the Christian as the Trinitarian communion of Persons, and by the Muslim as the submission to Allah.

To be sure, the precise character of that transcendence is too important an issue to be treated within the limits of this paper. Under the conditions of interreligious dialogue, we are able to acknowledge that all religions in differing degrees acknowledge the truth of transcendence--and especially those of Biblical Paternity. Now transcendence must, at the least, refer to that which is not confined to human subjectivity and human collectivity. The new configuration must resituate the integrity of each person within a context that breaks through the human horizon, both the individual and the social. Contemporary environmental movements promote an initial recognition of this need, but their attempts come to rest in the cosmos, placing the person in the ecology of the environing world. Adequate transcendence, however, must be more radically open, more than intracosmic.

Both a part of the cosmos as individuals, yet transcending it as persons,[106] each human being is called to receive from and respond to that Fullness of Being that is the Source of those very features that compose each person's most intimate existential presence and dignity.

Trinity College, University of Toronto
John Paul II Institute, Washington

---

[106]Cf. Jacques Maritain, *The Person and the Common God* (1947), University of Notre Dame Press, Indiana, 1966.

Chapter VIII

Iranian Institute of Philosophy

Gholamreza Aavani

ETHICS AND POLITICS WITHIN THE CONFINES OF RELIGION

There can be no doubt about the significance of religions in the individual and the collective life of humankind from time immemorial to the present. Every religion is an integral whole or a totality comprising a sacred doctrine, that is, a body of perennial truths believed by the adherents of that religion, and a method which makes it possible for the believers of that religion to attain the ultimate goal inculcated by that religion. This ideal goal to be attained, is variously called in different religions: spiritual enlightenment, salvation, realization, second birth, the kingdom of God, heavenly bliss, Beatitude, and so on.

Faith, needless to say is a condition *sine qua non* in every religion, without which religion itself becomes impossible. Moreover the basis of religious life is the practice of such virtues such as veracity, love of God, love of neighbor, charity, humility, trust in God, penitence, devotion, worship and so on. There are moreover some taboos in religions, which are violations of sacred doctrine or sacred practice. These are classified as cardinal and venial sins, which are more or less identical in almost all religions. Besides, every religion deems its founder as a paragon par excellence to be emulated and imitated.

Modernity, brushing aside religion as an individual and private affair, somehow relegates religion to human subjectivity. Neglecting the ultimate becoming of man, this reduces him to his terrestrial existence, totally forgetting his Heavenly and Divine vocation.

Modern political theory and ethics are based on secularism, that is, a total neglect of the Divine dimension of human existence. In my article, I try to argue that the application of certain secular theories especially in the political and ethical domains are incompatible with the very essence and spirit of religion.

The question posed in this paper is whether secular ethics and politics can be reconciled with the spirit of religion, granted that man is by nature a moral and political being. But before we are able to set our feet on secure soil, we must try to answer some preliminary questions without which the problem at issue would not find a satisfactory answer. What do we mean by religion; is religion predicated homonymously or synonymously. What are the ingredients of a true religion. Are ethics and politics among the essential attributes and the constituents of a religion, or are they marginal and peripheral elements which a religion can dispense with. What is the ultimate goal in religion, if any?

THE NATURE OF RELIGION

Religion, to begin with, is not a homonymous term, that is one word stipulated for quite diverse meanings, otherwise discourse about religion would be impossible: it is rather a synonymous term, that is a single term having exactly the same and identical meaning in its multifarious instantiations. Grammatically speaking this is a truism for which we can find many instances in our routine daily experience. But such grammatical platitudes have deeply-rooted metaphysical and ontological foundations without which they would not even be conceivable, which in this case is the universal principle of the manifestation of unity in multiplicity. Ours world is a spatio-temporal continuum which by its very nature demands multiplicity and diversity. A fact which is unique in time is not unique in space and inversely. So everything we behold in our universe is multiple in nature, even if it appears to be unique. Such multiplicity we observe in individuals, species, genera, substances, colors, races and languages. To take but the latter example each person speaks his own language and each language appears in its own sphere as the language, but none the less language in all these instances has a singular meaning and function. This argument would apply as well in the case of religion. It would be astonishing and indeed absurd if this multiplicity did not occur in the religious sphere.

Sacred Doctrine and Method

Every religion is an integral whole or a totality comprising a sacred doctrine, that is a body of perennial truths believed by the adherents of that religion, and a method, which is a way of union and which makes possible for the believers of that religion the attainment to the ultimate goal inculcated by that religion. The sacred doctrine is believed in a religion to be absolute and perennial by nature, having nothing in it of the nature of contingency. In all religions, the doctrine is concerned with making a distinction between the absolute and the relative, the *atma* and the *maya*, the creator and the creature, the beyond-being and being, or in most religions between God and the world. To deny the absolute or to relativize it (i.e. to downgrade it to a relative status) or to absolutize the relative and that which is contingent by nature, or to identify the absolute with the relative, is to commit a great metaphysical error and a manifest violation of the sacred doctrine in the religion concerned. The doctrine, moreover, is considered in every religion to be sacred and divine and hence inviolable, representing the eternal and primordial truth in the human order. It is as a matter of fact the highest truth that the human intelligence can attain by the aid of revelation and through Divine Grace. Lacking the sacred doctrine, by whatever designation it be called in each religion, is deemed ignorance (or *avidya*) pure and simple. Hence the doctrine has a saving function in each religion. Heathens or pagans who are not in possession of the doctrine are doomed to eternal damnation and the possessors of the doctrine are apportioned an abode of bliss and beatitude.

Every religion, in addition, requires a method, which is the way of attainment, and realization which ultimately ends in beatific vision and salvific union. Without a method religion would be a mere abstraction. Method, in other words, is the conformity and submission of the human will to the exigencies of the sacred doctrine.

Moreover, the method in each religion is associated with prayers, sacred rites liturgies litanies and certain other sacred practices.

Three Essential Concomitants

One could also say that knowledge, love and virtue (good deeds) are the three intrinsic concomitants of every religion which are correlated with the three distinctive features of human beings, that is, the Divine intellect, will and speech. The Divine intelligence has as its object, the total truth as manifested in the sacred doctrine; the human will has as its proper object, the submission to, and the deliberate choice of, the absolute as revealed in the sacred doctrine. It is fundamentally a choice between the outward and the inward, between the absolute and the relative between the permanent and the impermanent, between Heaven and earth, or between God and the world. Such a choice would be impossible without the voluntary submission of the human will which in itself necessitates love of God. This love in itself is a reversal or a conversion of an initial perversion resulting from man's fallen nature; a moreover, it must be continually renewed in order to counterbalance the love of the ego and the attachment to the world. Love of God, on the other hand, is a function of faith, without the intrinsic integrity of which love would not be real. Hence faith is the condition *sine qua non* in every religion. Stated counterpositively, unbelievers are deprived of the mysteries and the blessings of faith.

Faith and Virtues

In religion, intellectual qualification is not valid unless it is accompanied by moral qualification, or in other words by virtues and pious deeds. Faith in itself implies all the spiritual qualities such as patience, perseverance, trust, hope, gratitude, confidence, generosity, charity, love of neighbor, etc. Each virtue, on the one hand, is a realization and a reflection of a Divine quality in man, granted that man is an image of God. Virtue, on the other hand, is not a mere mental and conceptual abstraction; but rather, as its etymology implies, it is a spiritual power embedded in the human soul. Religiosity goes hand in hand with the practice of virtue, without which religion loses much of its flesh and substance.

Belief in the Hereafter

In all religions the present life is not the end of the story. This life is only a transitory phase in man's spiritual perfection. Death, in religion is not the termination of life, but the starting-point of a new life determined by the words, acts, deeds, beliefs and states achieved in this life. Belief in Heaven and hell (and in some religions, purgatory) is taken for granted. There might be some difference in the details about the destiny of man in the future life; some might believe in a sort of transmigration and metempsychosis and others not; but all the same it makes no difference as regards the existence rather than the modality of the future life. It makes all the difference whether one believes or not in its existence.

Cardinal and Venial Sins

The idea of sin is a key concept in every religion. We know of no religion in which "sin" does not play a fundamental role. The highest sin in every religion is the repudiation of the sacred doctrine, which is from the religious point of view a blatant metaphysical error, or it might be a violation of the orthoproxy or the sacred practice. Such sins as atheism, fornication, burglary, theft, dishonesty are universally condemned in all religions. Each sin is an obvious violation of a corresponding virtue and each sin would hamper the spiritual perfection of man.

Imitation and Emulation of the Founder of the Religion

In each religion, the founder is the embodiment par excellence of that religion and a paragon to be imitated and emulated. He is the balance in which should be measured all the deeds, thoughts and beliefs of the believer. He is the standard of the orthodoxy and the orthoproxy in each religion. So the principle of *imitatio Christi* applies *mutatis mutandis* in all religions. *Imitatio Buddii* would be a rule in Buddhism as Imitatio Muhammadi would be in Islam. In some religions, beside, the founder of the religion takes on a metaphysical and ontological significance. For Buddhists the Buddha nature pervades everything in the universe. For Taoists for whom Lao-Tze is the personification, the Tao is manifested in everything. For Christianity, Christ as the Logos is the origin who causes the existence of the universe. For Muslim mystics, the Muhammadan Reality is called the

Integral Ismuthean Reality (Barzakh-i-Jami'), that is the isthmus or the intermediary reality between the Divine Reality and the created reality order. Be it as it may, emulation and imitation of the spiritual character of the founder is of paramount importance and deliberate deviation therefrom is considered heresy: By imitation, of course is not meant a sort of blind imitation; rather it means a conscious and a conscientious following, or as some Muslim divines have allegorically expressed, it is to trace with compunction the footsteps of the founder of the respective religion.

Man Made for God

One of the latent principles tacitly implied in all religions is that man exists primarily for Heaven or for God and not for this world. Man, in other words is the image of God but the world is the image of man. God (or Heaven for that matter) alone can fill up the existential vacuum in man. From God alone, man can secure his moral and existential perfection. The heart of man, as certain Muslim scholars would say, is the throne of the Compassionate. God (or Heaven) has created man for himself, as he has created the world for man.

A point particularly emphasized in the Abrahamic religions, especially Islam is that man is the pontifex or the vicegerent of God on earth. A man of faith, from this perspective is one who does whatever pious function he does, as a deputy of God, be he a craftsman, a farmer, a ruler, a teacher or what else.

RELIGION AND BEING-IN THE-WORLD

Religion is intimately interwoven with our experience of being in this world. We usually speak about this world and the next or the other world. Now it is time to ask as to what we mean by "this world". It is, simply stated, our experience of reality from birth to death. Our present world starts from the moment we are born and ends the instant we die. In certain languages such as Persian and Arabic an equivalent expression for being born is "to come to this world" and of dying, "to go out of" or to "leave" the world. So "this world" is the horizon of our being in the present life. Nay, it constitutes our very "Dasein" in the present life. It should not, however be forgotten that our present "Dasein" takes place on this planet, i.e. earth, which has made our very "Dasein" or this experience of being-in-the-world possible. Our planet, in other words, is unique in this regard that it is the very condition necessary for the fulfillment and the realization of our very being-in-the-world. It is the prior condition for the Divine pontificity and vicegerency of man.

Religion and Secularism

Being-in-the-world does not and should not be construed to mean worldliness. The world viewed *sub specie aeternita* is divine and from the vantage point of the sacred doctrine the world cannot but be the manifestation of the Divine principle. For the Christian sages of the Middle Ages every entity in the universe was the *vestigio dei*, that is a sign of God as every human being was an imago Dei (an image of God). According to the teachings of the Glorious Quran everything within and without is a sign or a manifestation of God: "whithersoever you turn there is the face of Allah". Everything is the face of God in the sense that it is a manifestation (zuhūr) of God by which He is known. Again in Taoism each thing is an aspect or a manifestation of the Tao. In Hinduism too, the world is conceived as *maya*, that is an ephemeral and phenomenal reality which gives us the illusion of being the Absolute reality but by its very illusiveness hides and veils the Absolute Reality. From a spiritual point of view, secularism is wrong and fallacious in that it gives primacy and priority to the phenomenal order at the expense of the ultimate Reality. Secularism is a sort of paganism in that it accords an absolute status to what is relative and contingent by nature.

Secularism and Modernity

One can trace back the roots of secularism in the modern period in such cultural and intellectual currents as humanism, modern rationalism, empiricism and generally speaking other modern and contemporary currents of thought and also in such trends as scientism, machinism, modern technology and so on. As to humanism, it presupposes a sort of anthropomorphism, in a Protagorean vein this makes man, rather than God, the measure and the centre of everything. Faith not only gives us the belief that God is the alpha and omega of reality; is turns this belief into a certainty through the vision of God as the originating source of every reality.

Modern rationalism too, goes hand in hand with a secularist viewpoint. What should one say about a reason (*ratio*) cut off from the Divine intellect (*intellectus*) which alone is capable of comprehending the total truth. What should one say of the rationalism of a Descartes who relegates the human intellect to the abysmal chaos of subjectivism and reduces the order of matter to pure quantity. What should one say of a philosophers such as Kant whose capricious presuppositions make speculative and metaphysical truths (and hence the science of religion) impossible. How could we reconcile the agnostic doctrine of a Hume or modern Analytical philosophers with the sacred doctrine. How can we reconcile the modern science (which is of the order of the *scientia*) with sapiential wisdom (or with *Sapientia*). How can the *homo faber* of modern technology be transformed into the *homo sapiens* of the ancient wisdom or the *homo sanctus* of the Divine religions. This transformation no doubt requires, to use again the Christian terminology, a second birth, that is being born into a second kingdom, the kingdom of the spirit or the kingdom of Heaven. Secularism in short is deprived, and divested of the right to be born a second birth into the kingdom of God; to remain faithful to its tents, it must ever stay within the confines of physical birth.

IS ETHICS POSSIBLE WITHOUT RELIGION?

Modern philosophers have tried to lay the groundwork for a metaphysics of morals on a merely secular basis, that is, without recourse to religion. "Indeed what does human society become if it is deprived of a law founded upon the authority of God". Frithjof Schuon the great expounder of the *religio perennis* asking this vital question, answers it in the negative. The unbelievers having a "restricted and partially false idea of human nature" believe that it suffices to replace the religious law with the civil law founded upon common interest. Now the opinion of "free-thinkers" about the public good depends upon their scale of values, upon their conception of man and hence upon their meaning of life. But these philosophies having been based on individual tastes and idiosyncrasies

change with tastes, they follow the downward slope of history, because as soon as man is detached from his reason for existence, rooted in God, he can only slide downwards, in conformity with the law of gravity which is valid for the human order as well as for the physical order, notwithstanding the periodic renewal effected by the religions the sages and the saints.

For great sages such as Augustine, the very fact that there are universal necessary laws is itself sufficient proof for the existence of God, otherwise whence would they derive their universality and their necessity. That would apply equally to the laws of ethics and to an authentic moral code. Even some modern sages have gone to the extent of claiming that without Divinity, there can be no authority and without authority there would be no efficacy and that no permanent moral and social life is possible without a religious message. If there is morality in any sense in a secular society, it is not "... possible ... except for a brief period which without admitting it, is still living off the residues of a disavowed heritage."

Secularism adapts principles which are Divine by nature and reduces them to the lowest and the basest degree possible. Take, for example, the idea of moral "conscience" which according to some traditional Muslim thinkers is "the very voice of God in man." Secularism restricts it to the mundane and secular plane, whereas if listened to "the voice of consciousness" can awaken in man a fervent ardor for truth, love and liberation.

In Islam, as in other Abrahamic religions and in religions in general, God is the Law-giver and the supreme legislator. The Divine Law is all-encompassing in the sense that it embraces every aspect of the human life down to the minute details including the whole compass of human life from birth to death. Thereby the Divine Law sanctifies the whole of human life. Since Divine creativity is absolute in the sense that it leaves no entity in any sphere untouched, so is the Divine Law integral and total in the sense that it pervades every facet of human life. Hence, in the religious domain, one cannot talk, logically speaking, of the sacred and the secular. In religion every aspect of human life -- be it individual or social -- is immersed in Divine Grace.

Life is imbued with a Divine Meaning, nay God becomes the very meaning of life. The Law (Halukhah in Judaism, Shari'ah in Islam, Dharma in Hinduism or Tao in Taoism) is a road to the Absolute Reality and a way to ultimate union which ends in the final liberation, felicity and eternal beatitude.

RELIGION AND SECULAR POLITICS

Of all the religions of the world, it has been the lot of Christianity to undergo the challenge of secularism and to be undermined and almost devastated by it. We are not going to elaborate on the causes which brought about this torrent in the West; whatever the causes, it was propped up and cherished by the great minds of the Modern Period. Being a by-product of modernism, it went along with its other concomitants such as humanism, individualism, collectivism, mercantilism, historicism, economism, scientism, technicalism, physicalism, materialism and other-isms which mushroomed overnight in the academic and the non-academic circles. These were the aberrations of man as turned away from God and sacred doctrine.

In the political sphere certain notions which in a religious context had a spiritual significance, were divested of their religious and sacred nature and imbued with a secular hue. Such is for example, the idea of nationhood which in traditional communities was directly associated with the spiritual and Heavenly abode of man and never invested with a purely mundane and secular attire. In a traditional and religious community one's nation was inextricably bound up with man's source of being, from which he was severed as the result of the original fall and was ever eager to retie himself to that primordial fount. For the traditional man the idea of "nation," as everything else here below, was an effusion of the Divine source and as such had a sacred significance.

But in the modern and secular context, nationhood is deprived of such holy and religious connotations; nationalism has become so wide-spread and deep-rooted that the adoration of one's nation has replaced the worship of God.

Another idea which is of paramount significance is the idea of democracy which in the modern sense is a western political idea. But with regard to democracy certain points should be borne in mind and clarified. First in the religious worldview everything is authenticated only in so far as it fits the "Divine Economy" as delineated by revelation in question and in so far as it justifies the ways of God to men. How does democracy fit into, in this “Divine Economy.” Second, tyranny, injustice and oppression are universally condemned in all religions because they are the violations of the Divine justice, Divine truth, Divine love and the Divine wisdom as manifest in the cosmic order. Religion, being based on Divine truth, justice, wisdom and love is diametrically opposed to any kind of injustice and tyranny which are the hallmarks of ignorance. But religions throughout history have had their own ways for combating tyranny and their own established institutions for their purpose.

Third, in all traditional religions everything is valid only in so far as it has the sanction of God. Now the question is: can democracy have the sanction of God. Is it in agreement with the ends of Divine revelation? If it does comply with the tenor of the revealed religions and the sacred doctrine it should be accepted. But then the question is "How can we link an idea which in its origin is secular by nature to a revelation which envisages everything from a Divine vantage point?"

Fourth: those who propound and propagate democracy are not all saints and sages who do everything for God and for the utter love for humankind. Democracy, even if true epistemically, has become an ideology and a political gadget in the hands of secular politicians who are ready to fight anyone who is not ready to condescend to their vested interests. There is a crusade for democracy in the same way that Christians in the middle Ages crusaded against Muslims in the hope of converting them to Christianity. Even if the west has become secularized, something of the same crusading spirit has remained, this time to spread democracy and capitalism in other lands irrespective of whether it is in the interests of the people concerned and of whether they further the interests of revealed religions. It is this aspect of playing the so-called "nasty politics" which is abhorrent to truly liberal minds.

Professor of Philosophy
Director, Iranian Institute of Philosophy
Tehran, Iran

Chapter IX

Western Democracy from the Viewpoint of Islamic Studies

S.M. Mohaghegh Damad

Comparing Islam with Christianity as institutionalized in the Church, one finds a very important difference concerning the issue of politics: in the history of Christianity, after the Church had appeared next to the worldly power seem as the rational and mundane form of politics, i. e. of handling the earthly affairs of the people, the Church raised another issue, namely the "divine power manifested on earth ".

In Islam it is not like this at all. In Islam power took a worldly appearance right from its beginning and nothing ever evolved that could be called the "divine power manifested on earth".

The prophet's way of living amongst the people caused power to take on a popular and earthly character and prevented power from becoming heavenly and divine. The form of the prophet's social and political leadership is, according to Islamic sources, entirely popular and human. It is based on very important institutions and principles imbedded within the core teachings of Islam. The basic teachings of Islam were such that the power that took shape under the prophet himself was based on profane institutions and had in no way any heavenly character. The following are some of these institutions:

1. *The rule of the umma:* The use of the expression "umma" instead of any other word to denominate a superior center endowed with the power to rule indicates the specifically Islamic way of administration. In the time of the prophet and even immediately after him the term "state" ("daula") in its present meaning was not yet coined. Even though the Quran does mention this word, it is not taken in the everyday political usage of this word. What is meant is "dowla" (with "o") in the sense of an issue that is handed over among the people. The Quranic "umma" is different from the expression "milla" in the modern sense of "nation". By using this term, the Quran distinguished the society of the believers from other social groups of the time, the most important of which were structures like the "qabīlah" (tribe). The right to rule given to the umma results from the following tenets:

2. *Responsibility for our destiny:* According to Islamic teachings, man is the viceroy of God on earth, which means that God has made him responsible for the leadership and progress in the world he is living in. On this basis the theory of "popular authority" takes shape.

3. *The allegiance (beyaah)*: This is a kind of election that is performed by the people and afterwards confirmed and enacted by God. In other words, it is a mutual agreement and concord. Everyone can participate in political activities via the alligance. Within the structure of the society in which a man is living, this process is a

tradition that has been established according to the following Quranic verse in the time of the prophet in order to create an adequate structure of power:

لقد رضى الله عن المومنين اذيبايعونک تحت الشجرة (فتح/18)

After the death of the prophet (pbuh) the same tradition has been followed by his successors.

4. *Summons to the good and dissuasion from evil*: This principle, one of the most important Islamic teachings, not only concerns the usual relationship of the people in their everyday life in society, but first and foremost it contains the idea of popular observation and criticism of the ruling power.

5. *The principle of council (shoora):* In holy Quraan there are two verses about council.One is the verse acording to which the chapter is named“chapter of council"
(*soorat ul-shooraa*)

ISLAM AND DEMOCRACY

Islam does not mean possess a specific plan for political structure, but in Islamic teachings and doctrines there are certain institutions that in praxis lead the society towards a kind of government that is characterized by being mundane and popular. Thus, in the first days this kind of government took on the title "Islamic". But this title did not mean that it was a holy and heavenly entity or that it is designed and offered by God. Rather, it was seen as a kind of administration whose form and methods would be acceptable to the Muslims and in accordance with the tenets of Islam or at least adjustable to them. In the history of Islam it can often be seen that Muslims prevented the corruption of power on the basis of these very principles they learned and deduced from Islam. And if some groups attempted to consecrate power and give it a non-popular and non-worldly character, they were faced with the opposition of other groups who, pointing to the above mentioned principles, prevented this attempt.

This, in the Seffin war, after Ali (pbuh) had accepted the verdict, some of his supporters turned their back on him on the ground of the slogan that says: God alone can issue a verdict. They had wanted to declare the act of governing a divine matter. But Ali in answering them said:

> "This is a correct saying, but they interpret it in a bad way. Yes, to issue a verdict is indeed a right reserved for God, but they say that social rule and administration, too, is a divine matter, whereas a people needs a ruler, whether a bad one or a good one."

Ali, being a learned man in Islamic teachings and versed in the exegesis of the Qur'an and the sunna, says that no one by misinterpreting Quranic verses should try to give government a heavenly image. Ruling in the sense of administering people's earthly affairs is a mundane matter and a concern of the people. A ruler is a person chosen by the populace to rule, whether he be righteous ("bar") or unrighteous ("dissolute" fajer).

In other words, the key to accepting the kind of power that relies upon the people and to rejecting any power that has no basis in the populace is for Muslims a matter that lies within the teachings of Islam. This assertion is proved by the rising number of democratic powers in the course of history among Islamic societies. History is full of evidence showing that in whatever region Islam gained influence and spread, the form of government has gradually changed in the direction of becoming more and more popular.

Iran is a case study. This country has been the cradle of royal governments that is of powers which in no way had arisen from the populace. The kings saw their power as resulting from "divine farrah" (divine charisma) and they would present themselves as "the shadow of God" ("zell-ol-lah"). The people in a way worshiped the kings.

After Islam was established in Iran, its inherited culture and continuing tendency was to consecrate power and to consider that society had to be divided into classes. But after the establishment of Islam and due to its teachings the character of being divine was gradually erased from power and the stress was put on the equality of all men.

The people of Iran by the guidance of this kind of teaching in due course effaced sanctity from the rulers and looked upon them, whether they were suppressors or not, as men like themselves. It is interesting to see that later in certain periods of history the ruling powers, using all kinds of propaganda, violence and hypocrisy, tried to revive the aura of past sovereigns for themselves. They would present themselves as a heavenly creature, something perfectly special and, like God, totally non-responsible. In the same vein, they would proclaim that their orders to the people had to be obeyed without questione, since they were given in the name of God.

Even though in the short run they did have some success, after a time the Iranian people recognized their ignorance, regretted their past attitude and started to criticize the power. Historical analysis shows that the awakening of the people as well as their awareness often developed with the help of enlightening religious insights. Accordingly, it evolved on the basis of principles to be found in Islamic teachings. The criticisms uttered against the monarchs used exactly those terms and expressions of such Islamic teachings.

The reign of the Safavids (1501-1729) in Iran had for some time a totally sacred aura. The members of this dynasty called themselves "pīr" (master) and "muršed" (mentor) of the people as well as God's representatives, and the populace believed them for quite some time. But gradually the truth was revealed and the people turned their back on them to such an extent that they even accepted the abolition of the rule of hypocrisy by foreign intruders.

After the Safavids the Afshars led by Nadir Shah (1735-1747) gave a rationalistic character to power again. They managed the country's affairs with political prudence and, relying on an experienced and strong military, drove the aliens out of the country (1738).[107]

The consent to a rationalistic view of power had gone so far that in the Zand period (1747-1779) Karim Khan (1750-1779), the founder of the Zand dynasty, refused to call himself a sultan but rather adopted the title of "Representitive of the people". If we look at this title closely, we find that at this point in time the idea of the legitimacy of popular government was dwelt upon for the first time. The sovereign relies on the people for his power and does not want to justify it with some divine "farrah" (charisma) or give it a sacred outlook.

During the Qajar period (1779-1925) the former attitude of consecrating power customary in the early Safavid times returned to a certain degree. The rulers preferred to take on religious and divine titles. But those acquainted with Iranian history know that under the guidance of the ulema the Iranian people succeeded in organizing and advancing the constitutional movement, an upheaval that in view of the theme of the present article deserves to be looked at somewhat more closely.

During the constitutional movement (1897) two religious groups lined up against each other. Both sides were led by high ranking ulema. One fraction favored a constitutional government that would propagate civil liberties, the legislation of laws, a parliamentary body, free elections and popular sovereignty. This fraction considered all these institutions to be in accordance with

---

[107] L. Lockhard, *Nadir Shah,* trans. By Mosfeg Hamedani, Tehran, 1987, pp. 20-23.

the tenets of the religion. The other side, however, supported the existing despotism and claimed that those institutions were not religious. Of course the Iranian government of the time favored the latter group and resisted the idea of freedom. Ultimately, the Iranian parliament, the Majlis, was even bombarded by the infantry of the ruling king, Mohammad Ali Shah. But despite the fact that the ruling power supported the advocates of despotism and would continue to crush the constitutionalists, the people's resistance under the guidance of the leading ulema living in Najaf and Iran was finally successful and the ruling power had to surrender to the people. The constitution was drawn up and enacted by the leading ulema (1898). In the constitution all the power was put in the hands of the people. Everything depended on the decision of the parliament as well as the representatives elected by the people. According to the constitution the throne had the sole function of upholding national unity. Judicial courts were established that had to issue their verdicts on the basis of parliamentary laws. Religious scholars in the parliament had to make sure that the laws be in accordance with the dogmas of Islam.

The opposition to the constitutional movement could not survive in view of the demands and the resistance of the people from all over Iran and collapsed. The head of the opponents, Sheikh Fazlallah Nouri (1900), one of the most high ranking ulema of his time was arrested by the Mojahedeen who conquered Tehran. He was sentenced on the same day on charges of opposing the constitutional movement that was considered to be the embodiment of religious-nationalistic demands and of slaughtering the constitutionalists. Still on that day he was tried as a "corruptor on earth" and a "fighter against God" and was hanged (30.07.1900). The astonishing point about this affair is that after the sentence was carried out the people not only did not voice any protest but even rejoiced about it.

This author does not deny that the idea of constitutionalism in Iran was influenced by the spread of democracy in western societies. But my point is that Iranian Muslims in consultation with, and under the guidance of, the ulema did not view such an idea as opposed to their religion. And this attitude resulted from principles and rules inherent in the teachings of Islam itself.

The ulema of Najaf had explicitly issued a fatwa saying "it is a religious necessity that in the era of absence of Imam the rule of the Muslims be in the hands of the Islamic public."[108]

THE ISLAMIC REVOLUTION OF IRAN (1979)

In the time immediately preceding the revolution the Iranian people did not consider the ruling power as conforming to the principles and teachings of Islam. Therefore the devout people protested against it from a religious standpoint. Their demands centered around three principles: a) freedom, b) independence and c)

---

[108] Cited from Jusof Eshkewary, “Sarg” newspaper, Tehran, 05/08, 2004, p. 2.

Islamic republicanism. All three of these elements that form the basis for a popular and rational government rest on Islamic teachings. The leader of this movement was Imam Khomeiny (pbuh), the great scholar of Islam. The people that gave their property and their lives for these goals understood those principles as religious demands. In other words they believed that according to Islamic maxims they should have a government that secures people's freedom, independence and political participation.

Imam Khomeiny on the same day of his return to the country after years of exile in his first speech promised a government fully dependent on the vote of the people. Such a government he proclaimed legitimate and Islamic. He even declared the existing constitution that provided for a -- albeit parliamentary -- monarchy to be illegitimate on the basis of the fact that it was drawn up by former generations in totally different national and international circumstances.

In the deed he issued appointing Mr. Mehdi Bazargan prime minister, the Imam announced that the legitimacy of his own power rested on the will of the people.

CONCLUSION

In societies influenced by Islam gradually the idea of worldly governance on the basis of rationality has also gained momentum. Even if these societies resisted this idea for a certain period of time, they ultimately accepted it, nevertheless. Some concrete examples proving this claim to the following: Malik Fahd, the king of Saudi

Arabia, in an interview he gave to the Kuwaity journal "Assiyassiah" on June 28th 1992 openly declared:" The democratic system governing the world in no way suits the countries of our region...We have our own religion which establishes a perfect order and is a perfect religion. Within the sphere of Islam elections are meaningless...free elections are not adequate for our country, the kingship of Saudi Arabia."

But since this view was the private opinion of the king of Saudi Arabia and not that of the thinkers of the Islamic world, we saw that only 12 years later municipal elections have been held in that country.[109] And one can be sure that this trend will grow even stronger in the future.

Sultan Qabus, the king of Oman, said in an interview with a Dutch newspaper in 1993:" Islam is essentially democratic. We believe in equal rights...We think that the citizens must be able to express their opinions freely. This is the spirit of Islam in its pure form."

Yemen, the southern neighbor of Saudi Arabia, held general elections on April 27th 1993 that according to foreign observers were totally free. As a result of that election a coalition government comprised of three political parties, including the Socialists and the Islamic Party, came to power.

These were some examples of the general acceptance of democratic principles in the world of Islam.

But still one has to bear in mind that Islam and probably all theistic religions, on the one hand, and the

---

[109] *Ibid.*

phenomenon of democracy, on the other hand, are in some way incompatible with each other. The present democracies of the West are anthropocentric. The result of such a principal characteristic is that man strives for total freedom of his will. To put it in another way, no one must impose any thought on him from outside; he must be free to walk along the way he chooses. This concept is not compatible with the idea ofthe humankind being led by divine prophets. Under divine guidance by God's prophets man concedes to God's will and knows that he is in God's hands; whereas according to the anthropocentric view and the freedom that goes with it, following the western interpretation no law that man has not legislated himself is obligatory to him, since there is no obligation other than his own will. But in religions the individual laws that are given by God are mandatory.

These differences do exist, but at the same time the experience of some Islamic countries including Iran can be taken to indicate that some form of compatibility is possible, especially concerning democratic structures in public affairs and in management.

The constitution of the Islamic Republic of Iran provides for democratic institutions of various forms. In its preamble the principle of "šawrā" (consultation) in Islam is pointed out and the holy verse is cited. Councils on rural and municipal levels, the parliament -- which in Iran is explicitly called the "Consultative Parliament" -- the election of the president as well as the Council of the Experts and numerous further institutions are all in accordance with regulations in democratic societies. But this constitution has been furnished with a vehicle to ensure the Islamic character of the whole political order; it is called the "Council of the Guardians" (šawrā-je negahbān) and its function is to prevent any deviation of the parliamentary laws from Islamic dogmas.

Of course, it should be conceded that in these kinds of societies, despite the serious efforts of the fathers of the constitution to achieve cooperation, harmony and peace between the objectives of all sides and to secure their interests, quarrels have not yet ended. A confrontation between the principles and tenets of democracy, on the one hand and the defenders of the Shari'a, on the other hand, still exists. But by trusting in the potential of the order of Islamic rights, by applying the principle of continuous Ijtihad (based on rational and reasoned judgments of religious scholars acquainted with the realities of their times), and by observing the central principles and goals of the religion of Islam, a democratic order can be achieved and religious standards achieved.

It is necessary to point out that at present the West sees itself as the forerunner of democracy. The United States sometimes even wants to justify its military operations in the Middle East in the name of establishing democratic orders. But the Islamic people, especially the Iranian society, cannot believe this claim and views it with at least skepticism. This suspicion and uncertainty has several reasons but the main one is the fact that in the past century all liberation movements of the Islamic countries have been suppressed by the West and dictatorial governments established by western countries have ruled in the region for decades.

About half a century ago the national movement of Gamal Abd el Nasser (nasserism) in Egypt was crushed by the West (the US and England). Equally, in Iran the national movement led by Dr. Mossadegh and the Shiite clergy to attain political and economic independence met with opposition of the West. Eventually the democratic, legitimate and popular government of Dr. Mossadegh was toppled through a coup d'etat under the pretext of the spread of communism. The West later conceded its direct role in this coup. There are solid documents proving this claim in the book *Collected Secret Documents of the Secret Relation between Iran and the US*, and there is no doubt as to the credibility.

For convincing hard proof in this regard, see the official and so far "Completely Classified" U.S. Government diplomatic documents giving full account of how U.S. and U.K. Intelligence Agencies have brought about the clandestine overthrow of the only democratically elected and constituted government in Iran: "Foreign Relations of the United States" 1952-1954; Volume X, IRAN, Department of State; Washington D.C.

A number of these so far "secret" or "top secret" classified documents, only recently translated into Persian, prove beyond any shadow of doubt the subversive activities of the West in Iran, under the pretext of combating communis:

Top Secret U.S. Department of State Documents No. 9, 11, 35 concerning the initial position of the U.S. Government opposing previous policies and activities of U.K. in Iran.

Top Secret U.S. Government Document concerning discussions in U.S. National Security Council in Republican Administration (No. 394, 431, 462), U.S. President presiding.

Top Secret U.S. Government Document No. 98, conversation of U.S. Ambassador and Shah in Tehran, concerning removal of Iranian cabinet by any measure.

Documents No. 392-501 concerning negotiations on dividing the oil revenues after toppling the Iranian Government in August 1953, in a manner which satisfies foreign national interests fully and disregards Iranian legitimate rights and proven claims.

The Islamic people believe that the West, far more than being concerned with human values and interests or with human rights, thinks of its own narrow, material and economic interests.

In the second Gulf war as well, when the US marched into Iraq in defense of Kuwait, the Iraqi Shiites after years of suppression by Saddam Hossein rose up in favor of the American forces. But the incumbent President, Mr. Bush sr., left them alone in the middle of the struggle and reached a settlement with Saddam, inflicting heavy damages on the Shiites. After rebuilding his suppressive forces, Saddam again came to the area and began a genocide of the Shiites.

Head, Department of Islamic Studies
Academy of Sciences, Tehran, Iran
(Doshisha University Cismor, Nov. 10, 2004)

Chapter X

Islam and Human Rights

Ali Asgariyazdi

The struggle for universal human rights order is not a modern one. In fact, Islam promoted the universality of the human rights fourteen centuries ago. Islam does not limit human rights to certain aspects, as does the UDHR-Universal Declaration of Human Rights, but stands for human rights in all aspect of life.

HUMAN RIGHTS IN ISLAM

Muslims believe that human rights are bestowed from a Divine, transcendent powers, namely, Allah. So human rights existed before the United Nations appeared. Over 1400 years ago Islam declared that human rights are both universal and permanent and must be recognized, promoted, and defended by all people.

Islam views human rights as part of a religious way of life. Historically, many concepts of human rights were emphasized in divine religions such as Islam, Christianity and Judaism. Islam designed a matchless version of human rights before the United Nations declared them. In this context 'matchless' means that the Islamic concepts are universal, reasonable, acknowledgeable and practicable by most of the world's peoples.

Since human rights are innately universal, and Islam is also universal in thought and practice, its message is able to provide a firm substructure for human rights.[110]

---

[110] The Oxford History of Islam further expands on the universality of Islam's message:

"The universality of religious experience is an important premise of the Qur'an's argument against the profane of secular life. Taking a different tack from the hadith (the corpus of prophetic traditions that provides detailed instructions on how to act as a Muslim in specific ritual or moral contexts), the Qur'an is less concerned with defining creedal boundaries than with affirming the universal obligation to believe in one God. The Qur'an thus speaks of broad verities of religious experience to which every human being can relate. Similarly, when dealing with religious practices, the Qur'an is less concerned with the details of ritual than with the meaning that lies behind the rituals it prescribes. The details of ritual practice, which serve to define Islam for most believers, are usually left for tradition to define. By speaking in a transcendental voice and presenting a discourse that is relevant to human experience in general, the Qur'an overcomes the cultural limitations of the Arab civilization in which it was originally revealed and makes its message accessible to people of different cultural backgrounds. This universalism has never been more important than in the present day, when the majority of Muslims are South or Southeast Asian in origin and when only one-fifth of them are Arabs.

"Such a transcendence of culture is necessary for any religion that aspires to universal validity. As the vehicle for the word of God, it is necessary for the Qur'an to overcome linguistic and cultural differences and express itself in a metalanguage that can be understood when it's original Arabic is translated into a non-Semitic language such as English or Indonesian. An example of this metalanguage can be found in the tripartite model of knowledge previously discussed. Despite the exceptionalism of postmodern philosophy, which accentuates cultural boundaries by hypostasizing the notion of difference, the comparative study of human societies

There are two basic elements on which Islam's views on human rights are based. The first and most significant element is the existence of One God (Allah). In the Qur'an , Allah commands all people to respect and

---

reveals that most people—whatever their experiences and regardless of variations in culture—think in similar ways and have similar wants and needs. Responding to this fact, the Qur'an seeks to establish a common foundation for belief that is based on such shared perceptions and experiences. Over and over again, the Qur'an reminds the reader to look behind the familiar of mundane things of the world, such as the signs of God in nature, the practical value of virtue, and the cross-cultural validity of fundamental moral principles. What is good for Muslims is meant to be good for all human beings, regardless of gender, color, or origin..." (Esposito, 67)

Esposito, Joseph, "The Oxford History of Islam", Oxford University Press, 1999.

- The opening paragraph to a chapter entitled "European Colonialism and the Emergence of Modern Muslim States" in the Oxford History of Islam explains the universality of Islam's message:

"There are today more than fifty Muslim states, extending from the Atlas Mountains in the West to the Malay Archipelago in the East, and from Sub-Saharan Africa to the steppes of Central Asia. They include some of the most populous countries in the world, such as Indonesia, Nigeria, Bangladesh, and Pakistan, as well as some of the smallest such as the Maldives and the Comoros. Some are strong states with effective government institutions; others, like Bosnia-Herzegovina, enjoy only a precarious existence. Some, like Mali and Bangladesh, are poor; others, like Libya, Brunei, Turkmenistan, and Saudi Arabia, are endowed with great natural wealth; still others, like Malaysia—the world's seventh most exporting country in 1997—owe their wealth to successful industrialization. Some Muslim states are ethnically uniform; others include sizable ethnic, linguistic, or religious minorities. Nearly the entire spectrum of social, economic, ideological, institutional, and political expressions are represented in these states..." (Esposito, 549)

promote human rights. So, respect for human rights is expected from all believing Muslims in all aspects of their life.

The second element is the universal equality of human beings, which is the basis for Islam's recognition of human justice and equality, two essential principles of human rights. This means that all humans are equal in the sight of God. Islam has no concept of ethnic or other differences. Equality among all people, whether Muslims or not, male or female, has always been the most important human right promoted by Islam. In the view of Islam, discrimination in all its forms is rejected.

Some of the most significant aspects of human rights were advocated by Islam as early as 1400 years ago.

The basic rights that Islam recognizes for all people are:

- Respect: Deep respect and reverence for human life in all its aspects. This right includes, the right of privacy or the security of private life, the right to protection against any aggression, the right to protection of property, the right to the protection of honor and esteem, and respect for religious opinion and sentiments.
- Freedom: This contains such rights as: the right to choose one's religion, the right to have any belief, freedom of thought and speech, the right to asylum, the rights of minorities, the right to participate in the conduct and management of public affairs, the right to free

association, and the right to freedom of movement and residence.
- Equality: This covers many such rights as education, the rights of women, the right to enjoy equal opportunities.
- Justice for all people: This fourth right embraces such subordinate rights as the right to a fair trial, the right to protest against authorities, and so on.

These are four basic human rights in the view of Islam, each of them having several branches.

This paper elaborates some of these rights according to the Qur'an ic verses. We will see the schematic order of human rights in Islam.

DEEP RESPECT AND REVERENCE FOR HUMAN LIFE IN ALL ITS ASPECTS

One of the most important of human rights is to enjoy life and its basic necessities. In this regard the Holy Qur'an says: "... if anyone killed a person not in retaliation of murder, or (and) to spread mischief in the land - it would be as if he killed all mankind, and if anyone saved a life, it would be as if he saved the life of all mankind."[111]

---

[111]- أنَّهُ مَن قَتَلَ نَفسًا بِغَيْرِ نَفسٍ أَوْ فَسَادٍ فِي الأَرْضِ فَكَأَنَّمَا قَتَلَ النَّاسَ جَمِيعًا وَمَنْ أَحْيَاهَا فَكَأَنَّمَا أَحْيَا النَّاسَ(5:32)

The propriety of taking life in reprisal for murder or for spreading corruption can be decided only by a competent court of law. The Qur'an makes clear: "... and kill not anyone whom Allah has forbidden, except for a just cause (according to Islamic law). This He has commanded you that you may understand." Our Prophet, peace be upon him and his descendants, has declared homicide as the greatest sin after polytheism. He says: "The greatest sins are to associate something with Allah and to kill human beings."[112]

In all these verses of the Qur'an the word 'soul' *(nafs)* has been used in general terms without any particular indication, such as specific race or gender. That includes all people. Islam has recognized the 'Right to Life' as a whole for all people around the world.

Islam has recognized also the right to possess the basic necessities of life, the right of the needy to help. The Holy Qur'an says: "And in their properties there was the right of the beggar, and the *Mahrûm* (the poor who does not ask the others)."[113] In this verse, the Qur'an has not only limited the right to who asks for help, but has also laid down that if a Muslim comes to know that a certain man is without the basic necessities of life, then, regardless of his sex, nationality, race, religion, etc., whether he asks for help or not, it is his duty to provide all the help that he can afford.

Along with security of life, Islam has with equal clarity conferred the right of security of ownership of

---

[112] وَلَا تَقْتُلُوا النَّفْسَ الَّتِي حَرَّمَ اللَّهُ إِلَّا بِالْحَقِّ ذَلِكُمْ وَصَّاكُمْ بِهِ لَعَلَّكُمْ تَعْقِلُونَ(6:151) .

[113] وَفِي أَمْوَالِهِمْ حَقٌّ لِلسَّائِلِ وَالمَحْرُومِ(51:19)

property, that is, the right to protection of property. The Holy Qur'an goes so far as to declare that the taking of people's possessions or property is prohibited unless done by lawful means: The law of Allah categorically declares: "And eat up not one another's property unjustly (in any illegal way e.g. stealing, robbing, deceiving, etc.), nor give bribery to the rulers (judges before presenting your cases) that you may knowingly eat up a part of the property of others sinfully."[114]

Right of Privacy-The Sanctity and Security of Private Life: Islam recognizes the sanctity of privacy and stresses on the right of every citizen in an Islamic state to be free from undue intrusion on the privacy of his life. The Holy Qur'an says: "Do not spy on one another" (49:12). "O you who believe! Enter not houses other than your own, until you have asked permission and greeted those in them, that is better for you, in order that you may remember." [115]

The right of a person to protect his or her honor is one of the most important rights. Our Prophet (peace be upon him and his descendants) during the Hajjat-al-vedae (Farewell *Hajj)* said: not only Muslims are prohibited from taking the life and property of other Muslims, but they should refrain from any invasion on their honor and respect. The Holy Qur'an says:

---

[114] وَلاَ تَأْكُلُوا أَمْوَالَكُم بَيْنَكُم بِالْبَاطِلِ وَتُدْلُوا بِهَا إِلَى الْحُكَّامِ لِتَأْكُلُوا فَرِيقًا مِّنْ أَمْوَالِ النَّاسِ بِالإِثْمِ وَأَنتُمْ تَعْلَمُونَ.(2:188)

[115] يَا أَيُّهَا الَّذِينَ آمَنُوا لَا تَدْخُلُوا بُيُوتًا غَيْرَ بُيُوتِكُمْ حَتَّى تَسْتَأْنِسُوا وَتُسَلِّمُوا عَلَى أَهْلِهَا ذَلِكُمْ خَيْرٌ لَّكُمْ لَعَلَّكُمْ تَذَكَّرُونَ.(24:27) .

O you who believe! Let not a group scoff at another group, it may be that the latter are better than the former; nor let (some) women scoff at other women, it may be that the latter are better than the former, nor defame one another, nor insult one another by nicknames. How bad is it, to insult one's brother after having Faith [i.e. to call your Muslim brother (a faithful believer) as: "O sinner", or "O wicked", etc.]. And whosoever does not repent, then such are indeed *Zalimûn* (wrong-doers, etc.).

O you who believe! Avoid many suspicions, indeed some suspicions are sins. And spy not, neither backbite one another. Would one of you like to eat the flesh of his dead brother? You would hate it (so hate backbiting). And fear Allah. Verily, Allah is the One Who accepts repentance, Most Merciful. [116]

Under Islamic law, if it is proved that someone has assaulted the honor of another person, the offender will be punished.

RESPECT FOR RELIGIOUS SENTIMENTS

It is ordered by Allah in the Holy Qur'an : "And insult not those whom they (disbelievers) worship besides

---

[116] يَا أَيُّهَا الَّذِينَ آمَنُوا اجْتَنِبُوا كَثِيرًا مِّنَ الظَّنِّ إِنَّ بَعْضَ الظَّنِّ إِثْمٌ وَلَا تَجَسَّسُوا وَلَا يَغْتَب بَّعْضُكُم بَعْضًا أَيُحِبُّ أَحَدُكُمْ أَن يَأْكُلَ لَحْمَ أَخِيهِ مَيْتًا فَكَرِهْتُمُوهُ وَاتَّقُوا اللَّهَ إِنَّ اللَّهَ تَوَّابٌ رَّحِيمٌ <12> يَا أَيُّهَا النَّاسُ إِنَّا خَلَقْنَاكُم مِّن ذَكَرٍ وَأُنثَى وَجَعَلْنَاكُمْ شُعُوبًا وَقَبَائِلَ لِتَعَارَفُوا إِنَّ أَكْرَمَكُمْ عِندَ اللَّهِ أَتْقَاكُمْ إِنَّ اللَّهَ عَلِيمٌ خَبِيرٌ. (49:11-12)

Allah, lest they insult Allah wrongfully without knowledge".[117] If a person or a group of people hold certain beliefs which you feel is not worthy because you consider them wrong, it is not justifiable for you to use abusive language to them and injure their feelings. Islam teaches its followers to hold debates and discussions with the followers of others Ibrahimic religions in full respect.

And argue not with the people of the Scripture (Jews and Christians), unless it be in (a way) that is better (with good words and in good manner, inviting them to Islamic Monotheism with His Verses), except with such of them as do wrong, and say (to them): "We believe in that which has been revealed to us and revealed to you; our *Ilah* (God) and your *Ilah* (God) is One (i.e. Allah), and to Him we have submitted (as Muslims).[118]

Islam has also given people the right to freedom of association and the right to form parties or organizations. This right in Islam is not subject to spreading evil. We have not only been given the right to spread righteousness and virtue, but also, we have been ordered to exercise it. The Holy Qur'an declares:

The believers, men and women, are *Auliya'* (helpers, supporters, friends, protectors) of one another, they enjoin (on the people) *Al-Ma'rûf* (i.e. Islamic Monotheism

---

[117] وَلاَ تَسُبُّوا الَّذِينَ يَدْعُونَ مِن دُونِ اللهِ فَيَسُبُّوا اللهَ عَدْوًا بِغَيْرِ عِلْمٍ(6:108)

[118] وَلَا تُجَادِلُوا أَهْلَ الْكِتَابِ إِلَّا بِالَّتِي هِيَ أَحْسَنُ إِلَّا الَّذِينَ ظَلَمُوا مِنْهُمْ وَقُولُوا آمَنَّا بِالَّذِي أُنزِلَ إِلَيْنَا وَأُنزِلَ إِلَيْكُمْ وَإِلَهُنَا وَإِلَهُكُمْ وَاحِدٌ وَنَحْنُ لَهُ مُسْلِمُونَ.(29:46)

and all that Islam orders one to do), and forbid (people) from *Al-Munkar* (i.e. polytheism and disbelief of all kinds, and all that Islam has forbidden); they perform *As-Salat* (*Iqamat-as-Salat*) and give the *Zakat*, and obey Allah and His Messenger. Allah will have His Mercy on them. Surely Allah is All-Mighty, All-Wise.[119]

No one can deny this right to the people... It is equally a right of, and an obligation on, an individual to attempt to stop evil, whether this evil is performed by an individual, a group of people or government. Furthermore, he should openly condemn the evil and point to the goodness and morally correct.

The Holy Qur'an has described this quality of the Faithful in the following words:

Those (Muslim rulers) who, if We give them power in the land, (they) order for *Iqamat-as-Salat*. [i.e. to perform the five compulsory congregational *Salat* (prayers) (the males in mosques)], to pay the *Zakat* and they enjoin *Al-Ma'rûf* (i.e. Islamic Monotheism and all that Islam orders one to do), and forbid *Al-Munkar* (i.e. disbelief, polytheism and all that Islam has forbidden) [i.e. they make the Qur'an as the law of their country in all the

---

119. وَالْمُؤْمِنُونَ وَالْمُؤْمِنَاتُ بَعْضُهُمْ أَوْلِيَاء بَعْضٍ يَأْمُرُونَ بِالْمَعْرُوفِ وَيَنْهَوْنَ عَنِ الْمُنكَرِ وَيُقِيمُونَ الصَّلاَةَ وَيُؤْتُونَ الزَّكَاةَ وَيُطِيعُونَ اللّهَ وَرَسُولَهُ أُوْلَئِكَ سَيَرْحَمُهُمُ اللّهُ إِنَّ اللّهَ عَزِيزٌ حَكِيمٌ.(9:71)

spheres of life]. And with Allah rests the end of (all) matters (of creatures). [120]

EQUALITY

Islam not only recognizes the principle of equality between human beings, regardless of their sex, color, race or nationality, it even makes it an important reality. All human beings are the descendants from one father, Adam, and one mother, Eve. The Qur'an says the differences are to enable people only to know each others. In other words, the divisions of human beings into nations, races, groups and tribes, in view of Qur'an , are for the people to be able to recognize each other. Therefore, the people of one race or nation may meet and be acquainted with people belonging to another race or nation. "O mankind! We have created you from a male and a female, and made you into nations and tribes, that you may know one another". [121]

This division of human being is neither meant for arrogance of one nation over others, nor for one nation to treat another with rudeness. According to the Qur'an ic teachings spiritual values are the only criteria for the superiority of one man over another in God's eye. The Qur'an says: "Verily, the most honorable of you with Allah is that who has *At-Taqwa* ". [122]

---

[120] الَّذِينَ إِن مَّكَّنَّاهُمْ فِي الْأَرْضِ أَقَامُوا الصَّلَاةَ وَآتَوُا الزَّكَاةَ وَأَمَرُوا بِالْمَعْرُوفِ وَنَهَوْا عَنِ الْمُنكَرِ وَلِلَّهِ عَاقِبَةُ الْأُمُورِ (22:41).

[121] أَيُّهَا النَّاسُ إِنَّا خَلَقْنَاكُم مِّن ذَكَرٍ وَأُنثَى وَجَعَلْنَاكُمْ شُعُوبًا وَقَبَائِلَ لِتَعَارَفُوا (49:13)

[122] إِنَّ أَكْرَمَكُمْ عِندَ اللَّهِ أَتْقَاكُمْ إِنَّ اللَّهَ عَلِيمٌ خَبِيرٌ.(49:13)

Therefore, the superiority of one man over another is only on the basis of Allah-consciousness, purity of character and high morals, and not because of his color, race, language or nationality. Accordingly, people are not justified in their arrogance over other human beings. No one has any superiority over others. This has been thus exemplified by the Prophet (peace be upon him and his descendants) in one of his sayings: "No Arab has any superiority over a non-Arab, nor does a non-Arab have any superiority over a black man, or the black man any superiority over the white man. You are all the children of Adam, and Adam was created from clay." In this manner 1400 years ago, Islam established the principle of equality of all human beings and rejects all distinctions based on color, race, language or nationality

Equality before the Law: Islam believes that all people are equal before the law. As far as Muslims are concerned, there are clear teachings in the Holy Qur'an that the all people are equal in their rights and obligations: "The believers are nothing else than brothers (in Islamic religion). So make reconciliation between your brothers..."[123]

This religious brotherhood and the uniformity of their rights and duties is the base of equality in Islamic society. The position of non-Muslim citizens in an Islamic State has been well expressed by Imam Ali (peace be upon him and his descendants): "They have accepted our protection only because their lives are like our lives and their properties are like our properties". In other words,

---

[123] إِنَّمَا الْمُؤْمِنُونَ إِخْوَةٌ فَأَصْلِحُوا بَيْنَ أَخَوَيْكُمْ وَاتَّقُوا اللَّهَ لَعَلَّكُمْ تُرْحَمُونَ(49:10) .

their lives and properties are as dear and therefore protected as the lives and properties of Muslims.

JUSTICE

Justice is a very important and valuable right which Islam has recognized for human. The Holy Qur'an says: "...and let not the hatred of some people in (once) stopping you from *AlMasjidalHaram* (at Makkah) leads you to transgression (and hostility on your part). Help you one another in *AlBirr* and *AtTaqwa* (virtue, righteousness and piety); but do not help one another in sin and transgression..." [124]

In another verse the Qur'an teach us: "O you who believe! Stand out firmly for Allah and be just witnesses and let not the enmity and hatred of others make you avoid justice. Be just: that is nearer to piety..."[125] And we also see this notion in this verse: O you who believe! Stand out firmly for justice, as witnesses to Allah, even though it be against yourselves, or your parents, or your kin, be he rich or poor, Allah is a Better Protector to both (than you). So follow not the lusts, lest you may avoid justice, and if you distort your witness or refuse to

---

124 وَلاَ يَجْرِمَنَّكُمْ شَنَآنُ قَوْمٍ أَن صَدُّوكُمْ عَنِ الْمَسْجِدِ الْحَرَامِ أَن تَعْتَدُواْ وَتَعَاوَنُواْ عَلَى الْبرِّ وَالتَّقْوَى وَلاَ تَعَاوَنُواْ عَلَى الإِثْمِ وَالْعُدْوَانِ وَاتَّقُواْ اللّهَ(5:2)

125 يَا أَيُّهَا الَّذِينَ آمَنُواْ كُونُواْ قَوَّامِينَ لِلّهِ شُهَدَاء بِالْقِسْطِ وَلاَ يَجْرِمَنَّكُمْ شَنَآنُ قَوْمٍ عَلَى أَلاَّ تَعْدِلُواْ اعْدِلُواْ هُوَ أَقْرَبُ لِلتَّقْوَى وَاتَّقُواْ اللّهَ إِنَّ اللّهَ خَبِيرٌ بِمَا تَعْمَلُونَ.(5:8)

give it, verily, Allah is Ever Well Acquainted with what you do".[126]

Therefore, the point is made clear that Muslims have to be just not only to their friends, but also to their enemies. Consequently, Islam's invitation to justice is not limited to her followers, or to the people of a particular tribe, nation, race or faith, but also it includes all human beings.

Another right that Islam has bestowed to human beings is the right to protest against government dictatorship. The Qur'an says: "Allah does not like that the evil should be uttered in public except by him who has been wronged. And Allah is Ever All Hearer, All Knower."[127] This means that Allah strongly disagrees with language that reviles or discredits, but that the person who has been the victim of injustice or tyranny has the right to protest strongly and to raise the voice of his protest.

Freedom of Religion

Islam gives the right to all people whether to accept Islam or not. Islam does not try to force others to believe in God. The Holy Qur'an says: "There is no compulsion in religion. Verily, the Right Path has become distinct from the wrong path. Whoever disbelieves in *Taghût* and

---

[126] يَا أَيُّهَا الَّذِينَ آمَنُوا كُونُوا قَوَّامِينَ بِالْقِسْطِ شُهَدَاءَ لِلَّهِ وَلَوْ عَلَى أَنفُسِكُمْ أَوِ الْوَالِدَيْنِ وَالأَقْرَبِينَ إِن يَكُنْ غَنِيًّا أَوْ فَقِيرًا فَاللَّهُ أَوْلَى بِهِمَا فَلاَ تَتَّبِعُوا الْهَوَى أَن تَعْدِلُوا وَإِن تَلْوُوا أَوْ تُعْرِضُوا فَإِنَّ اللَّهَ كَانَ بِمَا تَعْمَلُونَ خَبِيرًا (4:135)

[127] لاَ يُحِبُّ اللَّهُ الْجَهْرَ بِالسُّوءِ مِنَ الْقَوْلِ إِلاَّ مَن ظُلِمَ وَكَانَ اللَّهُ سَمِيعًا عَلِيمًا (4:148)

believes in Allah, then he has grasped the most trustworthy handhold that will never break. And Allah is All-Hearer, All-Knower." [128]

CONCLUSION

This is a brief description of those rights which 1400 years ago Islam firmly recognized for human beings, the contemporary world could not produce more just and equitable laws than those given fourteen centuries ago.

---

[128] لاَ إِكْرَاهَ فِي الدِّينِ قَد تَّبَيَّنَ الرُّشْدُ مِنَ الْغَيِّ فَمَنْ يَكْفُرْ بِالطَّاغُوتِ وَيُؤْمِن بِاللّهِ فَقَدِ اسْتَمْسَكَ بِالْعُرْوَةِ الْوُثْقَىَ لاَ انفِصَامَ لَهَا وَاللّهُ سَمِيعٌ عَلِيمٌ. (2:256)

PART IV

DISTINCTION, RELATION, SEPARATION? THE PROPER INTERFACE OF RELIGION AND THE POLITICAL ORDER

Chapter XI

The Idea of Political Pluralism

William A. Galston

INTRODUCTION: A SKETCH OF LIBERAL PLURALISM

We often use the phrase "liberal democracy," but we do not always think about it very carefully. The noun points to a particular structure of politics in which decisions are made, directly or indirectly, by the people as a whole; and more broadly, to an understanding of politics in which all legitimate power flows from the people. The adjective points to a particular understanding of the scope of politics, in which the domain of legitimate political decision-making is seen as inherently limited. Liberal governance acknowledges that important spheres of human life are wholly or partly outside the purview of political power. It stands as a barrier against all forms of total power, including the power of democratic majorities.

The question then arises, how are we to understand the nature and extent of limits on government. The signers of the Declaration of Independence appealed to the self-evidence of certain truths, among them the concept of individuals as bearers of rights that both orient and restrict governmental power. Today, individual rights represent an important (some would say dominant) part of our moral vocabulary. The question is whether they are sufficient to explain and justify the full range of constraints we wish to impose on the exercise of public power, for example, the limits on government's right to intervene in the internal affairs of civil associations and faith-based institutions.

In a recent book, *Liberal Pluralism*,[129] I argue that we must develop a more complex theory of the limits to government. In this endeavor, three concepts are of special importance. The first is *political pluralism*, an understanding of social life that comprises multiple sources of authority--individuals, parents, civil associations, faith-based institutions, and the state, among others--no one of which is dominant in all spheres, for all purposes, on all occasions.

Political pluralism is a politics of recognition rather than construction. It respects the diverse spheres of human association; it does not understand itself as creating or constituting those activities. Because so many types of human association possess an identity not derived from the state, pluralist politics does not presume that the inner structure and principles of every sphere must mirror those of basic political institutions. For example, in filling positions of religious authority, faith communities may use, without state interference, gender-based norms that would be forbidden in businesses and public accommodations.

---

[129] William A. Galston, *Liberal Pluralism: The Implications of Value Pluralism for Political Theory and Practice* (New York: Cambridge University Press, 2002).

The second key concept is *value pluralism*, made prominent by the late British philosopher Isaiah Berlin. This concept offers an account of the moral world we inhabit: while the distinction between good and bad is objective, there are multiple goods that differ qualitatively from one another and which cannot be ranked-ordered. If this is the case, there is no single way of life, based on a singular ordering of values, that is the highest and best for all individuals. This has important implications for politics. While states may legitimately act to prevent the great evils of human existence, they may not seek to force their citizens into one-size-fits-all patterns of desirable human lives. Any public policy that relies upon, promotes, or commands a single conception of human good or excellence is on its face illegitimate.

The third key concept in my account of limited government is *expressive liberty*. Simply put, this is a presumption in favor of individuals and groups leading their lives as they see fit, within the broad range of legitimate variation defined by value pluralism, in accordance with their own understandings of what gives life meaning and value. Expressive liberty may be understood as an extension of the free exercise of religion, generalized to cover comprehensive conceptions of human life that rest on non-religious as well as religious claims.

The concept of expressive liberty yields an understanding of politics as an instrumental rather than ultimate value. Politics is purposive (which is why the critical phrase "in order to" immediately follows "We the People"); we measure the value of political institutions and practices by the extent to which they help us attain the ends for which they were established. In a liberal pluralist regime, a key end is the creation of social space within which individuals and groups can freely pursue their distinctive visions of what gives meaning and worth to human existence. There is a presumption in favor of the free exercise of this kind of purposive activity, and a liberal pluralist state bears and must discharge a burden of proof whenever it seeks to restrict expressive liberty.

This standard for state action is demanding, but hardly impossible to meet. While expressive liberty is a very important good, it is not the only good, and it is not unlimited. In the first place, the social space within which differing visions of the good are pursued must be organized and sustained through the exercise of public power; to solve inevitable problems of coordination among divergent individuals and groups, the rules constituting this space will inevitably limit in some respects their ability to act as they see fit. Second, there are some core evils of the human condition that states have the right (indeed the duty) to prevent; to do this, they may rightly restrict the actions of individuals and groups. (According to the U.S. Supreme Court, religious groups have a right to practice animal sacrifice. Does anyone believe that it would be legitimate for them to practice human sacrifice, or that the state would act wrongly if it intervened in the sacrificial practices of a neo-Aztec cult?) Third, the state cannot sustain a free social space if its very existence is jeopardized by internal or external threats, and within broad limits it may do what it necessary to defend itself against destruction, even if self-defense restricts valuable liberties of individuals and groups. A free society is not a suicide pact.

Liberal pluralists, then, endorse the essential conditions of public order, such as the rule of law and a public authority with the capacity to enforce it. They also endorse what may be called a "minimal universalism"—that is, the moral and practical necessity of organizing public life so as to ward off, to the greatest extent possible, the great evils of the human condition, such as tyranny, genocide, mass starvation, and deadly epidemics.[130] (I call the human condition characterized by the absence of the great evils as one of basic decency.) This minimal universalism overlaps with contemporary movements for universal human rights and provision of basic needs.

So understood, liberal pluralist government is both limited and robust. In securing the cultural conditions of its survival and perpetuation, for example, it may legitimately engage in civic education, carefully restricted to the public essentials--the virtues and competences that citizens will need to fulfill diverse roles in a liberal pluralist economy, society, and polity. One thing above all is clear: because the likely result of liberal pluralist institutions and practices will be a highly diverse society, the virtue of tolerance will be a core attribute of liberal pluralist citizenship. This type of tolerance does not mean wishy-washiness or the propensity to doubt one's own position, the sort of thing Robert Frost had in mind

---

[130] For a development of this point, see Stuart Hampshire, *Justice Is Conflict* (Princeton: Princeton University Press, 2000).

when he defined a liberal as someone who cannot take his own side in an argument. It does not imply, or require, an easy relativism about the human good; indeed, it is compatible with engaged moral criticism of those with whom one differs. Toleration rightly understood means the principled refusal to use coercive state power to impose one's views on others, and therefore a commitment to moral competition through recruitment and persuasion alone.

Liberal pluralism is (in the terms John Rawls made familiar) a "comprehensive" rather than "political" theory. It makes sense, I believe, to connect with one believes to be the best account of public life with comparably persuasive accounts of morality, human psychology, and the natural world. As a practical matter, of course, it makes sense to seek overlapping consensus. Politics as we know it would come to a halt if cooperation required agreement, not only on conclusions, but on premises as well. But philosophical argument, even concerning politics, need not mirror the structure of public life. A political philosopher may assert that X is true, and foundational for a particular understanding of a good, decent, or just society, without demanding that all citizens affirm the truth of X. Indeed, the founders of a political regime may publicly proclaim what they take to be moral, metaphysical, or religious truths as the basis of that regime without insisting that all citizens assent to those truths. In the United States, naturalizing citizens affirm their loyalty to the Constitution, not the Declaration of Independence, and all citizens pledge allegiance to the republic for which the flag stands, not

Locke or Hutcheson. So I disagree with Martha Nussbaum when she suggests that making public claims about foundational truths somehow signals disrespect for those who dissent.[131] Disrespect requires something more--namely, the use of coercive state power to silence and repress dissenters. Respect requires, not parsimony in declaring truth, but rather restraint in the exercise of power. By limiting the scope of legitimate public power, liberal pluralism does all that is necessary to secure the theoretical and institutional bases of respect.

WHY POLITICAL PLURALISM?

I turn now to the main focus of this essay---political pluralism, understood as a distinctive empirical account of human society that also supports a specific normative account of political authority.

A liberal democracy is (among other things) an invitation to struggle over the control of civil associations. State/society debates have recurred over the past century of U.S. history, frequently generating landmark Supreme Court cases. While the specific issues vary, the general form is the same. On one side are general public principles that the state seeks to enforce; on the other are specific beliefs and practices that the association seeks to protect. *Boy Scouts of America v. Dale*[132] is

---

[131] Martha Nussbaum, "Political Objectivity," *New Literary History* 32, 4 (2000): 883-906.
[132] 530 U.S. 640 (2000).

the latest chapter in what will no doubt be a continuing saga.

Within the U.S. constitutional context, these issues are often debated in terms such as free exercise of religion, freedom of association, or the individual liberty broadly protected under the 14th amendment. Rich and illuminating as it is, this constitutional discourse does not go deep enough. It is necessary to reconsider the understanding of politics that pervades much contemporary discussion, especially among political theorists, an understanding that tacitly views public institutions as plenipotentiary and civil society as a political construction possessing only those liberties that the polity chooses to grant and modify or revoke at will. This understanding of politics makes it all but impossible to give serious weight to the "liberal" dimension of liberal democracy.

The most useful point of departure for the reconsideration of politics I am urging is found in the writings of the British political pluralists and pluralist thinkers working in the Calvinist tradition.[133] This pluralist movement began to take shape in the 19th century as a reaction to the growing tendency to see state institutions as plenipotentiary. This tendency took various practical forms in different countries: French

---

[133] For the British tradition, see Paul Q. Hirst, ed., *The Pluralist Theory of the State: Selected Writings of G. D. H. Cole, J. N. Figgis, and H. J. Laski* (London: Routledge, 1989). For the Calvinist tradition, see James W. Skillen and Rockne M. McCarthy, eds., *Political Order and the Plural Structure of Society* (Atlanta: Scholars Press, 1991).

anticlerical republicanism; British parliamentary supremacy; the drive for national unification in Germany and Italy against subordinate political and social powers. Following Stephen Macedo (though disagreeing with him in other respects), I shall call this idea of the plenipotentiary state "civic totalism."[134]

Historically, one can discern at least three distinct secular-theoretical arguments for civic totalism. (Theological arguments, which raise a different set of issues, are beyond the scope of these comments.) The first is the idea, traced back to Aristotle, that politics enjoys general authority over subordinate activities and institutions because it aims at the highest and most comprehensive good for human beings. The *Politics* virtually begins with the proposition that "all partnerships aim at some good, and . . . the partnership that is most authoritative of all and embraces all the others does so particularly, and aims at the most authoritative good of all. That is what is called . . . the political partnership." (For present purposes, whether this statement is an adequate representation of Aristotle's full view is a matter we may set aside.)

Hobbes offered a second kind of justification for civic totalism: any less robust form of politics would in practice countenance divided sovereignty--the dreaded

---

[134] For the full account of our agreement and (mainly) disagreement, see my review of Macedo's latest book, *Diversity and Distrust: Civic Education in a Multicultural Society* (Cambridge, MA: Harvard University Press, 2000), recently published in *Ethics* 112, 2 (January 2002): 386-391.

imperium in imperio, an open invitation to civic conflict and war. Sovereignty cannot be divided, even between civil and spiritual authorities (*Leviathan*, "Of Commonwealth," ch. 29). In Hobbes' view, undivided sovereign authority has unlimited power to decide whether, and under what conditions, individuals and associations would enjoy liberty of action. No entity, individual or collective, can assert rights against the public authority. Indeed, civil law may rightfully prohibit even the teaching of truth, if it is contrary to the requirements of civil peace (*Leviathan*, "Of the Kingdom of Darkness," ch. 46; cf. "Of Commonwealth," ch. 17).

A third argument for civic totalism was inspired by Rousseau: civic health and morality cannot be achieved without citizens' wholehearted devotion to the common good. Loyalties divided between the republic and other ties, whether to civil associations or to revealed religious truth, are bound to dilute civic spirit. And the liberal appeal to private life as against public life will only legitimate selfishness at the expense of the spirit of contribution and sacrifice without which the polity cannot endure. Representing this tradition, Emile Combes, a turn-of-the-century premier in the French Third Republic, declared that "There are, there can be no rights except the right of the State, and there [is], and there can be no other authority than the authority of the Republic."[135]

I do not wish to suggest that these three traditions converge on precisely the same account of civic totalism.

---

[135] Quoted by J.N. Figgis in Hirst, op. cit., p. 112.

A chasm divides Hobbes and Rousseau from Aristotle. To oversimplify drastically: Greek religion was civil, offering support for the institutions of the polis. The post-classical rise of revealed religion-especially Christianity-ruptured the unity of the political order. Much renaissance and early modern theory sought to overcome this diremption and restore the unity of public authority. Hobbes and Rousseau wrote in this "theological-political" tradition and tried in different ways to subordinate religious claims to the sovereignty of politics.

For this reason, among others, Hobbes and Rousseau were less willing than was Aristotle to acknowledge the independent and legitimate existence of intermediate associations. They were drawn instead to a doctrine, originating in Roman law and transmitted to modernity through Bodin among others, according to which intermediate associations existed solely as revocable "concessions" of power from the sovereign political authority. Individuals possessed no inherent right of association, and associations enjoyed no rights other than those politically defined and granted. In short, intermediate associations were political constructions, to be tolerated only to the extent that they served the interests of the state. This Roman-law stance may be contrasted to the view of early Calvinists that a civil association required no special fiat from the state for its existence. As Frederick Carney puts it, "Its own purposes, both natural and volitional, constitute its *raison d'etre*, not its convenience to the state."[136]

These three traditions may seem far removed from the mainstream of contemporary views. Doesn't the liberal strand of "liberal democracy" qualify and limit the legitimate power of the state? Isn't this the entering wedge for a set of fundamental freedoms that can stand against the claims of state power?

The standard history of liberalism lends support to this view. The rise of revealed religion created a diremption of authority and challenged the comprehensive primacy of politics. The early modern wars of religion sparked new understandings of the relation between religion and politics, between individual conscience and public order, between unity and diversity. As politics came to be understood as limited rather than total, the possibility emerged that the principles constituting individual lives and civil associations might not be congruent with the principles constituting public institutions. The point of liberal constitutionalism, and of liberal statesmanship, was not to abolish these differences but rather, so far as possible, to help them serve the cause of ordered liberty.

---

[136] Carney, "Associational Thought in Early Calvinism," in D. B. Robertson, ed., *Voluntary Associations: A Study of Groups in Free Societies* (Richmond, VA: John Knox Press, 1966), p. 46.

THE TOTALIST TEMPTATION

Despite this history, many contemporary theorists, including some who think of themselves as working within the liberal tradition, embrace propositions that draw them away from the idea of limited government and toward civic totalism, perhaps against their intention. Some come close to arguing that if state power is exercised properly---that is, democratically---it need not be limited by any considerations other than those required by democratic processes.

Jurgen Habermas offers the clearest example of this tendency. He insists that once obsolete metaphysical doctrines are set aside, "there is no longer any fixed point outside the democratic procedure itself." But this is no cause for worry or regret: whatever is normatively defensible in liberal rights is contained in the discourse-rights of "sovereign [democratic] citizens."[137] The residual rights not so contained constitute, not bulwarks against oppression, but rather the illegitimate insulation of "private" practices from public scrutiny.

An eminent American democratic theorist, Robert Dahl, is tempted by Habermas's stance. He characterizes as "reasonable" and "attractive" the view that members of political communities have no fundamental interests, rights, or claims other than those integral to the democratic process or needed for its preservation. The only limits to the legitimate scope of democratic power

---

[137] Quoted and discussed in John Rawls, *Political Liberalism* (New York: Columbia University Press, 1996), p. 379.

are the requisities of democracy itself. Put simply: a demos that observes the norms of democratic decision-making may do what it wants.[138]

Unlike Habermas, Dahl is not entirely comfortable with restricting the domain of rights to the conditions of democracy. He concedes that this proposal raises a "disturbing" question: what about interests, rights, and claims that cannot be adequately understood as aspects of the democratic process but which nonetheless seem important and defensible? What about fair trials, or freedom of religion and conscience? Without definitively answering this question, Dahl examines the various ways in which the defense of rights may be institutionalized, concluding that those who would temper democratic majorities with "guardian" structures such as courts bear a heavy burden of proof that they rarely if ever discharge successfully. The most reliable cure for the ills of democracy is more democracy; the resort to non-majoritarian protections risks undermining the people's capacity to govern itself.[139]

John Rawls presents the most complex case of the phenomenon I call the totalist temptation. He asserts that "the values of the special domain of the political . . . normally outweigh whatever values may conflict with them."[140] Why is this the case? Rawls offers two reasons. First, political values are very important; they determine

---

[138] Robert Dahl, *Democracy and Its Critics* (New Haven: Yale University Press, 1989), pp. 182, 183.

[139] Dahl, op. cit., pp. 183-192.

[140] Rawls, *Political Liberalism,* pp. 139, 157.

social life and make fair cooperation possible. Second, conflict between political and nonpolitical values can usually be avoided, so long as political values are appropriately understood.[141]

Rawls famously maintains that justice is the preeminent political value, the "first virtue of social institutions" and that "laws and institutions no matter how efficient and well-arranged must be reformed or abolished if they are unjust."[142] Nonetheless, he asserts, consistent with the liberal tradition, that the principles of justice do not directly regulate institutions and associations--such as churches and families--within society.[143] (Principles of justice do affect these institutions indirectly, via the influence of just background institutions.)

The difficulty is to explain why, within the structure of Rawls's theory, the principles regulating the basic structure of society should not be applied directly to institutions such as churches and the family. Taken literally, many of these background principles would seem to warrant such interventions. For example, imbalances in parenting responsibilities can affect women's "fair equality of opportunity." Does this mean, as Rawls seems to suggest, that "special provisions of

---

[141] Rawls, *Political Liberalism*, pp. 139-140.

[142] Rawls, *A Theory of Justice* (Cambridge, MA: Harvard University Press, 1971), p. 3.

[143] Rawls, *Justice as Fairness: A Restatement*, ed. Erin Kelly (Cambridge, MA: Harvard University Press, 2001), p. 10.

family law" should prevent or rectify this imbalance?[144] If the family is part of the basic structure of society, as Rawls now claims, why does he judge it "hardly sensible" that parents be required to treat their children in accordance with the principles directly governing the basic structure?[145]

The ambiguous status of the family reflects a deeper structural problem in Rawls's account. At one point he offers a formulation that seems promising: We distinguish between the point of view of citizens and of members of associations. As citizens, we endorse the constraints of principles of justice; as association members, we want to limit those constraints so that the inner life of associations can flourish. This generates a "division of labor" that treats the basic structure and civil association as being, so to speak, on a par with one another.[146]

But on closer inspection, it turns out that there's a hierarchical relation after all, with the principles of justice serving as trumps. Otherwise put, the basic structure constitutes the end, and the various associations are in part means to that end. So, for example, "the treatment of children must be such as to support the family's role in upholding a constitutional regime."[147] But what if (say)

---

[144] Rawls, *Justice as Fairness*, p. 11.

[145] Rawls, *Justice as Fairness*, p. 165. To complicate matters further, on one and the same page (10), Rawls seems to characterize the family both as part of the basic structure of society and as an institution within the basic structure. I don't see how it can be both, and it makes a huge difference which it is.

[146] Rawls, *Justice as Fairness*, p. 165.

[147] Ibid.

religious free exercise includes teachings and practices that don't do this? (Imagine a religious group that has no intention of altering the public structure of equal political rights for women but teaches its own members that women shouldn't participate in public life.)

Rawls is certain (quite sensibly in my view) that "We wouldn't want political principles of justice to apply directly to the internal life of the family."[148] The reasoning appears to be that various associations have inner lives that differ qualitatively from that of the political realm, so that political principles would be "out of place." This then raises a question: why aren't political, nonpolitical associations understood as related horizontally rather than vertically? Why can't nonpolitical associations be seen as limiting the scope of politics at the same time that the basic structure of politics constrains associations? Rawls's apparent answer runs as follows: the sphere or domain of the nonpolitical has no independent existence or definition, but is simply the result (or residuum) of how the principles of justice are applied directly and indirectly. In particular, the principle of equal citizenship applies everywhere.

In one sense, this is clearly true. If an association uses coercion to prevent some of its members from exercising their equal political rights, the state must step in to enforce them. But the more usual case is that the association organizes itself according to norms (of membership or activity) that are inconsistent with principles of equal citizenship. What is the state's

---

[148] Ibid.

legitimate power in the face of these dissenting practices? Is it so obvious that the legitimate activities of nonpolitical associations should be defined relative, not to the inner life of those associations, but rather to the principles of the public sphere? Can we not say something important about the distinctive natures of individual conscience, friendship, families, communities of faith or inquiry, and shouldn't those primary features of our social life have an effect on the scope of political principles, not just vice versa? Even if justice is the "first virtue" of public institutions and enjoys lexical priority over other goods of the public realm (a debatable proposition), it does not follow that the public realm enjoys comprehensive lexical priority over the other forms of human activity and association.[149]

THE PLURALIST ALTERNATIVE

It is in the context of questions such as these that political pluralism emerges as an alternative to all forms of civic totalism. Political pluralism, to begin, rejects efforts to understand individuals, families, and associations simply as parts within, and of, a political whole. Relatedly, pluralism rejects the instrumental/teleological argument that individuals, families, and associations are adequately understood as "for the sake of" some political purpose. For example,

---

[149] For much more on civic totalism, see William A. Galston, *The Practice of Liberal Pluralism* (New York: Cambridge University Press, 2004), chapter 3.

religion is not (only) civil and in some circumstances may be in tension with civil requirements. This is *not* to say that political communities must be understand as without common purposes. The political order is not simply a framework within which individuals, families, and associations may pursue their own purposes. But civic purposes are not comprehensive and do not necessary trump the purposes of individuals and groups.

Political pluralism understands human life as consisting in a multiplicity of spheres, some overlapping, with distinct natures and/or inner norms. Each sphere enjoys a limited, but real, autonomy. It rejects any account of political community that creates a unidimensional hierarchical ordering among these spheres of life. Rather, different forms of association and activity are complexly interrelated. There may be local or partial hierarchies among subsets of spheres in specific context, but there are no comprehensive lexical orderings among categories of human life.

For these reasons, among others, political pluralism does not seek to overcome, but rather endorses, the post-pagan diremption of human loyalty and political authority created by the rise of revealed religion. That this creates problems of practical governance cannot be denied. But pluralists refuse to resolve these problems by allowing public authorities to determine the substance and scope of allowable belief (Hobbes) or by reducing faith to civil religion and elevating devotion to the common civic good as the highest human value (Rousseau). Fundamental tensions rooted in the deep structure of human existence cannot be abolished in a stroke but must rather be acknowledged, negotiated, and adjudicated with due regard to the contours of specific cases and controversies.

Pluralist politics is a politics of recognition rather than of construction. It respects the diverse spheres of human activity; it does not understand itself as creating or constituting those activities. Families are shaped by public law, but that does not mean that they are "socially constructed." There are complex relations of mutual impact between public law and faith communities, but it is preposterous to claim that the public sphere creates these communities. Do environmental laws create air and water? Many types of human association possess an existence that is not derived from the state. Accordingly, pluralist politics does not presume that the inner structure and principles of every sphere must (for either instrumental or moral reasons) mirror the structure and principles of basic political institutions.

A pluralist politics is however responsible for coordinating other spheres of activity, and especially for adjudicating the inevitable overlaps and disputes among them. This form of politics evidently requires the mutual limitation of some freedoms, individual and associational. It monopolizes the legitimate use of force, except in cases of self-defense when the polity cannot or does not protect us. It understands that group tyranny is possible and therefore protects individual against some associational abuses. But pluralist politics presumes that the enforcement of basic rights of citizenship and of exit rights, suitably understood, will usually suffice. Associational integrity requires a broad though not unlimited right of groups to define their own membership, to exclude as well as include, and a pluralist polity will respect that right

VARIETIES OF ARGUMENTS FOR POLITICAL PLURALISM

The core of my thesis is that different forms of human activity and association generate different kinds of claims, both to liberty and authority, and that no single ensemble of claims dominates the rest for all purposes or in all circumstances. As a distinctive form of activity and association, politics both makes claims and is limited in various ways by claims deriving from other sources. The question is how to justify this thesis.

Joseph Raz offers an argument for limited political authority based on two premises: the idea of responsibility as the core of human agency; and an understanding of political authority as derived from the consent of individual agents. Raz contends that while individuals can legitimately transfer responsibility for some aspects of their lives to others, they cannot abandon responsibility altogether without undermining agency. Thus, he concludes, "Only limited government can be legitimate."[150]

Limited how, exactly? Raz argues that a doctrine specifying the content of limited government would have two parts. The first is instrumental: delegating

---

[150] Joseph Raz, ed. *Authority* (New York: New York University Press, 1990), p. 12.

responsibility to government lacks a rationale in areas where individuals can act for themselves as efficiently and effectively as others can act for them. The second principle of limitation is avowedly non-instrumental: it consists of all those matters regarding which "it is more important to act independently than to succeed in doing the best." Raz remarks, laconically, that he "feel[s] the need for a substantive account of this category," an account he does not provide.[151] Any effort to do so would quickly encounter, inter alia, well-worn debates about the justification of paternalism---that is, the category of interventions in which considerations of an agent's well-being trump those of responsibility or autonomy.

Much liberal thought grounds limits to government on some conception of individual rights. While this line of argument has considerable merit, it is also incomplete. It is not easy to move from the concept of rights to a specific conception. Most American can recite the Declaration's famous litany of life, liberty, and the pursuit of happiness; few realize that the words "among which are" precede this triad, raising but not answering the question concerning the content of these unnamed additional rights. Similarly, the Ninth Amendment cautions that "The enumeration in the Constitution of certain rights shall not be construed to deny or disparage others retained by the people." But what exactly are these retained rights?

The language of individual rights goes astray, moreover, not when it claims to be *a* source of limits on

---

[151] Raz, p. 13.

governmental authority, but when it presents itself as the *sole* source. I take seriously the idea of individual inviolability, rightly understand, and I shall defend in detail one aspect of inviolability---namely, freedom of conscience. But I want to suggest that we may do better to proceed more empirically, by considering the diverse forms of human sociability and association.

For example, family obligations can limit the scope of political authority. Sophocles' *Antigone* revolves around primordial imperatives of kinship that stand opposed to the imperatives of patriotic loyalty. The fact that one of Antigone's brothers was slain in battle against his own city does not justify Creon's effort to prevent her from burying him. To be sure, Antigone is as deaf to Creon's legitimate concerns for his city as he was to her family ties. Still, the playwright presents the disaster that befalls Creon as the direct result of his extension of political authority beyond its rightful limits.

American constitutional law endorses the proposition that family ties limit political authority because the status of parenthood generates a sphere of authority. For example, the famous case of *Piece v. Society of Sisters*, the Supreme Court rejected the right of a public authority (in this case, the state of Oregon) to require all parents within its jurisdiction to send their children to public schools. In justifying its stance, the Court declared that

> The fundamental theory of liberty upon which all governments in this Union repose excludes any general power of the State to standardize its children by forcing

them to accept instruction for public school teachers only. The child is not the mere creature of the State; those who nurture him and direct his destiny have the right, coupled with the high duty, to recognize and prepare him for additional obligations.[152]

This does not mean, of course that family activities are immunized from political regulation. The *Pierce* court explicitly recognized a substantial degree of legitimate governmental regulation of the family, including its educational decisions. For example, the deep theory of liberty on which the court relied allows the state to require "that all children of proper age attend *some* school."[153] It is the task of what might be called pluralist casuistry to distinguish legitimate from illegitimate assertions of political authority over families.

Consider another example. U.S. law and jurisprudence limit the sway of public authority over religious associations. I have always made reference to the commonplace that these associations may establish their own criteria for their religious offices, general public norms of nondiscrimination to the contrary notwithstanding. But these limits go even deeper. As Laurence Tribe observes, courts and other agencies of the U.S. government "may not inquire into pervasively religious issues."[154] The rationale for this restriction goes

---

[152] 268 U.S. 510 (1925), at 535.

[153] 268 U.S. 510 (1925), at 534; emphasis mine.

[154] Tribe, *American Constitutional law, Second Edition* (Mineola, NY: Foundation Press, 1988), p. 1227.

beyond prudential fears of entanglement and political divisiveness. It reflects, as well, the belief that doctrinal and scriptural interpretation are beyond the competence and rightful authority of political power.

Democratic polities have not always acknowledged these limits. Well into the 20th century, the British House of Lords operated on the premise that property was contributed to religious bodies pursuant to an "implied trust" framed by the doctrines and practices of those bodies prevailing at the time of the donation. When doctrinal disputes and schisms occurred, the Lords did not hesitate to adjudicate property claims on the basis of their own interpretation of the litigants' fidelity to those doctrines and practices, an intrusion against which British pluralists such as Figgis protested bitterly but to no avail.

As early as 1872, however, U.S. courts abandoned the implied trust doctrine in favor of the rule that whenever the ordinary principles of contract and property law did not resolve disputes within religious association, courts should defer either to the majority in congregational churches or to the highest authority in hierarchical churches. The Court's argument for this position was rooted in principle as well as prudence:

> The law knows no heresy, and is committed to the support of no dogma, the establishment of no sect. The right to organize voluntary religious associations to assist in the expression and dissemination of any religious doctrine, and to create tribunals for the decision of controverted questions of faith within the association,

and for the ecclesiastical government of the individual members, congregations, and officers within the general association, is unquestioned. All who unite themselves to such a body do so with an implied consent to this government, and are bound to submit to it. But it would be a vain consent, and would lead to the total subversion of such religious bodies, if any one aggrieved by one of their decisions could appeal to the secular courts and have them reversed. It is of the essence of these religious unions, and of their right to establish tribunals for the decisions of questions among themselves, that those decisions should be binding in all cases of ecclesiastical cognizance, subject only to the appeals as the organism itself provides for.[155]

There is, in short, a sphere of religious authority distinct from, and limiting, the scope of rightful political authority.[156]

This is not exactly a new idea. In the familiar New Testament story of the silver coin, Jesus responds to a politically charged inquiry about paying taxes to Rome with the maxim, "Pay Caesar what is due to Caesar, and pay God what is due to God."[157] The task of tracing the

---

[155] *Watson v. Jones*, 80 U.S. 679 (1872), at 728-29. While this case was decided on the basis of common law, 80 years later the Court rendered a parallel decision based on the First Amendment. See *Kedroff v. Saint Nicholas Cathedral*, 344 U.S. 94 (1952).

[156] For a parallel discussion, see Nancy L. Rosenblum, *Membership & Morals: The Personal Uses of Pluralism in America* (Princeton: Princeton University Press, 1998), pp. 80-83.

[157] Matthew 22:15-22; Mark 12:13-17; Luke 20:20-26.

line between God's realm and Caesar's has challenged political thought, secular and theological, for two millennia. But the difficulty of this task does not obviate its necessity, once we acknowledge the independent force of religious claims.

FREEDOM OF CONSCIENCE

I now turn, in detail, to the idea of individual conscience as an important source of pluralist limits on state authority. To frame this inquiry, I begin by recalling an important but largely forgotten episode in U.S. constitutional history: a rapid and almost unprecedented turnabout by the Supreme Court on a matter of fundamental importance. I begin my tale in the late 1930s.

Acting under the authority of the state government, the school board of Minersville, Pennsylvania had required both students and teachers to participate in a daily pledge of allegiance to the flag. In the 1940 case of *Minersville v. Gobitis*[158], the Supreme Court decided against a handful of Jehovah's Witnesses who sought to have their children exempted on the grounds that this exercise amounted to a form of idolatry strictly forbidden by their faith. With but a single dissenting vote, the Court ruled that it was permissible for a school board to make participation in saluting the American flag a condition for attending public school, regardless of the conscientious objections of parents and students. Relying on this

[158] 310 U.S. 586 (1940).

holding and quoting liberally from the majority's decision, the West Virginia State Board of Education issued a regulation making the flag salute mandatory statewide. When a challenge to this action arose barely three years after *Gobitis*, the Court reversed itself by a vote of 6 to 3.[159] To be sure, during the brief interval separating these cases, the lone dissenter in *Gobitis* had been elevated to Chief Justice and two new voices, both favoring reversal, had joined the court, while two supporters of the original decision had departed. But of the seven justices who heard both cases, three saw fit to reverse themselves and to set forth their reasons for the change.

This kind of abrupt, explicit reversal is very rare in the annals of the Court, and it calls for some explanation. A clue is to be found, I believe, in the deservedly well-known peroration of Justice Jackson's majority decision overturning compulsory flag salutes:

> If there is any fixed star in our constitutional constellation, it is that no official, high or petty, can prescribe what shall be orthodox in politics, nationalism, religion, or other matters of opinion or force citizens to confess by word or act their faith therein. If there are any circumstances which permit an exception, they do not now occur to us. We think the action of the local authorities in

---

[159] *West Virginia v. Barnette*, 319 U.S. 624 (1943).

> compelling the flag salute and pledge transcends constitutional limitation on their power and invades the sphere of intellect and spirit which it is the purpose of the First Amendment to our Constitution to reserve from all official control.[160]

I want to suggest that the protected "sphere of intellect and spirit" and the antipathy to forced professions of faith to which Jackson refers enjoy a central place in the development of American political thought and in liberal political theory more generally. Expounded under the rubric of "conscience," not least by James Madison, it provides one of the clearest examples of limits to legitimate state power understood as inherent rather than constructed. It is to Madison's exposition of this concept that I now turn.

Consider, first, the language that Madison drafted for inclusion in the Virginia Declaration of Rights (1776), asserting:

> That religion, or the duty which we owe our CREATOR, and the manner of discharging it, can be directed only by reason and conviction, not by force or violence; and therefore, that all men are equally entitled to enjoy the free exercise of religion, according to the dictates of

---

160 319 U.S. 642.

> conscience, [unpunished and unrestrained by the magistrate, Unless the preservation of equal liberty and the existence of the State are manifestly endangered]; And that it is the mutual duty of all to practice Christian forbearance, love, and charity towards each other. (Madison's proposal for the Virginia Declaration of Rights, June 1776; brackets indicate words deleted in the final version adopted)

Note that by removing reservations against rights of conscience based on the good order of society, the Virginia Convention's revision of Madison's proposal had the effect of making those rights even stronger, less contingent on circumstances, than Madison had suggested. Still, through most of American history, some version of Madison's caveat has prevailed. In a line of cases extending back to 1878, the Supreme Court has distinguished between religious belief, which enjoys total immunity from state action, and religious practices, which may be regulated or even prohibited if they run afoul of basic individual or social interests that government has a duty to protect.

In *Cantwell v. Connecticut*[161], the Court expounded this distinction with exceptional clarity. The religion clause of the First Amendment embraces two concepts--freedom to believe and freedom to act. The first is absolute but, in the nature of things, the second cannot be. Conduct

---

161 310 U.S. 296 (1940).

remains subject to regulation for the protection of society. . . In every case the power to regulate must be so exercised as not, in attaining a permissible end, unduly to infringe the protected freedom.[162]

In subsequent cases the Court refined this doctrine: the state interests in the name of which basic liberties are restricted must be "compelling" (basic and urgent), and the means must be narrowly drawn so as to minimize the intrusion on liberty.[163]

To return to the development of Madison's thought: In his famous "Memorial and Remonstrance" (1785), coauthored with Thomas Jefferson and directed against a Virginia proposal to publicly fund teachers of Christianity, Madison further explained the basis of his stance on freedom of conscience:

> We remonstrate against the said Bill 1. Because we hold it for a fundamental and undeniable truth, "that Religion or the duty which we owe to our Creator and the manner of discharging it, can be directed

---

[162] 310 U.S. 303-304.

[163] Some commentators believe that this standard was significantly relaxed by the Court's decision in *Employment Division v. Smith*, 494 U.S. 872 (1990). In this case, five members of the Court held that it was acceptable for the state of Oregon to enforce its drug laws against the use of peyote in Native American religious rites. The five-member majority could not agree, however, on the grounds for this holding, and the case remains bitterly contested in both legislative and judicial forums.

only by reason and conviction, not by force or violence." The Religion then of every man must be left to the conviction and conscience of every man; and it is the right of every man to exercise it as these may dictate. This right is in its nature an unalienable right. It is unalienable, because the opinions of men, depending only on the evidence contemplated by their own minds cannot follow the dictates of other men: It is unalienable also, because what is here a right toward men, is a duty toward the Creator. It is the duty of every man to render to the Creator such homage and such only as he believes to be acceptable to him. This duty is precedent, both in order of time and degree of obligation, to the claims of Civil Society. Before any man can be considered as a member of Civil Society, he must be considered as a subject of the Governour of the Universe: And if a member of Civil Society, who enters into any subordinate Association, must always do it with a reservation of his duty to the General Authority; much more must every man who becomes a member of any particular Civil Society, do it with a saving of his allegiance to the Universal Sovereign. We maintain therefore that in matters of Religion, no mans right is abridged by the institution of Civil Society

> and that Religion is wholly exempt from its cognizance. True it is, that no other rule exists, by which any Question which may divide a Society, can be ultimately determined, but the will of the majority; but it is also true that the majority may trespass on the rights of the minority.

Madison's efforts continued at the national level during the early constitutional period. Indeed, two of the amendments that Madison drafted for inclusion in the Bill of Rights, one of which would have been binding on the states, made explicit reference to "rights of conscience." For example, Madison's initial draft of what become the religion clauses of the First Amendment read:

> The civil rights of none shall be abridged on account of religious belief or worship, nor shall any national religion be established; nor shall the full and equal rights of conscience be in any manner, or in any pretext, infringed. (amendment to the Constitution drafted by Madison for inclusion in the Bill of Rights, June 8, 1789)

Over the next century, the Supreme Court played at most a minor role in protecting what we now understand as the basic civil rights of individuals. During the decades after the Civil War, the Court increasingly deployed a broad construction of individual property rights against the states while typically leaving political and civil liberties under the aegis of state power -- a jurisprudential strategy that reached its peak in the famous (for some, infamous) 1905 decision of *Lochner v. New York*.[164] Legal commentators and dissenting justices began asking how these two tendencies could be reconciled.

In 1920, for example, the case of *Gilbert v. Minnesota* came before the Supreme Court.[165] Gilbert, a pacifist, had criticized American participation in World War One. He was convicted under a state statute prohibiting advocacy or teaching that interfered with or discouraged enlistment in the military. While the Court's majority declined to extend Fourteenth Amendment liberty guarantees to Gilbert, Justice Brandeis dissented, writing:

> I have difficulty believing that the liberty guaranteed by the Constitution, which has been held to protect [a wide property right], does not include liberty to teach, either in the privacy of the home or publicly, the doctrine of pacifism ...I cannot believe that the liberty guaranteed by the 14th Amendment includes only liberty to acquire and to enjoy property.[166]

Over time, the Court's unwillingness to abandon its doctrine of broad economic rights helped create the basis

---

[164] 198 U.S. 45 (1905).
[165] 254 U.S. 325 (1920).
[166] 254 U.S. 343.

for a broader understanding of constitutionally protected and enforceable liberties. Consider the controversy sparked a Nebraska law which, reflecting the nativist passions of the First World War era, prohibited instruction in any modern language other than English. Acting under this statute, a trial court convicted a teacher in a Lutheran parochial school for teaching a Bible class in German. In *Meyer v. Nebraska*[167]the Supreme Court struck down this law as a violation of the Fourteenth Amendment's liberty guarantee. Writing for a seven-member majority, Justice McReynolds declared:

> That the State may do much, go very far, indeed, in order to improve the quality of its citizens, physically, mentally, and morally, is clear; but the individual has certain fundamental rights which must be respected. A desirable end cannot be promoted by prohibited means.[168]

I now jump forward eight years, to 1931. In that year, the Supreme Court handed down its decision in the case of *U. S. v. Macintosh.*[169] The facts were as follows: Douglas Clyde Macintosh was born in Canada, came to the U.S. as a graduate student at the University of Chicago, and was ordained as a Baptist minister in 1907. He began teaching at Yale in 1909 and in short order became a member of

---

[167] 262 U.S. 390 (1923).
[168] 262 U.S. 401.
[169] 283 U.S. 605 (1931).

the faculty of the Divinity school, Chaplain of the Yale Graduate School, and Dwight Professor of Theology. When World War One broke out, he returned to his native Canada and volunteered for service on the front as a military chaplain. He reentered U.S. in 1916 and applied for naturalization in 1925. When asked whether he would bear arms on behalf of his country, he said he would not give a blanket undertaking in advance without knowing the cause for which his country was asking him to fight or believing that the war was just, declaring that "his first allegiance was to the will of God." After he was denied naturalization, he went to court.

The government argued that naturalization was a privilege, not a right, that the government has the right to impose any conditions it sees fit on that privilege, that the exemption of native-born citizens from military service on grounds of conscience was a statutory grant, not a Constitutional right, and that the Congress had not provided such statutory exemption for individuals seeking naturalization. The lawyers for Macintosh argued that our history makes it clear that conscientious exemption from military service was an integral element of the rights of conscience, guaranteed by the First Amendment that inhere in individuals and that in any event this was one of the rights reserved to the people by the Ninth Amendment.

By a vote of 5 to 4, a deeply divided Court decided in favor of the government. The case turned both on matters of statutory construction and on broader considerations. Writing for the majority, Justice Sutherland said:

> When [Macintosh] speaks of putting his allegiance to the will of God above his allegiance to the government, it is evident, in light of his entire statement, that he means to make *his own interpretation* of the will of God the decisive test which shall conclude the government and stay its hand. We are a Christian people . . ., according to one another the equal right of religious freedom, and acknowledging with reverence the duty of obedience to the will of God. But, also, we are a Nation with the duty to survive; a Nation whose Constitution contemplates war as well as peace; whose government must go forward upon the assumption, and safely can proceed upon no other, that qualified obedience to the Nation and submission and obedience to the laws of the land, as well those made for war asthose made for peace, are not inconsistent with the will of God.[170]

Writing for the four dissenters, Chief Justice Hughes began by offering an argument based on statutory construction, but like Sutherland, he did not end there. Hughes framed the broader argument this way:

---

[170] 283 U.S. 625.

Much has been said of the paramount duty to the State, a duty to be recognized, it is urged, even though it conflicts with convictions of duty to God. Undoubtedly that duty to the State exists within the domain of power, for government may enforce obedience to laws regardless of scruples. When one's belief collides with the power of the State, the latter is supreme within its sphere and submission or punishment follows. But, in the forum of conscience, duty to a moral power higher than the State has always been maintained. The reservation of that supreme obligation, as a matter of principle, would undoubtedly be made by many of our conscientious and law-abiding citizens. The essence of religion is belief in a relation to God involving duties superior to those arising from any human relation . . . . One cannot speak of religious liberty, with proper appreciation of its essential and historic significance, without assuming the existence of a belief in supreme allegiance to the will of God. . . . [F]reedom of conscience itself implies respect for an innate conviction of paramount duty. The battle for religious liberty has been fought and won with respect to religious beliefs and practices, which are not in conflict with good order,

> upon the very ground of the supremacy of conscience within its proper field. What that field is, under our system of government, presents in part a question of constitutional law and also, in part, one of legislative policy in avoiding unnecessary clashes with the dictates of conscience. There is abundant room for enforcing the requisite authority of law as it is enacted and requires obedience, and for maintaining the conception of the supremacy of law as essential to orderly government, without demanding that either citizens or applicants for citizenship shall assume by oath an obligation to regard allegiance to God as subordinate to allegiance to civil power.[171]

This debate between the proponents of political sovereignty and the advocates of parallel religious and political authority brings me back at long last to the dueling court decisions with which I began this section. As we will see, *Gobitis* and *Barnette* bring into play a number of issues much debated among students of jurisprudence and political theory during the past decade: the clash between history-based and principle-based interpretations of constitutional norms; the roles of courts and legislatures in a constitutional democracy; the competition between parents and the state for control of

---

[171] 283 U.S. 633-634.

education; the appropriate contents and limits of civic education. The deepest issue is the relative weight to be given to claims based upon individual liberties and those based upon social order and cohesion. Legal doctrines of presumption, burden of proof, and tests ("rational basis," "compelling state interests," "clear and present danger") serve as proxies for competing moral intuitions and judgments.

Writing for the majority in the Pennsylvania case, Justice Frankfurter offered an argument in favor of a democratic state whose legitimate powers include the power to prescribe civic exercises such as the flag salute. He began by locating the controversy in a complex field of plural and competing claims: liberty of individual conscience versus the state's authority to safeguard the nation's civic unity. The task is to "reconcile" these competing claims, which means "prevent[ing] either from destroying the other." Because liberty of conscience is so fundamental, "every possible leeway" should be given to the claims of religious faith. Still, Frankfurter reasoned, the "very plurality of principles" prevents us from establishing the "freedom to *follow* conscience" as absolute.[172]

The next issue concerns the meaning of these clashing principles. Frankfurter suggested that in considering the judicial enforcement of religious freedom we are dealing with a "*historic* concept."[173] That is, we should not look at its underlying logic or principles, but rather and only at

---

[172] 310 U.S. 591-594; italics mine.
[173] 310 U.S. 594; italics mine.

the way this concept has been applied in the past. We may well wonder whether this constitutes an adequate account of constitutional interpretation. ("Cruel and unusual"?) But even if it were, it would not necessarily support Frankfurter's conclusion. He insisted that "Conscientious scruples have not, in the course of the long struggle for religious toleration, relieved the individual from obedience to a general law not aimed at the promotion or restriction of religious belief."[174] But (as a number of commentators quickly pointed out) the *Cantwell* decision handed down just two weeks before *Gobitis* had done precisely that: it exempted individuals (in fact, Jehovah's Witnesses) engaged in religious activities from regulations not facially aimed at restricting free exercise, but rather at preventing fraud.

Still, Frankfurter insisted, "The mere possession of religious convictions which contradict the relevant concerns of a political society does not relieve the citizen from the discharge of political responsibilities."[175] On its face, this premise is fair enough; but raises the question of what must be added to "mere possession" to create a valid claim against the state. When (if ever) does the Constitution require some individuals to be exempted from doing what society thinks is necessary to promote the common good? Conversely, what are the kinds of collective claims that rightly trump individual reservations?

---

[174] Ibid.
[175] 301 U.S. 594-595.

Frankfurter offers a specific answer to the latter, as follows: Social order and tranquility provide the basis for enjoying all civil rights--including rights of conscience and exercise. Indeed, all specific activities and advantages of government "presuppose the existence of an organized political society." Laws that impede religious exercise are valid when legislature deems them essential to secure civic order and tranquility. National unity is the basis of national security--a highest-order public value (as we would now say, a compelling state interest). National unity is secured by the "binding tie of cohesive sentiment," which is the "ultimate foundation of a free society." This sentiment, in turn, is fostered by "all those agencies of the mind and spirit which may serve to gather up the traditions of a people, transmit them from generation to generation, and thereby create that continuity of a treasured common life which constitutes a civilization."[176]

If the cultivation of unifying sentiment is a valid end of government action, Frankfurter concluded, then courts should not interfere with legislative determinations of appropriate means. We do not know what works and what does not; we cannot say for sure that flag salutes are ineffective. In judging the legislature, we may use only the weakest of tests: is there any basis for the means the legislature has chosen to adopt? If there is, the courts must stay out.[177] But if satisfying the weakest test is enough, then the countervailing claims cannot be that

---

[176] 301 U.S. 595-596.
[177] 301 U.S. 597-598, 599-600.

important after all. So religious free exercise, which at the beginning of the opinion is characterized as "so subtle and so dear" as to require every possible deference, is reduced to a near-nullity by the end.

Frankfurter was aware that the thrust of his argument stood in tension with the Court's holding in *Pierce*. To square the circle, he offered a tendentious reinterpretation of that decision as defending diverse opinions about how to socialize children.[178] But as we have seen, the *Pierce* court cited, not the fact of diversity, but rather a fundamental theory of liberty, as the basis for its decision--precisely the kind of general claim against the state that Frankfurter was anxious to sidestep. It is hardly surprisingly to learn that while still a law professor, Frankfurter inveighed against *Pierce* when the decision was first handed down, on the grounds that a Court that deployed fundamental principles of liberty against state regulation of education could deploy comparable principles against state regulation of the economy. If you like *Pierce*, his reasoning went, you must accept *Lochner*. And that is a cost that outweighs the gains.[179] It is perhaps understandable that Frankfurter could not foresee the emergence of a new jurisprudence that would reorder the relation between religious and economic regulation. But that is no excuse for deliberately understating the evident force of conscience-based claims.

---

[178] 301 U.S. 598-599.

[179] Felix Frankfurter, "Can the Supreme Court Guarantee Toleration?" 43 *The New Republic* 85 (1925).

Toward the conclusion of his opinion, Frankfurter touched on an issue that figures centrally in our current debates--the right of public authorities "to awaken in the child's mind considerations . . .contrary to those implanted by the parent."[180] He is right to suggest that the bare fact of a clash with parents does not suffice to render a state's action illegitimate. But who seriously thinks that parental claims are always trumps? The thesis is rather that there are certain classes of claims that parents can interpose against state authority---especially when the state employs particularly intrusive means in pursuit of public purposes. Recall that what was at stake in *Gobitis* was not just the right of the state to require civic education; it was the state's power to compel students to engage in affirmations contrary to conscientious belief. It is not unreasonable to suggest that compelling the performance of speech and deeds contrary to faith is a step even graver than prohibiting activities required by faith and places the state under an even heavier burden to justify the necessity of its coercion.

Frankfurter endorsed no such principle. Quite the reverse: to foster social order and unity, he asserted, the state "may in self-protection utilize the educational process for inculcating those almost unconscious feelings which bind men together."[181] And if the state gets it wrong? Frankfurter answered this question, and concluded his opinion, with a profession of faith in the democratic process: It is better to use legislative processes

---

[180] 301 U.S. 599.
[181] 301 U.S. 600.

to protect liberty and rectify error, rather than transferring the contest to the judicial arena. As long as the political liberties needed for effective political contestation are left unaffected, "education in the abandonment of foolish legislation is itself a training in liberty [and] serves to vindicate the self-confidence of a free people."[182] There is clearly some wisdom in this position, which is enjoying a modest resurgence today. What it overlooks is the cost---especially to the most affected individuals and groups---of waiting for a democratic majority to recognize its mistake.

Remarkably, *Gobitis,* decided with but a single dissenting vote in 1940, was overruled just three years later in *West Virgina v. Barnette* by a stunning 6 to 3 margin. I turn now to Justice Jackson's majority opinion, a highlight of which we have already encountered.

Jackson did not question that state's right to educate for patriotism and civic unity. But in his view, what was at stake was not education, rightly understood, but something quite different: “Here . . .we are dealing with a compulsion of students to declare a belief."[183]

> [C]ensorship or suppression of expression of opinion is tolerated by our Constitution only when the expression presents a clear and present danger of action of a kind the State is empowered to prevent and punish. It would seem that involuntary affirmation

---

[182] Ibid.
[183] 319 U.S. 630.

> could be commanded only on even more immediate and urgent grounds than silence. But here the power of compulsion is invoked without any allegation that remaining passive during a flag salute ritual creates a clear and present danger that would justify an effort even to muffle expression. To sustain the compulsory flag salute we are required to say that a Bill of Rights which guards the individual's right to speak his own mind, left it open to public authorities to compel him to utter what is not in his mind.[184]

The issue, Jackson asserted, is not one of policy, that is, of effectiveness of means in pursuit of a legitimate end such as national unity. The prior question is whether the state possesses the rightful power to promote this end through compulsion contrary to conscience, a power the *Gobitis* majority assumed to inhere in our constitutional government. If it does not, then the issue is not exempting dissenters from otherwise valid policies, but rather reining in a state that is transgressing the bounds of legitimate action.[185]

Jackson insisted that limited government is not weak government. Assuring individual rights strengthens government by bolstering support for it. In the long run, individual freedom of mind is more sustainable and

---

[184] 319 U.S. 633-634.
[185] 319 U.S. 635-636.

powerful than is "officially disciplined uniformity."[186] "To believe that patriotism will not flourish if patriotic ceremonies are voluntary and spontaneous instead of a compulsory routine is to make an unflattering estimate of the appeal of our institutions to free minds."[187]

> Limited government is not simply a wise policy, Jackson argued; it is also a matter of constitutional principle: The very purpose of a Bill of Rights was to withdraw certain subjects from the vicissitudes of political controversy, to place them beyond the reach of majorities and officials and to establish them as legal principles to be applied by the courts. One's right to life, liberty, and property, to free speech, a free press, freedom of worship and assembly, and other fundamental rights may not be submitted to vote; they depend on the outcome of no elections.[188]

Limitations on government affect means as well as ends. There is no question that government officials and institutions may seek to promote national unity through persuasion and example. "The problem is whether under our Constitution compulsion as here employed is a

---

[186] 319 U.S. 637.
[187] 319 U.S. 641.
[188] 319 U.S. 639.

permissible means for its achievement."[189] It is in this context that Jackson penned his famous words about the fixed star in our constitutional constellation, the sphere of intellect and spirit that our laws protect from all official interference.

Justice Frankfurter, the author of the majority opinion in *Gobitis,* penned a lengthy dissent, a personal *apologia* whose tone of injured dignity was set by its opening sentence: "One who belongs to the most vilified and persecuted minority in history is not likely to be insensible to the freedoms guaranteed by our Constitution."[190] But he declared that what was at stake was not a constitutional question but rather a policy judgment. In this arena, courts should override legislatures only if reasonable legislators could not have chosen to employ the contested means in furtherance of legitimate ends. As a general proposition, there is a presumption in favor of legislatures, and legislation must be considered valid if there exists some rational basis for connecting it to a valid public purpose.[191]

Exceptions to this presumption arise when the state employs constitutionally prohibited means. But the mandatory flag salute was not of this character. The state action at issue, Frankfurter asserted, was not intended to promote or discourage religion, which was clearly forbidden. Rather, it was "a general non-discriminatory civil regulation [that] in fact [but not as a matter of

---

[189] 319 U.S. 641.
[190] 319 U.S. 646.
[191] 319 U.S. 646-651.

intended effect] touches conscientious scruples or religious beliefs of an individual or a group."[192] In such cases, it is the legislature's role to make accommodations, not the court's. Frankfurter argued that Jefferson and those who followed him wrote guarantees of religious freedom into our constitutions. Religious minorities as well as religious majorities were to be equal in the eyes of the political state. But Jefferson and the others also knew that minorities may disrupt society. It never would have occurred to them to write into the Constitution the subordination of the general civil authority of the state to sectarian scruples. . . . The constitutional protection of religious freedom terminated disabilities, it did not create new privileges. It gave religious equality, not civil immunity. Its essence is freedom from conformity to religious dogma, not freedom from conformity to law because of religious dogma. . . . The essence of the religious freedom guaranteed by our Constitution is this: no religion shall either receive the state's support or incur its hostility. Religion is outside the sphere of political government. This does not mean that all matters on which religious organizations or beliefs may pronounce are outside the sphere of government.[193]

Many other laws (e.g., compulsory medical measures) have employed compulsion against religious scruples, but courts have not struck them down:

---

[192] 319 U.S. 651.
[193] 319 U.S. 653-654.

> Law is concerned with external behavior and not with the inner life of man. It rests in large measure upon compulsion. . . . The consent on which free government rests in the consent that comes from sharing in the process of making and unmaking laws. The state is not shut out from a domain because the individual conscience may deny the state's claim.[194]

Indeed, Frankfurter asserted, it was wrong to describe the mandatory flag salute as compelled belief:

> Compelling belief implies denial of opportunity to combat it and to assert dissident views. Such compulsion is one thing. Quite another matter is submission to conformity of action while denying its wisdom or virtue with ample opportunity for seeking its change or abrogation.[195]

Frankfurter concluded his dissent with a profession of political faith. Liberal democracy is more a matter of active, self-governing citizens than of protective or tutelary courts:

> Of course patriotism cannot be enforced by the flag salute. But neither can the

---

[194] 319 U.S. 655.
[195] 319 U.S. 656.

> liberal spirit be enforced by judicial invalidation of illiberal legislation. . . Only a persistent positive translation of the faith of a free society into the convictions and habits and actions of a community is the ultimate reliance against unabated temptations to fetter the human spirit.[196]

JURISPRUDENCE, MORAL INTUITION, AND POLITICAL THEORY

I am not a legal historian. I have told this tale, not for its own sake, but with moral intent. I want to use these materials as a basis for testing our judgments about two questions. First: looking at the judicial bottom-line---the "holding"---are we more inclined to favor the outcome in *Gobitis* or in *Barnette*? Second: what kinds of broader principles underlie our judgment concerning these specific cases?

It is easy to sympathize with Frankfurter's dismay at the deployment of judicial review to immunize concentrated economic power against public scrutiny; with his belief that democratic majorities should enjoy wide latitude to pursue the common good as they see it; with his belief that the requirements of social order and unity may sometimes override the claims, however worthy, of individuals, parents, civil associations, and religious faith; and with his conviction that the systematic substitution of judicial review for democratic self-

---

[196] 319 U.S. 670-671.

correction can end by weakening citizenship itself. Nonetheless, I believe (and I am far from alone), that Frankfurter's reasoning in *Gobitis* was unsound, and his holding unacceptable. There are certain goods and liberties that enjoy a preferred position and are supposed to be lifted above everyday policy debate. If liberty of conscience is a fundamental good, as Frankfurter acknowledges, then it follows that state action interfering with it bears a substantial burden of proof. A distant harm, loosely linked to the contested policy, is not enough to meet that burden. The harm must be a real threat; it must be causally linked to the policy in question; and the proposed remedy must do the least possible damage to the fundamental liberty, consistent with the abatement of the threat. The state's mandatory pledge of allegiance failed all three of these tests. *Gobitis* was wrongly decided; the ensuing uproar was a public indication that the Court had gone astray; and the quick reversal in *Barnette*, with fully half the justices in the new six-member majority switching sides, was a clear indication of the moral force of the objections.

We now reach my second question: is our judgment on these cases a particularized moral intuition, or does it reflect some broader principles? The latter, I think. What Justice Jackson termed the "sphere of intellect and spirit" is at or near the heart of what makes us human. The protection of that sphere against unwarranted intrusion represents the most fundamental of all human liberties. There is a strong presumption against state policies that prevent individuals from the free exercise of intellect and spirit. There is an even stronger presumption against compelling individuals to make affirmations contrary to their convictions. (These presumptions drove Madison's understanding of freedom of conscience, discussed earlier in this essay.) This does not mean that compulsory speech is always wrong; courts and legislatures may rightly compel unwilling witnesses to give testimony and may rightly punish any failure to do so that does not invoke a well-established principle of immunity, such as the bar against coerced self-incrimination. Even here, the point of the compulsion is to induce individuals to tell the truth as they see it, not to betray their innermost convictions in the name of a state-administered orthodoxy.

It is easy for polities---even stable constitutional democracies---to violate these principles. In that obvious empirical sense, fundamental liberties are political constructions. But that democratic majorities can deprive minorities of liberty, often with impunity, does not make it right. Like all politics, democratic politics is legitimate to the extent that it recognizes and observes the principles that limit the exercise of democratic power. The liberties that individuals and the associations they constitute should enjoy in all but the most desperate circumstances go well beyond the political rights that democratic politics requires. We cannot rightly assess the importance of politics without acknowledging the limits of politics. The claims that political institutions can make in the name of the common good coexist with claims of at least equal importance that individuals and civil associations make, based on particular visions of the good for themselves or for humankind. This political pluralism may be messy and conflictual; it may lead to confrontations not conducive to maximizing public unity and order. But if political pluralism, thus understood, reflects the complex truth of the human condition, then the practice of politics must do its best to honor the principles that limit the scope of politics.

There is an ambiguity that I must now address. My announced topic in this section is freedom of conscience. But what is "conscience," anyway? For James Madison and other 18th century thinkers, the term clearly pointed toward religious conviction. Although Justice Jackson's sphere of intellect and spirit includes religion, it encompasses much else besides. So is conscience to be understood narrowly or expansively?

We may approach this question from two standpoints, the constitutional and the philosophical. Within constitutional law, both the narrow and expansive views have found proponents among able interpreters of the First Amendment. On the narrow side, Laurence Tribe argues that "The Framers . . . clearly envisioned religion as something special; they enacted that vision into law by guaranteeing the free exercise of *religion* but not, say, of philosophy or science."[197] Christopher Eisgruber and Lawrence Sager object that "To single out one of the ways that persons come to understand what is important in life, and grant those who choose that way a license to disregard legal norms that the rest of us are obliged to obey, is to defeat rather than

---

[197] Laurence Tribe, *American Constitutional Law; Second Edition* (Mineola, NY: Foundation press, 1988), p. 1189.

fulfill our commitment to toleration."[198] In effect, they argue that we must read the religion clauses of the 1st Amendment in light of the Equal Protection clause of the 14th.

We see this debate playing out in a fascinating way in the evolution of the jurisprudence of conscience-based exemptions from the military draft. Section 6(j) of the WWII-era Universal Military Training and Service Act made exemptions available to those who were conscientiously opposed to military service by reason of "religious training and belief." The required religious conviction was defined as "an individual's belief in a relation to a Supreme being involving duties superior to those arising from any human relation, but [not including] essentially political, sociological, or philosophical views or a merely personal moral code."

In the case of *United States v. Seeger* (1965), however, the Court broadened the definition of religion by interpreting the statue to include a "sincere and meaningful belief which occupies in the life of its possessor a place parallel to that filled by the God of those admittedly qualifying for the exemption."[199] In five years later, in *Welsh v. United States*, a Court plurality further broadened the reach of the statute to include explicitly secular belief that "play the role of a religion and function as a religion in life." Thus, draft exemptions

---

[198] Christopher L. Eisgruber and Lawrence G. Sager, "The Vulerability of Conscience: The Constitutional Basis for Protecting Religious Conduct," 61 *University of Chicago Law Review* (1994): 1315.
[199] 380 U.S. 163 (1965), at 176.

could be extended to "those who consciences, spurred by deeply held moral, ethical, or religious beliefs, would give them no rest or peace if they allowed themselves to become a part of an instrument."[200]

For our purposes, the real action takes place in the penumbra of the plurality's opinion. Justice Harlan, who provided the fifth vote for the expansive reading of conscientious exemption, argued in a concurring opinion that while the plurality's interpretation of the statutory language was indefensible, the Court could and should save the statute by engaging in an explicit act of reconstruction. The reason: it would be a violation of both the Establishment and Equal Protection clauses for Congress to differentiate between religious and nonreligious conscientious objectors.[201] This is the judicial precursor of the Eisgruber/Sager position.

For their part, the three dissenters argued that while Harlan was right as a matter of statutory construction, he was wrong as a matter of constitutional interpretation. They wrote that "neither support nor hostility, but neutrality, is the goal of the religion clauses of the First Amendment. 'Neutrality,' however, is not self-defining. If it is 'favoritism' and not neutrality to exempt religious believers from the draft, is it 'neutrality' and not 'inhibition' of religion the compel religious believers to fight when they have special reasons for not doing so, reasons to which the Constitution gives particular recognition? It cannot be denied [the dissenters

---

[200] 398 U.S. 333 (1970), at 339, 344.
[201] 398 U.S. 345, 356-57.

concluded] that the First Amendment itself contains a religious classification"-Lawrence Tribe's point exactly.[202]

To shed light on this dispute, it is useful to move outside the realm of constitutional adjudication and raise more general considerations. There are, I suggest, two features of religion that figure centrally in the debate about religiously-based exemptions from otherwise valid laws. First, believers understand the requirements of religious beliefs and actions as central rather than peripheral to their identity; and second, they experience these requirements as authoritative commands. So understood, religion is more than a mode of human flourishing. Regardless of whether an individual experiences religious requirements as promoting or rather thwarting self-development, their power is compelling. (In this connection, recall the number of Hebrew prophets---starting with Moses---who experience the divine call to prophetic mission as destructive of their prior lives and identities.

My suggestion is that at least in modern times, some individuals and groups who are not religious come to embrace ensembles of belief and action that share these two features of religious experience---namely, identity-formation and compulsory power. It does not seem an abuse of speech to apply the term conscience to this experience, whether religious or non-religious. My concept of expressive liberty functions, in part, to support the claim that conscience in this extended sense enjoys a rebuttable presumption to prevail in the face of

---

[202] 398 U.S. 372.

public law. In this respect, though not others, I find myself in agreement with Rogers Smith when he writes that

> the only approach that is genuinely compatible with equal treatment, equal protection, and equal respect for all citizens is treating claims of religious and secular moral consciences that same. Fully recognizing the historical, philosophical, and moral force of claims for deference to sincere conscientious beliefs and practices whenever possible, I would place all such claims in a 'preferred position' as defined by modern constitutional doctrines: governmental infringements upon such conscientious claims would be sustainable in court only if it were shown that they were necessary for compelling government interests."[203]

What are the kinds of collective interests that suffice to rebut the presumption in favor of individual conscience? I can think of at least two. First, the state cannot avoid attending to the content of conscience. Deep convictions may express identity with compulsory

---

[203] Rogers M. Smith, "'Equal' Treatment? A Liberal Separationist View," in Stephen V. Monsma and J. Christopher Soper, eds., *Equal Treatment of religion in a Pluralistic Society* (Grand Rapids, MI: Eerdman's, 1998) , p. 193.

power and nonetheless be deeply mistaken in ways that the state may rightly resist through the force of law. And second, even if the content of an individual's conscientious claim is not unacceptable in itself, its social or civic consequences may expose it to justified regulation or even probibition.

It may well be possible to add other categories of considerations that rebut the presumptions of conscience. In practice, the combined force of these considerations may warrant more restriction than accommodation. My point is only that the assertion of a conscience-based claim imposes a burden on the state to justify its proposed interference. There are many ways in which the state may discharge that burden, but if my position is correct, Justice Frankfurter's argument in *Gobitis* is not one of them. It is not enough to say that whenever a state pursues a general good within its legitimate purview, the resulting abridgement of conscience may represent unfortunate collateral damage but gives affected individuals and groups no legitimate grievance or cause of action. Claims of conscience are not trumps, but they matter far more than Frankfurter and his modern followers are willing to admit.

The ultimate reason is this: in a liberal democracy, the state is not an end in itself but rather a means to certain ends that enjoy an elevated status. The ability of individuals and groups to live in ways consistent with their understanding of what gives meaning and purpose to life (which I call expressive liberty) is one of those ends. This kind of liberty may rightly be limited to the extent necessary to secure the institutional conditions for its exercise. Beyond that point, the rightful relation of ends and means is turned on its head. That is the line a liberal democratic state ought not cross.

CONCLUSION

As I have defined it, political pluralism is the thesis that human life, individual and associational, consists in a heterogeneous variety of activities, each of which generates a distinctive ensemble of claims to respect and authority. Politics is but one of these activities. While it possesses distinctive competences and advances distinctive claims, its authority does not dominate every other type of activity.

I do not mean to suggest that there are neatly separated, hermetically sealed spheres, each of which is dominated by a single set of claims. For example, we have seen that parents and public institutions each exercise rightful authority over decisions concerning the education of children. (For some purposes, children share this authority as well.) We have also seen that the line between religious and political authority over social life can prove exceedingly difficult to draw. While there are many instances in which it appears reasonably clear which set of claims is to take priority, there are many others (perhaps the majority) in which claims qualitatively different in their content and source will vie for control, with no obvious principles for resolving the conflict. Indeed, part of the point of politics is to deal with such controversies, through bargaining, voting, and attending to particular circumstances. It is inevitable that these political decisions will reflect, not only path dependency, but also differences of natural endowment and social power. (Republican government, however perfect is no exception; Hobbes called democracy the "aristocracy of orators.") My point is only that once we recognize the diversity of authority claims, it becomes impossible to sustain the theory of civic totalism.

Must we acknowledge this diversity? My argument is that once we attend to some basic features of social life, it becomes far more plausible to affirm than to deny this diversity; the idea of a single dominant authority appears procrustean, even counterfactual. Political pluralism is an empirical social theory with normative force.

Chapter XII

Religious Violence or Religious Pluralism: The Essential Choice

William A. Galston

INTRODUCTION

The question of the hour is whether traditional Islam is compatible with democracy. Though important, that question is subordinate to another: whether Islamic traditionalists can make their peace with religious pluralism, whether their efforts to impose their practices on Muslims who reject them will engender unending conflict.

It is natural for Western observers to believe that the "irrationality" of religious violence is the problem and that rationality (or at least reasonableness) is the solution. I want to suggest a somewhat different approach. The diminution of religious violence in the West, I shall argue, is the product not so much of ideas as of concrete historical experiences that made populations more receptive to the reality of religious pluralism and the necessity of tolerance. These practices, in turn, lent support to the theory and institutions of liberal constitutionalism. The real issue today, therefore, is whether there are concrete processes underway within Islam that may over time make the politics of pluralism more acceptable and attractive, even to traditionalist Muslims unsympathetic to Western liberalism.

POLITICS, RELIGION, PLURALISM

Speaking broadly and schematically, there are three possible relations between political and religious authority. First, political authority may be comprehensively dominant over religion, which is seen as serving state power (and for this reason is often called "civil"). One of many difficulties with this position is that it subordinates the religious content of faith—its theological claims--to its civil consequences. Recent controversies in France over religious garb and symbols in public schools reveal the continuing compatibility between the civic republican tradition and the consignment of religion to civil status.

Second, and conversely, religious authority may coincide with, or comprehensively dominate, political authority, yielding some version of theocracy. This stance invariably represents the dominance of a particular faith at the expense of all others.

Third, political and religious authority may coexist without either enjoying a comprehensive dominance. One version of this position seeks to divide social life into different spheres, dominated by either politics or faith. (Maxims such as "Render unto Caesar what is Caesar's . . ." provide the basis for such an understanding.) It is hard to come by such neat surgical divisions, however. More typically, the coexistence model implies overlapping and conflicting claims, generating the need for both theoretical clarification and legal adjudication.

Few individual believers or faith communities can be satisfied with the civic republican approach, which embodies an ordering of values antithetical to most religious commitments. As the history of European nations such as France and Italy with deep civic republican traditions shows, the effort to demote religion to purely civil status is bound to spark political conflict and, on occasion, actual violence.

The theocratic option fares no better. Whatever may be the case for homogeneous communities espousing a single faith (few of any size do so), the theocratic impulse creates grave difficulties for societies with multiple faith communities. In circumstances of diversity, a serious religious establishment (as distinguished from, say, the increasingly symbolic role of the Church of England) will inevitably use legal coercion to impose its views on faith communities that conscientiously reject them. Here again, political conflict will tend to spill over into episodes of violent resistance.

That leaves the coexistence model, a mode of pluralism that implies horizontal rather than hierarchical relations, not only between political and religious authority claims, but also among faith communities. By definition, this option is bound to leave both theocrats and civic totalists dissatisfied, but it holds out the hope of reducing coercion to a manageable minimum. The problem of religiously related violence can be addressed best, not through secularism, but rather through institutionalized pluralism.

Compared to the 16th and 17th centuries, the level of religious violence originating in the West is low. It is natural for those who applaud this change to wonder how it happened, and whether it can serve as a template for reform in regions where religiously inspired violence remains high. And it is reasonable to conjecture that ways of thinking now pervasive in the West helped shape that template.

What is the relationship between the pluralist approach, the reduction of religious violence, and what the organizers of this conference have called "the Enlightenment"? For the purposes of this essay, I will presuppose what many deny—namely, that religion often serves as an independent source of conflict rather than as a rhetorical screen for violent antipathies spawned by oppression, deprivation, the memory of colonialism, or a deep sense of humiliation—not to mention very specific complaints. It is more gratifying and convenient for Americans to believe that we were attacked on September 11 because our adversaries "hate freedom" than because they oppose the presence of our troops in Saudi Arabia. At the least, we should remain aware of the possibility that our current concerns about religious terrorism reflect tensions considerably less exalted than faith-based disputes over the content of God's law.

With this caveat firmly in mind, we can begin to engage the announced topic of this conference. It is a mistake, I believe, to think of the Enlightenment (even in Europe, leaving aside the encounters of Christianity, Judaism, and Islam with Greek philosophy) as a single, unified historical phenomenon. We may identify a *radical*

Enlightenment, atheistic in theory and aggressively secularist in practice. The early days of the French Revolution revealed what the politics of radical Enlightenment actually meant, leading many who initially sympathized with the revolutionary impulse to recoil. Indeed, this history shows why the proposition that the Enlightenment is the remedy for sectarian violence is false on its face. The radical Enlightenment is in fact a form of sectarianism, and in the two centuries between the onset of the French Revolution and the fall of the Berlin Wall it occasioned some of the bloodiest violence the world has ever seen.

But there was also a moderate Enlightenment that wished to open a social space for free inquiry and religious diversity without denigrating or expunging specific faiths. The majority of the American founders fell in this category; those who did not (think of Tom Paine) tended to stand out.

I would argue that the proponents of moderate Enlightenment were in fact pluralists, even though they did not use the term. For example, James Madison's depiction of rights of religious conscience, which became canonical for American political thought and eventually American jurisprudence as well, rested explicitly on the coexistence of two different kinds of authority, neither of which straightforwardly trumps the other. To put the point more broadly: it is a mistake to see liberal constitutionalism as strictly supreme over, or subordinate to, claims based on religious conviction. It is sometimes the one, sometimes the other, and sometimes neither.

It is also a mistake to trace the reduction of religious violence in the West solely to the Enlightenment, however understood. Consider the theocratic argument, stripped to its essentials. IF (1) revealed religion X is true; and (2) to secure spiritual perfection or salvation, individuals and communities must live in accordance with that truth; and (3) law backed by coercive force is a permissible means of overcoming the inevitable resistance to living in that manner, THEN there is no objection in principle to establishing and enforcing religion X. But while a handful of daring Enlightenment thinkers such as Benedict Spinoza and Pierre Bayle were offering critiques of this argument's first two premises, the most effectual response focused on the third premise, for reasons that had little to do with the Enlightenment.

By 1640, a century of religious conflict had left Europe exhausted and disillusioned. Ordinary people as well as distinguished thinkers were moving toward the conclusion that coercion in matters of religion was unacceptable, even in the name of saving souls. Their experience had led them to an historic judgment: violence in the name of religion was a greater problem than the political, moral, and spiritual ills it purported to cure. Modern scholars as diverse as Judith Shklar and Leo Strauss have documented how European attitudes shifted against what Machiavelli was the first to call "pious cruelty."

While this judgment was at its core moral rather than theoretical, it sparked the development of new conceptions of religious toleration. Some argued that coercion in matters of faith was a contradiction in terms and therefore bound to fail. Others contended that Christianity, rightly understood, precluded such coercion. A few brave souls even speculated that precisely because it is given to mortals to see the divine only through a glass, darkly, there was more than one path to God and that religious controversies over which so much blood had been spilled should be regarded as matters of "indifference."

This thesis could, and did, verge on an approach to religion that reflected more directly the influence of the Enlightenment—the idea of "natural theology," or (in the title of Kant's notable contribution to the genre) religion within the limits of reason alone. But while this approach might vindicate the god and cosmos of the philosophers, it was bound to leave out most of what bound the pious to their particular faiths. Worse, it denied, tacitly if not explicitly, the core claim of most actual religions—that miraculous events of revelation or incarnation had pierced the barrier between God and man, making known truths beyond the bounds of reason. Even Kant felt impelled to remark that his famous critique of pure reason had limited reason's reach in order to make room for faith. It seems safest to say that while philosophy can try to understand the conflict between faith and reason, it cannot surmount or abolish that conflict. Because there is no final solution, any viable political response must somehow embody this tension without overcoming it. This is what liberal constitutionalism at its pluralist best is able to achieve.

"RELIGION" AND "VIOLENCE": SOME DISTINCTIONS

Up to now, I have conjured with "religion" and "violence" as undifferentiated concepts. At this stage of my argument, I need to offer some distinctions.

Religion

For my purposes, I want to propose three dimensions of variation among religions. (1) Religions differ in their basic structure. Some focus on inward states, while others give greater emphasis to external behavior, in the form of worship rituals as well as laws governing daily life. (2) Religions differ in the share of human existence over which they claim primary jurisdiction. Some view their domain as partial (Render unto Caesar what is Caesar's . . .), while others make totalizing claims to direct every aspect of life. (3) Some religions make universalistic claims, to be the one true faith for all human beings whoever and wherever they might be, while others are more particularistic.

My suggestion is that each of these dimensions bears on the ability of a specific religion to live with moral and religious plurality. In the first place, acceptance of pluralism comes more easily to religions that emphasize inner conviction, because they need ask little of politics beyond being left alone. By contrast, religions that take the form of law, as do traditional forms of Judaism and Islam, are forced to take seriously the content of public law. The terms of engagement between religious law and public law then become critical.

Second, religions that view their domain of jurisdiction as restricted are likely to coexist more comfortably with pluralism than are those with unlimited claims. Practitioners of a religion in which everything matters, from the consumption of food to the organization of politics, will feel compelled to use public power to mandate, or at least protect, their preferred practices. And this is bound to repress free expression and free exercise for other believers, not to mention nonbelievers, within that political community.

The difficulties for plurality engendered by comprehensive faith claims are deepened whenever a religion propounds the seamless unity of all existence. According to a leading traditionalist scholar of Islam, Seyyed Hossein Nasr, Islam rejects the distinction (characteristic of Christianity) between the religious and the secular, or the sacred and the profane: "In the unitary perspective of Islam, all aspects of life . . . are governed by a single principle." From this standpoint, the idea of a secular realm of freedom and plurality, independent of religion, is a leading modern example of the "mortal threat of 'polytheism'" against which Islam has struggled since its inception.[204]

Finally, universalistic religions are likely to have a less accommodating stance toward plurality, wherever it may appear. At the very least, they will proselytize, raising the hackles of religious communities subjected to their messengers. And if they view the use of more forceful

---

[204] Seyyed Hossein Nasr, *Islamic Life and Thought* (Chicago: ABC International Group, 2001), pp. 7, 14.

modes of conversion as limited only by prudential considerations rather than moral norms, then universalistic claims can be (and during the past two millennia, have been) translated into outright coercion.

My hypothesis is this: the more a religion expresses itself in external law the more extensive its scope, and the more universalistic its claims the less accommodating will be its stance toward plurality, and the more likely it will be to resort to violence to overcome or eliminate plurality. Thus, the universalism of many Protestant denominations is counterbalanced by their inward focus, and in some cases by more than prudential restraints on religious coercion as well. While classical rabbinic Judaism emphasizes external observance (and must therefore engage with public law), its claims are particularistic and (as we shall see) partial as well. Of all the "Abrahamic" faiths, my hypothesis suggests that Catholicism and Islam should have had a much harder time accepting plurality and eschewing violence; Islam the hardest of all, in that it holds *shari'ah* to express the direct, unalterable will of God to a greater extent than does civil or canon law for Catholics.

Violence

The distinctions between restricted and unlimited domains, and between particularist and universalistic faiths, allow us to distinguish between religious violence that is essentially *defensive* in nature and violence that is *offensive.*

Particularist faith with limited domains are content to withdraw from the arena of power, or to participate in it on equal terms with others, so long as they are free to practice their faith. They may not accept other faiths as equal to their own; they may deplore the copresence of "foreign" or "strange" gods within their political community. But they are prepared to accept competing practices, out of necessity, as the price for being left alone. They will resort to violence only to defend themselves against other religious communities or public power seeking to restrict the free exercise of their faith.

Offensive religions, by contrast, seek and use power to impose their way on others. Four characteristics of render them especially dangerous: their outlook is intolerant; their stance, uncompromising; their aspirations, totalist; their tactics, coercive when necessary. These are the faiths that pluralist societies and those seeking to build such societies have good reason to fear.

There is another distinction that I introduce more tentatively, as a speculation for discussion. Some religious violence is *instrumental*—that is, consciously and deliberately chosen as the most effective way of advancing the one true faith. By contrast, another kind of religious violence is *instinctive*, when believers spontaneously lash out at practices they experience as degraded or disgusting.

My hypothesis is that it is easier to deter instrumental violence (through incentives and disincentives that rational actors must consider) than to restrain instinctive violence. Religions that experience diverse practices—for example, in gender relations--as impure and defining are especially likely to be violence-prone. Consider the case of Sayyid Qutb, arguably the father of modern Islamist fundamentalism. As a graduate student at the University of Northern Colorado, he was revolted by what he felt to be the licentiousness of relations between young American men and women—a wanton intermingling (while dancing, for example) rather than the strict division ordained by God. Describing his U.S. experiences years later, his prose remains suffused with disgust. Radically divergent visions of gender relations may be close to the heart of the conflict between traditionalist Islam and social forces (within as well as outside the Islamic world) that have been influenced by Western modernity.

PLURALISM AND RELIGIOUS VIOLENCE: THREE CASE STUDIES

At the outset of this essay, I suggested that more than ideas (let alone something as diffuse as the Enlightenment) it is concrete historical experiences that prepare the ground for religious pluralism and tolerance. In this concluding section of my essay, I offer three case studies that illustrate this thesis.

The Transformation of Catholicism

Westerners troubled by what they regard as the exclusionary and anti-rational stance of traditional Islam would do well to remember that as recently as the 19th century, the Catholic Church was the most vehement antagonist of liberalism, pluralism, and the Enlightenment on earth.

From the early stirrings of liberalism in the eighteenth century through the mid-twentieth century, the opposition between official institutional Catholicism and liberalism was stark. The clash between natural law-based organicist monism and individualistic pluralism was at the heart of this historic opposition. As David O'Brien puts it,

> The problem of *Quadregesimo Anno* ... was that its proposed Christian social order would be difficult, perhaps impossible, to implement in a pluralistic society. How could differing interest groups be persuaded to subordinate group interests to the general welfare? More important, who would define the specific requirements of the common good? The church had always regarded the democratic answer of negotiation and compromise as incompatible with natural law. . . . Refusing to acknowledge the legitimacy of pluralism, [the popes prior to Vatican II] could hardly understand the necessarily messy, ambiguous ways of democratic politics.[205]

O'Brien's cool scholarly account does not wholly capture the texture of 19th century Catholic anti-pluralism. In 1864, Pope Pius IX promulgated an

---

205 David O'Brien, "A Century of Catholic Social Teaching," in John A. Coleman, ed., *One Hundred Years of Catholic Social Thought* (Maryknoll, NY: Orbis Books, 1991), pp. 19-20.

encyclical entitled *Quanta Cura* condemning (*inter alia*) popular sovereignty, freedom of speech, and liberty of conscience and worship. He also issued a "Syllabus of Errors," each of which he condemned as absurd on its face. Some examples: Error 11 reads, in part, "The Church . . . ought to tolerate the errors of philosophy, leaving it to correct itself." Error 15: "Every man is free to embrace and profess that religion which, guided by the light of reason, he shall consider true." Error 18: "Protestantism is nothing more than another form of the same true Christian religion, in which form it is given to please God equally as in the Catholic Church." Error 77: "In the present day, it is no longer expedient that the Catholic religion should be held as the only religion of the State, to the exclusion of all other forms of worship." Pius IX saved the worst, Error 80, for last: "The Roman Pontiff can, and ought to, reconcile himself and come to terms with progress, liberalism, and modern civilization."

Since then, of course, the gap between Catholicism and liberal modernity has narrowed significantly. Mainstream Catholicism has made its peace with constitutional democracy, rights of religious conscience, and individual liberties generally. Indeed, this reconciliation is now expressed in the language of principle rather than of regrettable necessity or *modus vivendi*.

In *Dignitatis Humanae* (1965), the Second Vatican Council's "Declaration on Religious Liberty," we find the Church invoking principles such as the "dignity of the human person" and the "human conscience" to support religious freedom and pluralism. We read that "the human person has a right to religious freedom." This means, in particular, that "all men are to be immune from coercion on the part of individuals or of social groups and of any human power, in such wise that no one is to be forced to act in manner contrary to his won beliefs, . . . within due limits."

The stance carried broad consequences for the Church's stance toward political life. To quote O'Brien once more:

> [John XXIII's] list of human rights included both the social and economic rights developed in the social encyclicals and the political and civil rights, including the right to religious liberty, about which the popes had long seemed more doubtful. Because they drew heavily on neo-scholastic philosophical categories, John's encyclicals recalled those of Leo XIII, but now these affirmations of human dignity and human rights were placed in a democratic context: individuals and states had the obligation to share responsibility for constructing institutions in which these rights could be protected. . . .[206]

Two of the most important reconciliations with liberalism have come in the areas of freedom of

---

[206] O'Brien, "A Century of Catholic Social Teaching," in Coleman, pp. 22-24.

expression and religious pluralism. Regarding freedom of expression, the *New Dictionary of Catholic Social Thought* observes that

> In *Pacem in terris* John XXIII abandoned the earlier papal emphasis on censorship and recognized a person's moral right to freedom in expressing and communicating his feelings. Though a person may think and speak incorrectly, the pope insisted that a distinction be made between error and the person who errs. Thus, errors must be rejected, but people in error must be allowed to speak so that they might break through their mistakes and make available to everyone occasions for the discovery of truth.[207]

Even more significant is the shift in the sphere of religious pluralism, which implies a fundamental shift in the relationship between the Church and public authority. Bryan Hehir notes that

> In the nineteenth century church-state controversies (Gregory XVI to Leo XIII), religious pluralism was an exception to be tolerated when it could not be overcome.... In the teaching of Vatican II religious pluralism was ... the accepted setting in

---

[207] Dwyer, *The Dictionary of Catholic Social Thought*, 623.

> which the church pursued its ministry in freedom, dependent only on its own resources and the quality of its witness.[208]

In our time, accordingly, the freedom of the Church is understood as requiring not a favored, publicly authorized position in society but only the protected ability to be socially engaged.[209]

For present purposes, the critical questions are these: How was such a radical transformation possible? What were the processes through which a church that began by demanding plenipotentiary power over the entire political and social order ended by accepting the authority of civil power and peacefully taking its place within religiously plural societies?

The 19th century problem was rooted in the clash between the Catholic Church and the vehemently anti-clerical radical Enlightenment. Conversely, a vital part of the solution can be traced to the Church's encounter with the moderate Enlightenment. The leaders of the burgeoning Catholic community in the United States had to come to grips with a polity that rejected religious establishment but not religion. As de Tocqueville noted, in post-revolutionary America (unlike post-revolutionary France), faith and freedom were not opposed. America was the land of religious liberty, but not of militant

---

[208] J. Bryan Hehir, "The Right and Competence of the Church in the American Case," in Coleman, p. 63.

[209] Hehir, "The Right and Competence," in Coleman, pp. 59-61.

secularism. While American Catholics experienced more than their share of bigotry, they also learned that religious pluralism at least allowed them the social space they needed to build their own systems of worship, education, and charity.

As American Catholic leaders reflected on these experiences, they grappled with the relation between liberal constitutionalism and traditional Catholic social thought. Thinkers such as John Courtney Murray developed new understandings of social liberty and freedom of conscience, rooted in the dignity of the human person, that could endorse individual rights without negating the classic Catholic concern for the common good. John F. Kennedy's election as the nation's first Catholic president symbolized the final closing of the breach between Catholicism and American citizenship. Just a few years later, American Catholics brought their interpretation of modernity to the Second Vatican Council and with the benign encouragement of Pope John XXIII, persuaded the entire Church to embrace it.

I tell this (vastly oversimplified) tale, not for its own sake, but rather to suggest one hopeful model for transforming today's antipluralist faiths from within. As Muslims immigrate in greater numbers to Western liberal democracies, it is at least possible that they will undergo experiences comparable to those of Catholics in America. To be sure, there is nothing in Islam that parallels the hierarchical unity of the Catholic Church. The feedback loops connecting Muslim experiences in the West to conceptions of Islam in the Muslim world are much more diffuse. Over time, nonetheless, increasing numbers of Muslims may decide that they can lead lives consistent with their faith even in polities whose laws they do not wholly control, and even in societies they are compelled to share with unbelievers.

Claims of Politics and Claims of Faith in Judaism

One might imagine that traditional Judaism would tend toward theocracy. One can certainly find examples of theocracy in the Bible.

If traditional Judaism were unequivocally theocratic, this would create a deep gulf between Judaism and liberal constitutional politics, which is emphatically anti-theocratic. There is a long line of Biblical and Talmudic interpretation, however, that leads to at least a qualified endorsement of secular government.

The discussion takes as its point of departure the establishment of kingship. Taken literally, the authority established by the laws of Moses was theocratic and, if the *Book of Judges* is to be taken as history, was exercised theocratically for an extended period. Gideon famously refused the people's demand that he become king over Israel: "I will not rule over you myself; nor shall my son rule over you; the Lord alone shall rule over you" (Judges 8:23) There was a problem, however; the Lord ruled, not directly, but through human intermediaries. What would happen when these theocratic authorities, the "judges," strayed from the true path? Samuel, the last of the judges, was a righteous man, but his sons were not: "they were bent on gain, they accepted bribes, and they subverted justice." The leaders of the people gathered to request that

Samuel "appoint a king for us, to govern us like all the other nations." Samuel resisted their demands, to no avail. The elders insisted that the administration of justice and the conduct of war made kingship necessary: "We must have a king over us . . . [to] rule over us and go out at our head and fight our battles." In the end, the Lord said to Samuel, "Heed their demands and appoint a king for them" (1 Samuel 8).

Although the Lord also tells Samuel that the people's demand for a king means that "it is Me they have rejected as their king," the Bible does not characterize kingship as wrong in the same way that idolatry is wrong. Indeed, the period before kings is linked to stories of strife and disorder. Without a king, "everyone did as he pleased." It seems that the establishment of non-theocratic authority was needed to prevent the Jewish people from swallowing one another alive. Rightly understood, kings can perform limited but critical non-theological functions: ensuring public order, administering justice, and safeguarding the people against external danger.

As the discussion of this matter developed during the Talmudic and medieval periods, kingship became a metaphor for secular government in general, not a particular form of political regime. Nissim Gerondi, a leader of the Barcelona Jewish community, argued explicitly for two "separate agencies," one to judge the people in accordance with Torah law, the other to uphold public order. The precedent for this, he insisted, was established during the Biblical period: "at a time when Israel had both Sanhedrin and king, the Sanhedrin's role was to judge the people according to just [Torah] law only and not to order their affairs in any way beyond this, unless the king delegated his powers to them." Gerondi accepted that the secular authority would need to use coercion "to enhance political order and in accordance with the needs of the hour," even if the application of force is "undeserved according to truly just [Torah] law." He went so far as to acknowledge that "some of the laws and procedures of the [gentile] nations may be more effective in enhancing political order than some of the Torah's laws." No matter; the king would correct these deficiencies, acting in the name of political order. The secular authority, in short, has one sphere of authority, religious leaders another; and the former need not always give way to the latter in cases of conflict. The aims of Torah law may be more elevated, but the aims of secular law may be more urgent. Sometimes efforts to achieve a spiritually good life must yield to the necessity of preserving life itself.[210]

Once the legitimacy of two authorities, one secular, the other religious, was accepted, a question necessarily arose concerning the relation between them. This question assumed particular urgency after the fall of the Jewish commonwealth and the dispersion of the Jews among the nations of the earth. Shmuel, an authority of

---

[210] For these quotations from Gerondi, see Walzer et al, eds., *The Jewish Political Tradition, volume one: Authority* (New Haven, Yale University Press, 2000), pp. 156-159. As an indication of Gerondi's enduring importance as the prime expositor of the "two authorities" view, note that Isaac Halevi Herzog argues for the rejection of British and Turkish law for the state of Israel through a critique of Gerondi's position.

the early Talmudic period, laid down a principle that became central to all subsequent discussion of this issue: "The law of the [secular] kingdom is law."

This might seem to give secular authority plenipotentiary power over the Jewish community subject to its jurisdiction. Over time, however, two important limitations emerged--one formal, the other substantive. In the *Mishneh Torah*, Maimonides articulated a version of the principle that we now call "equal protection," which he used to distinguish between genuine laws and arbitrary decrees:

> The general rule is: any law promulgated by the king to apply to everyone and not to one person alone is not deemed robbery. But whatever he takes from one particular person only, not in accordance with a law known to everyone but [rather] by doing violence to this person, is deemed robbery. [211]

To be valid, law must comply with the requirements of formal justice. When secular authority disregards these formal requirements, it exceeds its just powers and may be criticized, even resisted, if circumstances permit.

Alongside this formal restraint, there developed a substantive limitation on the content of secular law that Jews were require to obey. In the course of answering

---

[211] Maimonides, *Mishneh Torah,* Laws of Robbery and Lost Property 5:14.

questions posed by Napoleon to the Jews of France, Ishmael of Modena observed that "All the [interpreters of Shmuel's principle] have written that as long as the laws of the kingdom do not contradict Torah law, we must abide by them."[212] But what does it mean to "contradict" the Torah? The maximalist interpretation would be that civil law contradicts the Torah if, and to the extent that, it deviates from Torah law. To say this, however, would be to undermine virtually all civil law, contradicting the intention of the basic principle.

The most widely accepted interpretation, historically and down to the present, is that civil law is valid when it "does not contravene an explicit statement of the Torah."[213] Civil law loses its claim to be obeyed if it commands something that the Torah forbids, or forbids something that the Torah commands. It does not follow, however, that traditional Jews are always required to disobey civil law when such conflicts arise. A few civil demands (such as mandatory idolatry) must be resisted, to the death if need be. In most cases, however, it is permissible to take into account the severity of the consequences of disobedience.

The legal structures of traditional (rabbinic) Judaism, in short, developed over a period of nearly two millennia during which Jews were a nearly powerless minority in the states they inhabited. The religious practices, such as the rituals of the Temple, that presupposed Jewish

---

[212] Walzer et al., p. 451.
[213] Ovadyah Haddayah, "Does *Dina de-Malkhuta Dina* Apply to the State of Israel?," excerpted in Walzer et al, p. 477.

sovereignty in Israel fell into desuetude and were not revived - even after the reestablishment of a Jewish state in Israel in 1947.

During the founding period, to be sure, there were some traditionalists who urged the supremacy of religious over political authorities and who were bitterly disappointed when this failed to develop. Isaac Halevi Herzog, a prominent rabbinic authority who welcomed the establishment of the state, writes that he "aspired to create a powerful movement among us whose purpose would be to influence the future legislative council to include in the constitution a basic clause stipulating that the law of the state will be Torah law."[214] For him, it was "inconceivable that the laws of the Torah should allow for two parallel authorities."[215]

But not only were modernizing Jews opposed to state imposition of Torah law; so were many traditionalist Jews who did not see how a system predicated on millennia of political powerlessness could possibly serve as the legal framework for a modern state. The result was a political order in which secular and religious authorities uneasily coexist. The rabbinate exercises total control over the "private" laws of marriage and divorce for Jews. (Other faith communities within Israel enjoy similar prerogatives; within the state, no one has the opportunity to enter into a purely civil marriage.) The state exercises total control over civil functions such as economic regulation and national defense; Orthodox Jews use

---

[214] Walzer et al, p. 473.
[215] Walzer et al, p. 475.

political power to bend civil authority toward, e.g., enforcing Torah-based laws of kashrut and the Sabbath and granting religious students exemption from military service. And then there are constant boundary disputes over question such as "Who is a Jew?" the answer to which determines the scope of the famous Law of Return guaranteeing the rights of unimpeded immigration and instant citizenship to Jews everywhere. While it would be an exaggeration to say that Jewish orthodoxy has fully made its peace with democratic pluralism, there is a rough *modus vivendi* on many points.

Many, but not all. Citing their interpretation of God's promise to the Jewish people, some Orthodox leaders are inciting religious soldiers in the Israel Defense Forces to resist the lawful commands of officials representing a democratic majority. As we saw a decade ago, religious extremists are willing to slaughter Muslims at prayer, and even to assassinate an Israeli prime minister. There is no evidence that they have changed their minds in the interim. Thus, despite a sustained encounter with constitutional democracy and the European Enlightenment, Judaism continues to harbor elements of intolerant, fanatical violence. This fact offers grounds for doubting that enlightenment thought, or even the political institutions to which it gives rise at its best, will cure the ills of intolerance and violence in traditions far less well disposed toward the West.

Pluralism and Violence in Traditionalist Islam

Those who believe that there are many paths to God, or that it is not given to finite humans to know which is the right path to the Infinite God, will find it relatively easy to embrace religious pluralism. Islamic traditionalists cannot accept either of these beliefs. They may however believe that other faiths are on the same (right) path although they cannot reach the end--the one true faith. They may also believe that it is wrong to use coercion as an instrument of religious conversion.

Each of these beliefs finds textual support as well as opposition within Islam. For example, in the Koran we find the following: "Verily, those who believe and those who are Jews and Christians and Sabians, whoever believes in Allah and the Last day and do righteous good deeds shall have their reward with their Lord; on them shall be no fear, nor shall they grieve." And even more famously, the Koran declares that "There can be no compulsion in religion." In a recent article, Reza Aslan argues that

> Islam is and always has been a religion of diversity. The [Wahhabist] notion that there was once an original, unadulterated Islam that was shattered into heretical sects and schisms is a historical fiction. Both Shiism and Sufism in all their wonderful manifestations represent trends of thought that have existed from the very beginning of Islam, and both find their inspiration in the words and deeds of the Prophet. God

> may be One, but Islam most definitely is not.[216]

Much depends on the ability of the proponents of a genuinely Islamic pluralism to broaden public support for a generous and accommodating interpretation of their shared tradition.

This will not be easy, in part because there are important historical differences between Judaism and Islam that make traditionalist Muslims more receptive to theocratic claims than are most traditionalist Jews. Throughout the medieval and early modern periods, Jewish populations sought to maximize communal autonomy and to minimize conflict between the law of secular authorities and the commandments of the Torah. Efforts to enforce the fundamentals of the religion were invariably *defensive,* never offensive. And when, after World War II, Israel was established, it was barely thinkable that the religious law developed over centuries of political marginality in the diaspora could serve as civil legislation for the new state. For the most part, Orthodox communities and political parties in Israel ranked other goals ahead of the aspiration to rest civil legislation on Torah law, in part because applying it to political power wielded by a Jewish majority might well require sweeping revisions in the content of that law.

In contrast to Talmudic law, *Shari'ah* (the Muslim religious law founded on the Koran and the conduct and

---

[216] Aslan, "From Islam, Pluralist Democracies Will Surely Grow," *The Chronicle of Higher Education*, March 11 2005, B8.

statements of the Prophet) developed in an extended period during which Muslims wielded political power, often over populations that were overwhelmingly Muslim. The structure of that law thus reflects the expectation that it would have political as well as communal authority. As Khaled Abou El Fadl states, classical Muslim jurists described the best system of government as "the caliphate, based on *Shari'ah* law (which) fulfills the criteria of justice and legitimacy and binds governed and governor alike." The idea of a secular state in which *Shari'ah* is both distinct from and subordinate to political authority stands in uneasy relation to this ideal, and many Muslims experience that idea as an alien (Western) imposition.

For example, in 1959, Iraq's new revolutionary ruler, General Abd al-Karim Qasim, promulgated a Code of Personal Status that contradicted *Shari'ah* in areas such as polygamy and inheritance. Clerical resistance to the Code helped undermine General Qasim's regime, and the repeal of the Code was among the first acts of the new government that took power in 1963 following a successful coup. (After taking power, Saddam Hussein permitted practices that contradicted *Shari'ah* and encouraged a substantial degree of gender equality.)

Calls to ground civil law on *Shari'ah* and to recognize the jurisdiction of religious judges have a resonance in Islamic communities without parallel for most Jews, no matter how observant. In the wake of the recent Iraqi elections, the new Shia majority is pushing for the restoration of *Shari'ah*-based codes, especially in the area of family law. "Our position on the family status law is nonnegotiable. It will be based on *Shari'ah*," said Sheikh Kashef al Gatta, an influential Shiite politician who is expected to play a central role in drafting a new permanent constitution for Iraq. If this happens, traditionalist religious courts will make most decisions concerning marriage, divorce, inheritance, child custody, and the status of women. In this event, U.S. policy makers would be faced with an unpalatable choice between honoring the results of a democratic election and defending what most Americans regard as basic human rights. Said one U.S. official when asked about the possible majoritarian imposition of *Shari'ah*, "There is a vision of where we want Iraq to be that would make sense in terms of the resources we've put into this place and our overarching goal for democracy." The official's clear implication was that a coercive, theocratic family code would fail that test.[217]

It would be too hasty to conclude, however, that Islamic traditionalism must entail some form of theocracy or always take a violent and intolerant form. There are a number of political arrangements that might express an Islamic outlook without ceasing to respect pluralism. Clearly, Ataturk's severe, French Revolution-style anti-clericalism is not one of them. Nor is an American-style separation of church and state.

But one might well imagine an Islamic version of the Netherlands, a state in which a number of different faiths enjoy public funding and public standing, especially in

---

[217] Farnaz Fassihi, "Iraqi Shiite Women Push Islamic Law on Gender Roles," *The Wall Street Journal*, March 9 2005, A1.

the arena of education. Another possibility is a new version of the multi-confessional structure of the Ottoman Empire (reproduced to some degree in Israel), in which a dominant religious group shares civic space with other faiths that enjoy substantial autonomy and authority, especially over family law.

In short, there is no reason in principle why a moderate official "establishment" of Islam need eventuate in religious persecution and repression. As Noah Feldman, author of *After Jihad: America and the Struggle for Islamic Democracy,* has written

> If many in the West cannot imagine democracy without separation of church and state, many in the Muslim world find it impossible to imagine legitimate democracy with it. Fortunately, democracy does not require an absolute divide between religion and political authority. Liberty of conscience is an indispensable requirement of free government--but an established religion that does not coerce religious belief and that treats religious minorities as equals may be perfectly compatible with democracy.

Feldman is right, at least in principle. The most effectual cure for religious violence within Islam (or any other faith tradition, for that matter) is not grafting on some external concept of enlightenment, but rather mobilizing the resources within the faith that can open up social space for religious pluralism. But as the experience of early modern Europe shows, it can take a very long time indeed before the combatants conclude that the costs of religious violence exceed its benefits. In the process, instability reigns, and blood spills in profusion. It is not yet clear that the brave proponents of pluralism within Islam are speaking for anyone except themselves.

University of Maryland

Chapter XIII

Religion and Political Authority

William A. Galston

It is an honor to participate in this important conference, which does great credit to the organizers and to those who have traveled such a great distance to participate. To the delegation from Iran in particular, I say: you have extended your hand to us in dialogue, and we have an obligation to grasp it, without denying or evading the differences that divide us.

This morning, Professor Nasr asked: Who is authorized to formulate Islamic political theory? I do not know the answer, but I do know one thing: as a non-Muslim political theorist, it is not I who can offer some thoughts from an external perspective, but only Muslims can make the judgements that really matter.

Professor Nasr went on to pose two fundamental questions. The first was this: Who rules – God, the people, or both? This question raises a familiar difficulty: while in many religions, including Islam, God reveals principles and laws according to which the people should live, God typically "rules," not directly, but rather through intermediaries. So Professor Nasr's question leads to another: when God does not rule directly, who speaks for God? Who interprets God's laws and applies them to an endless variety of changing circumstances? There are three classic alternatives. The first is that the political leadership rules by "divine right" and has been invested by God with the authority, not just to enforce law, but to interpret it as well. The second is that a council of those who excel in learning and piety have special competence, and therefore authority, to interpret the law. The third is that the people as a whole have the right to do so. There is an ancient Latin saying – *vox populi*, the voice of the people is the voice of God. To state the obvious, each of these alternatives points to different structures of governance here on earth.

Professor Nasr's second question was this: What are the sources of governmental legitimacy? Every citizen of the United States who has studied our Declaration of Independence would give roughly the same answer: all legitimate government rests on the consent of the people, who are empowered to authorize political power. This is because God has endowed them with certain rights that do not change and which cannot be abridged. In effect, both God and the people contribute to governmental legitimacy.

Let me come at this issue from a slightly different angle by asking: What then are the signs of criteria of legitimacy? Here is the way I would answer. A legitimate government is one that serves all the people, not just some; one in which all members enjoy full and equal citizenship, regardless of ethnicity or religion; a government that respects the rights of minorities as well as the will of the majority, that honors the claims of individual conscience and embraces the principle that there can be no coercion in matters of religion.

Ayatollah Zanjani has raised another question: What is the relation, or difference, between Islamic democracy and liberal democracy? Because my understanding of Islamic democracy is so incomplete, I cannot fully respond. But I have spent a great deal of time studying the theory and practice of liberal democracy and wish to make a few points that may help answer Ayatollah Zanjani's query.

The theory of liberal democracy is shaped by its responses to three questions about government. The first concerns is proper *source*, which (as we have already seen) is held to be the people as a whole. The second concerns its *structure*. Here the guiding conception is that the people themselves rule, either directly or through representatives who they select, directly or indirectly, so that there is no governing institution that does not flow from, and reflect, the will of the people. The third concerns the *scope* of government. Liberals believe that legitimate government is limited government, that there are some matters that individuals and associations must be free to determine for themselves. In these areas, not even a 99 percent can rightly compel a minority to accept its will.

It is vital to understand that liberal democracy is not secular democracy. Liberalism stands for a particular relation between religion and politics, not for the abolition or marginalization of religion. Liberalism rejects both theocracy and secularism, embracing instead the idea that religion and politics are parallel sources of authority, interacting in complex ways.

While the United States is a liberal democracy, it is far from a godless or secular society. Indeed, it is the most religious of all the nations of the West. But its society contains hundreds of religions, not just one. That poses the question that virtually every nation on earth must answer – namely, how are its political institutions to deal with the fact of religious diversity? By refusing to give any particular religion a preferred political status, the United States tries to treat all religions equally. This is a sign of respect for religion, not indifference, and certainly not hostility.

These observations allow me to close with a question of my own: What are the resources on which Islam may draw to cope in its own way with religious pluralism? True scholars can answer, but I can at least contribute one important passage from the Quran:

> We have given a law and way of life to each of you. Had God wanted, he could have made you into one nation, but he wanted to see who are the more pious among you. Compete with each other in righteousness. All of you will return to God, who will tell you the truth in the matter of your differences.

I would suggest that any state, any political community, whether it be the United States or Iran, contains many "nations". The Quran seems to suggest that the political authorities of every political community should allow its nations to compete freely in developing their differing conceptions of religious truth and in performing deeds of goodness and mercy. It is for God, not man, to pronounce on their merits and to give each its due. That is exactly what liberals believe. If it is also what pious Muslim believe, then our politics need not be so different after all.

Chapter XIV

Religion, Ethics, and Liberal Democracy: A Possible Symbiosis?

Fred R. Dallmayr

The oral tradition of Islam—the so-called "*hadith*"—contains a statement by Prophet Muhammad regarding religious faith. In response to a question about the basic nature of such faith, the Prophet is reported to have said: "self-restraint and gentleness"—which is a surprising statement in many respects.[218] For one thing, the statement does not refer to any specific content of faith, to any religious doctrine or creed. In the language of some contemporary theologians, the saying is not concerned with *orthodoxy*, but rather with a proper mode of conduct or *orthopraxis*. More importantly still, the saying conflicts with an image, popular in the West, of Islam as a basically aggressive or belligerent faith—an image which, among its sponsors, has triggered an equally belligerent Islamophobia. To be sure, the Prophet's statement is not at all surprising if placed alongside central teachings of other world religions. Thus, in Buddhism, the path to liberation/salvation is said to be paved by self-abandonment or self-overcoming (*anatman*)—

---

[218] See Maulana Wahiduddin Khan, ed., *Words of the Prophet Muhammad: Selections from the Hadith* (New Delhi: Al-Risala Books, 1996), p. 3 (*hadith* of Muslim).

an effort which, in turn, ushers forth great gentleness or deep compassion (*karuna*), the willingness to assist "all beings however innumerable they may be." On their part, Christians may recall the so-called "beatitudes" when Jesus praised "the meek or gentle [*mites*], for they shall inherit the earth" and also the "merciful or compassionate [*misericordes*], for they shall obtain mercy." They may also recall the passage in Paul's letter to Timothy where he states that "God did not give us a spirit of timidity but a spirit of power and love and self-restraint."[219]

Sayings of this kind—which could be augmented by many others from different traditions—stand in sharp contrast with politics as practiced in most parts of the world; in fact, an unbridgeable gulf seems to separate the two domains. The gulf is clearly evident in modern Western societies where the process of "secularization" has tended to expurgate politics of any remnants of religious faith. The trend is particularly pronounced in modern liberal democracies, given their attachment to liberal "neutrality": the doctrine that politics or the public realm must be completely neutral or indifferent vis-à-vis religious (and other substantive) beliefs. In some cases, as is well known, the doctrine has been constitutionally stylized as a "wall of separation" which needs to remain "unimpregnable".

---

[219] See Matthew 5: 5, 7, and 2 Timothy 1: 7. For the Buddist notions of non-ego and compassion see, e.g., Masao Abe, *Zen and Western Thought*, ed. William R. LaFleur (Honolulu: University of Hawaii Press, 1985), pp. 176-178, 222-223.

The situation is aggravated by the invasion or colonization of the vacant public space by perspectives which are starkly at odds with, and even hostile to, religious as well as ethical teachings. Most prominent among these colonizing inroads is the equation of politics with private business or else with military warfare. Under the auspices of liberal market principles, politics or the public weal tends to be reduced to the dictates of economic self-interest, to the "maximization" of private benefits at the lowest possible cost—with little or no attention being given to ethical or religious concerns. Even more damaging to these concerns is the military colonization of politics. When politics is briskly defined as the confrontation between "friend and enemy", public affairs are placed under the aegis of military campaigns—perhaps with the proviso that "outright" warfare is simply the continuation of politics by other (more violent) means. Similar results derive from the equation of politics with power or struggle for power. When a leading international expert declares power to be "the universal and everlasting essence of all politics," he implicitly grants highest honors to the most powerful—while the sayings of Jesus and Muhammad are effectively expunged.[220]

---

[220] See Samuel P. Huntington, "Culture, Power, and Democracy," in Marc F. Plattner and Aleksander Smolar, ed., *Globalization, Power, and Democracy* (Baltimore: Johns Hopkins University Press, 2000), p. 5. The definition of politics in terms of a "friend-enemy" confrontation was introduced by Carl Schmitt, *The Concept of the Political*, trans. George Schab (New Brunswick, NJ: Rutgers University Press, 1976).

The point here is not to call into question liberal democracy or the separation of religion and politics—as long as by "religion" one means an established church or an official religious doctrine. Given the diversity of churches and religious creeds in modern societies, the public square can surely not be monopolized by one doctrine or clerical institution. However, things are different on the level of practical conduct. How can a Christian—someone who sincerely follows Jesus's teachings in his everyday conduct—be expected suddenly to forget about these teachings when entering the world of politics? Likewise, how can a Buddhist or a Muslim whose ordinary life is governed by self-restraint and compassion, be assumed to switch suddenly in politics to rampant self-interest and belligerence? Strictly applied, liberal doctrine in this respect seems to lead to a Chekyl-and-Hyde existence, in any case to large-scale social schizophrenia. The danger is all the greater given the "democratic" component of liberal democracy: the fact that ordinary people at large here are assumed to be the ultimate rulers and hence to function both as rulers and ruled, as politicians and private citizens.

Particularly in democracies, there is an urgent need to synchronize modes of conduct: that is, to encourage and enable people to apply congruent standards in their public and private lives, both as rulers and as ruled. Earlier phases of Western political thought still exhibited a strong concern with the moral character of "rulers," a concern manifest in an extensive literature dealing with the proper education of "princes." The present chapter, in its first section, reviews one prominent treatise taken from this literature: Erasmus's *The Education of a Christian Prince*, a text which will be compared briefly with similar writings found in other cultural traditions. The second part turns to a discussion of Erasmus's text by a leading contemporary democratic theorist (Norberto Bobbio) who concludes, regretfully, that some of its teachings are not applicable to "real-life" politics. By way of conclusion, I attempt to show that the teachings are indeed applicable to, and even required by, democratic politics, using as my chief witness the Mahatma Gandhi whose life-work illustrates the linkage of self-rule and compassion.

ERASMUS ON THE EDUCATION OF RULERS

Nurturing the moral character or fiber of rulers is a vital need at all times and places; yet, it is often disparaged for various reasons. For one thing, skeptics may refer to the absence or shortage of agreed-upon norms of conduct—a point which derives some plausibility from the evidence of cultural variations. However, the same skeptics are prone to protest, irrespective of cultural differences, whenever their own rights or personal interests are unfairly curtailed—and they will do so not merely on the basis of dislike, but on moral grounds. Another point frequently heard is that moral conduct cannot be legislated or imposed (so-to-speak) from "on high"—which again has some plausibility given the difference between properly motivated conduct and legally sanctioned or coerced behavior. However, the real issue here is not legislation of morals, but rather persuasion and education—an endeavor which is bound to be all the more effective if accompanied by the exemplary conduct of teachers. A further point often raised concerns the presumed traditionalism of the topic: the aspect that much of the literature in this field is tailored to the education of monarchs, princes, and other potentates. In a time of liberal democracy, one hears, this focus is basically obsolete—an objection which is profoundly mistaken. Precisely in a democracy where ordinary people are the ultimate rulers, the conduct and moral character of these rulers cannot be viewed as irrelevant. In fact, great vigilance on this score is needed at all times. Wherever the rulers of a regime are unjust, violent or corrupt, the welfare and even survival of populations are in jeopardy; in a democracy whose rulers exhibit the same character traits, the fate of minorities and dissenters is inevitably at risk.

In the traditional literature on the training of rulers—the so-called "mirror of princes" literature—Erasmus's *The Education of a Christian Prince* (*Institutio principis Christiani*, 1516) stands out for its simplicity and its eloquent but sober style. In his treatise, Erasmus does not seek to propagate radically new or unfamiliar moral standards; many of the views expressed can be found in earlier texts on the subject (stretching from antiquity to the Renaissance). On this score, his treatise is sometimes criticized as being conventional and insufficiently innovative. However, this criticism is hardly judicious. The book and its moral instructions were addressed to actual, not imaginary princes, that is, to political rulers or professional politicians—who, by and large, can be assumed to be slow learners. Confronting such rulers with unheard of or unfamiliar principles would scarcely make a dent in their behavior. By contrast, the chances of education are improved if instruction appeals to customary moral teachings and especially to principles which political rulers, in their better moments, might themselves approve or at least seem to cherish. Erasmus was not unaware of the advantages of the latter approach and deliberately adopted it in his political writings. As he noted in one of his letters, it was his belief that

> no other way of correcting a prince is as efficacious as offering the pattern of a truly good prince under the guise of flattery to them, for thus do you present virtues and disparage faults in such a manner that you seem to urge them to the former while restraining them from the latter.[221]

---

[221] P. S. Allen, *Opus epistularum Desiderii Erasmi* (Oxford: Clarendon Press, 1906), Ep. 179; cited from Lester K. Born, ed. and trans., *The Education of a Christian Prince, by Desiderius Erasmus* (New York: Columbia University Press, 1936), p. 6. As Born states, in view of the many traditional sources of Erasmus's treatise, "we can readily state that great originality in political thinking was not his contribution. . . . [However,] the mere fact that Erasmus did not originate—in fact could not have originated—most of the doctrines he expounded in no way militates against his importance in the world of political theory" (pp. 24-25). In his "Introduction," Born provides an overview of the "mirror of princes" literature from antiquity to the Renaissance (pp. 94-124). On this score, Erasmus's text clearly differs markedly from Nietzsche's goal of a radical "transvaluation of all values." In the political domain, Nietzsche's approach appears both

The historical context of the treatise was turbulent and fraught with grave dangers. As previously indicated, this was the time of the emerging European nation-states, with powerful national monarchies competing for preeminence. In addition to political rivalries, the age was ripe with religious, social, and economic conflicts—which, a century later, would throw Europe into a paroxysm of destruction. At the time of the book's first appearance, Spain was ruled by Philip I to whose son, prince Charles—the future Emperor Charles V—the text was dedicated. In England, Henry VIII was at the helm—an impetuous and headstrong ruler (to whom Erasmus, nonetheless, dispatched one of the first copies). France was under the reign of Francis I and Germany governed by a variety of princes. Barely a year after the book appeared, Charles was at war with Francis I; and England during the ensuing decades was steadily preparing for its decisive battle with Spain. In this context, educating political rulers was surely an uphill battle. As Thomas Morus wrote to his friend Erasmus: "How I wish Christian princes would follow good instructions! Everything is upset by their mad follies."[222] Mindful of this sobering situation, Erasmus starts his book by

---

too difficult (being accessible only to a select few intellectuals) and too easy—since most politicans naturally believe to be "beyond good and evil" (without having made even the first step toward self-overcoming or "overman").

222. Allen, *Opus epistularum*, Ep. 423; cited from Born, *The Education of a Christian Prince*, p. 27. As one should note, Thomas Morus's *Utopia* was published in the same year (1516).

appealing immediately to the most illustrious teachings on rulership, especially to Plato's *Republic* and the *Laws* which commend the greatest diligence in the training and education of rulers. In these writings, he says, Plato "does not wish them to excel all others in wealth, in gems, in dress, in statues and attendants, but in [philosophical] wisdom alone." Here wisdom does not mean being adept in disputing about abstract principles but rather having a mind "free from the false opinions and vicious predilections of the masses" and acting accordingly. Being free of false opinions and vicious impulses means not to be under their tyrannical sway—which also is a safeguard against becoming a tyrant or a ruler obsessed with lust for power or dominion. As Erasmus adds, addressing himself to Charles and other European rulers: "If you want to make trial of yourself with other princes, do not consider yourself superior to them if you take away part of their power or scatter their forces, but only if you have been less corrupt than they, less greedy, less arrogant, less wrathful, less headstrong."[223]

As can be seen, Erasmus was not opposed to competition as such, to a genuine "agon" about excellence, but to unjust and senseless power plays. To be able to switch from the latter to the former type of contest, political rulers have to undergo training aimed at fostering self-restraint and self-overcoming—a training which was a the heart of traditional teachings about virtue and character formation. Following the classical canon, Erasmus maintains that rulers should be people

---

[223] *The Education of a Christian Prince*, pp. 133-134, 150-151.

who excel in "the requisite kingly qualities of wisdom, justice, moderation, foresight, and zeal for the public welfare." In conformity with Seneca, the text distinguishes between three kinds of excellence or nobility—of which only the first one is truly admirable. This top kind is displayed in "virtue and good actions"; the second type reflects hearsay acquaintance with virtue, while the last one relies on kinship and the genealogy of wealth: "It by no means becomes a prince to swell with pride over this lowest degree of nobility, for it is so low that it is nothing at all, unless it has itself sprung from virtue." For a Christian ruler, in particular, training in virtue and self-overcoming involves sharing not in the glory but in the cross of Jesus. What is this cross? Erasmus asks, and responds: "I will tell you: follow the right, do violence to no one, plunder no one, sell no public office, be corrupted by no bribes." A ruler adhering to these maxims is bound to be not a scourge but a boon and a blessing to people. In the words of Plutarch, such a ruler has exalted and nearly divine qualities, for "his goodness makes him want to help all; his power makes him able to do so." Employing similar language, Erasmus's text compares a good ruler more to a "divine being" than to an ordinary mortal; for such a ruler is "sent by God above to help the affairs of mortals by looking out and caring for everyone and everything," holding the life of others "more dear than his own," even "at great risk to himself." Upon the moral qualities of such a ruler "depends the felicity of the country."[224]

---

[224] *The Education of a Christian Prince*, pp. 140, 151, 154, 157, 162-163.

Given the title of Erasmus's text, his admonitions are addressed first of all to the typical rulers of his time, that is, to "princes" or monarchs. In fact, in agreement with the dominant opinion of his age, Erasmus tended to view kingship or monarchy on the whole to be superior to other regimes—provided the qualities of the ruler were adequate for the task. Lacking these qualities, however—he agreed—monarchy was in grave danger of sliding into tyranny. The basic difference between these regimes resided in the ruler's treatment of the common people. Whereas a good prince treats the well-being of citizens as his paramount concern, a tyrant turns everything to "his own personal gain," thus subjugating and abusing his people. Moreover, the prince's goodness cannot remain a private judgment, but must be endorsed as such by the common people, that is, elicit the "consent of the governed." For "what is it which alone makes a prince," Erasmus asks pointedly, "if it is not the consent of his subjects?" In another bold statement, reminiscent of the Stoics, the text affirms that "nature created all men equal, and slavery was superimposed on nature—which fact even the laws of the pagans recognized." Christian people, in any event, cannot accept any ruler as absolute master, much less as slave master—because they recognize as their master only Jesus (whose lordship, however, is not based on subjugation, but on justice and grace). Heeding the teachings of the ancients as well as the example of Jesus, a good ruler must avoid being harsh, cruel, arrogant, and oppressive, and instead cultivate the virtues of kindness, equity, and mercy. The character traits which, in Erasmus's view, are "farthest removed from tyranny" are the qualities of "clemency, affability, fairness, courtesy, and kindliness," to which might be added "integrity, self-restraint, seriousness, and alertness." Again, Plato is invoked as a reliable witness who, in his *Republic*, demanded "a quiet and mild nature in a prince" and stated that "men of sharp and excitable nature are suited to a military career," but "entirely unfit for government."[225]

Although addressed to a "Christian prince"—specifically prince Charles—Erasmus's instructions are not narrowly confessional or even narrowly religious in character. On this score, as a learned "humanist," Erasmus differed markedly from some of the religious Reformers of his time who, reviving the older quarrel between Athens and Jerusalem, opted resolutely in favor of the latter. As he observes sharply: "To be a philosopher and to be a Christian is synonymous in fact; the only difference is in the nomenclature." This statement concurs entirely with his view of the meaning of Christian faith—a conception which was far removed from doctrinal orthodoxy and basically centered on inner disposition, practical conduct or *orthopraxis*. "Who is truly Christian?" the text asks, and responds: "Not he who is baptized or anointed, or who attends church. It is rather the man who has embraced Christ in the innermost feelings of his heart, and who emulates Him with his pious deeds."

In their practical conduct, princes or political rulers need to emulate the teachings of Jesus and the ancients—and not seek an alibi in the distinction between political

---

[225] *The Education of a Christian Prince*, pp. 161, 177, 183, 209, 233.

affairs, on the one hand, and philosophy and religion, on the other. Notwithstanding certain occupational differences, rulers like other people—and more so because of their preeminence—should cultivate the qualities of equity, kindness and self-restraint, rather than "slide back into the ways of Julius [Caesar] and Alexander the Great." Moreover, the virtues of equity and kindness must be practiced by rulers not only toward their own subjects or citizens, but also—and with particular diligence—toward outsiders or strangers. Again, Plato serves as witness:

> Although the prince must ever try to see that no one suffers any harm, still, according to Plato, in the case of strangers he should be even more careful than in the case of his own subjects to see that no harm befalls them; for strangers are deprived of all their friends and relatives and hence are more susceptible to mishaps. For this reason, they are said to have Jupiter as their special protector, who in this capacity is called *Xenius* [the wayfarer's god].[226]

Given his non-denominational and truly ecumenical outlook, Erasmus's observations on rulership can be readily compared with prominent views originating in different religious and cultural settings. In

---

[226] *The Education of a Christian Prince*, pp. 150, 153, 220.

the context of Islamic civilization, it seems appropriate to turn briefly to the great al-Farabi (870-950)—both because of his closeness to Plato and Aristotle and because of his effort to reconcile his religion with classical philosophical teachings (or Athens with Mecca). Among al-Farabi's numerous writings, the most pertinent here is a treatise called "The Aphorisms of the Statesman" (*Fusul al-Madani*) which seems to present his own views on rulership (rather than merely commenting on the ancients). To be morally commendable, the text defines rulership as the practice and continuous cultivation of virtues whose goal or result is the well-being and happiness of all inhabitants. "The true king [or ruler]," al-Farabi states, "is one whose aim and purpose . . . are such that he affords himself and the people of the city true happiness, which is the end and gist of the royal craft." The most prominent and important quality in a good ruler and a "virtuous city" is justice or equity, especially when the latter is joined with kindness, friendliness, and compassion. As the text states emphatically: When the segments or parts of the city are "united and bound together by sympathy," the city will be "controlled and maintained by justice and the actions of justice. . . . Justice follows upon sympathy."

These standards are entirely incompatible with a rulership geared toward self-enhancement or self-glorification, that is, toward political domination and conquest. Although military action may sometimes be justified for limited purposes and as a last resort, just rulership must never be identified with warfare as such. Thus, if a ruler makes war "for nothing else but for the sake of conquest," he engages in unjust war; similarly, "if he makes war or kills to appease rage, or for the pleasure he takes in sheer victory," he commits an injustice and forfeits the claim to just rule.[227]

Similar sentiments can also be found in East Asian traditions, especially in the long history of Confucian teachings. Among the many sayings ascribed to Confucius, one may recall the one about rulership, where he stated that a good ruler "loves his people" and a wise ruler "knows or understand them." At another time, the sage listed three requisites of good rulership: trust of the common people, adequate food, and sufficient weapons. When asked which of the three, if need be, he would forgo first, he responded "weapons," and which to forgo second, he said "food": "For from old, death has been the lot of all men; but a people that no longer trust its rulers is lost indeed." Despite modifications in detail, the sage's teachings were preserved intact through the centuries, finding a particularly strong resonance during the so-called "neo-Confucian" revival at the time of the Sung

---

[227] Al-Farabi, *Fusul al-Madani (Aphorisms of the Statesman)*, ed. D. M. Dunlap (Cambridge: At the University Press, 1961), pp. 40, 53, 57. As al-Farabi adds: "Similarly, if people have enraged him [the ruler] by some injustice, but what they deserve for that injustice falls short of war or killing, war and killing are undoubtedly unjust" (p. 57). On broadly Aristotelian grounds, the text distinguishes between virtue and "self-restraint" (p. 33)—which seems to suggest that virtue can become so habitual as no longer to need fostering (which does not concur with ordinary experience). For a somewhat different rendering of the text see Alfarabi, *The Political Writings*, trans. Charles E. Butterworth (Ithaca, NY: Cornell University Press, 2001), pp. 11-67.

dynasty. A prominent theme in this revival was the emphasis on self-restraint (or "self-rectification") as a requisite of good rulership—a theme which was developed in a number of texts dealing with the "Learning of Emperors and Kings" (or similar titles). Among neo-Confucian scholars, a particularly impressive figure was Chen Te-hsiu (1178-1235) who lived in the interval between al-Farabi and Erasmus. Following in the footsteps of Confucius, Chen stressed the importance of combining knowing and loving (or "mind and heart") and of placing both in the service of justice or equity. The basic standard of good rulership in his view could be summed up in this motto: "To cultivate fully one's mind-and-heart, and to be fairminded or equitable. In developing fully his mind-and-heart, the ruler will have no reason to be ashamed; if he is fair-minded, he will not be guilty of favoritism." On another occasion, Chen expressed the standard in these couplets:

> Discipline the self by incorruptibility.
> Pacify the people by humaneness (*jen*).
> Preserve the mind by impartial equity.
> Perform your duties with diligence.[228]

---

[228] See Wm. Theodore de Bary, *Neo-Confucian Orthodoxy and the Learning of the Mind-and-Heart* (New York: Columbia University Press, 1981), pp. 69, 85. For the sayings of Confucius see *Analects*, XII: 7 and XII: 22. Compare in this context also Roger T. Ames, *The Art of Rulership: A Study of Ancient Chinese Political Thought* (Albany, NY: State University of New York Press, 1994). Concentrating on the ninetieth book of the classical text *Huai Nan Tzu* (140 B.C.), Ames demonstrates the

NORBERTO BOBBIO'S "IN PRAISE OF MEEKNESS"

Classical teachings of this kind are no longer in vogue and have become nearly apocryphal in our time. Even people specializing in the study of politics are rarely, if ever, acquainted with traditional texts on rulership. As previously indicated, politics and political rule today tend to be equated with business affairs or with power plays, that is, with the pursuit of economic self-interest or else with a struggle for power which treats opponents as "enemies" (in a quasi-military sense). Even political philosophers—the supposed guardians of a long tradition—often dismiss concern with the qualities of rulership, either because of an excess of moral skepticism or because of a misguided attachment to liberal "neutrality" (as stated before). Fortunately, neglect is not universal and one can find voices remonstrating against the prevailing state affairs. For present purposes, attention will be focused on a prominent contemporary voice: the Italian political philosopher Norberto Bobbio. What makes the choice of Bobbio appealing is both his immense erudition and his deep concern with the fate of liberal democracy, demonstrated in his numerous publications as well as his public life.[229] On both

---

importance in classical rulership of the notion of "benefiting the people" (*li min*).

229 Norberto Bobbio is emeritus professor of legal and political philosophy at the University of Turin and senator-for-life in the

philosophical and political grounds, his credentials as a defender of liberal democratic principles and practices are unimpeachable and widely recognized. At the same time, he has never hesitated to hold up to democrats or democratic rulers the unflattering "mirror of princes," that is, the basic ethical standards of rulership and just conduct. While not explicitly predicated on religious grounds, his observations on this theme largely concur with past teachings, or at least mesh with them on the level of *orthopraxis*.

One of Bobbio's most recent writings is titled *In Praise of Meekness: Essays on Ethics and Politics*. As the subtitle indicates, the book struggles with the basic issue of the relation between moral standards and politics, an issue which has been vexed throughout history but has reached unprecedented acuteness in recent times due to the experiences of totalitarianism and genocide. In a central chapter devoted to the topic, Bobbio discusses a broad spectrum of possible positions ranging from rigid "monism" all the way to rigid "dualism"—where "monism" means either the reduction of politics to ethics or of ethics to politics, and "dualism" the thesis of an unbridgeable gulf. For a number of reasons, Bobbio finds himself unable or unwilling to subscribe to the first kind of monist coincidence; one of the chief reasons is

---

Italian Senate. Among his many publications, the following seem most pertinent here: *The Future of Democracy* (Cambridge, UK: Polity Press, 1987); *Democracy and Dictatorship* (Cambridge, UK: Polity Press, 1989); *Liberalism and Democracy* (London: Verso, 1990); *The Age of Rights* (Cambridge, UK: Polity Press, 1996).

precisely the rise of liberal democracy with its differentiation between religion and politics, church and "state" (which carries over into the distinction between private and public domains and the espousal of individual freedom of conscience). At the same time, he holds no brief for the collapse of ethics into power politics or for the doctrine of liberal neutrality predicated on a radical gulf. What emerges from his deliberations is a highly nuanced mode of mutual correlation which, while respecting individual freedom, does not release democratic politics into moral indifference. As Bobbio writes, with a glance at fashionable defenses of *realpolitik*: "An efficient government is not of itself a good government"—the latter being defined by the moral end of rulership, that is, the well-being of the governed. An efficient government may also be corrupt, where corruption—in line with venerable teachings—means that a ruler "has placed his personal interest before the collective interest, personal benefit before the common good." Wanton pursuit of "power for its own sake" is likewise corrupting, because it transforms a mere means into a final goal. Thus, even in liberal democracies, political action—which is "free or presumed to be so"—"does not escape the judgment whether it is right or wrong."[230]

One of the writers repeatedly mentioned in Bobbio's book is Erasmus, and especially his *Education of a Christian Prince*—a testimony to his own broadly humanist

---

[230] Bobbio, *In Praise of Meekness: Essays on Ethics and Politics*, trans. Teresa Chataway (Cambridge, UK: Polity Press, 2000), pp. 68-70.

leanings. Although close to the Renaissance thinker in many ways, Bobbio is hesitant to endorse the former's text wholeheartedly—mainly (it seems) because of an apprehension of appearing politically naïve or idealistic. In introducing Erasmus at one point, he refers to the German historian Gerhard Ritter who argued that there were two basic tendencies at the beginning of the modern age: one was the "realist current" represented by Machiavelli and the other the "idealist" strand typified by Thomas Morus who portrayed "the republican Utopia in which perfect peace rules with perfect justice."

As Bobbio adds, apparently endorsing the argument: "It must not be forgotten that Machiavelli wrote *The Prince*, regarded as the unsurpassed example of realist politics, at the same time as Erasmus wrote *The Education of a Christian Prince*, which is considered a similarly perfect example of idealist politics." Likewise, when presenting his spectrum of positions on the ethics-politics relationship, he offers Erasmus's text as an exemplar of the "monistic" variety which levels politics into ethics—contrasting this type sharply with Machiavelli's reverse monism. Almost a contemporary of Machiavelli's *The Prince*, he writes, "Erasmus's Christian prince is the reverse of the demonic face of power." The virtues extolled by Erasmus as standards of rulership are light years removed from Machiavelli's robust and realist notion of *virtú*: The former's "exclusively moral virtues have nothing to do with virtue understood in the Machiavellian sense."[231]

As stated, the contrast is somewhat puzzling. For one thing, it lacks the kind of nuances which Bobbio otherwise commends and exemplifies. Surely, Erasmus was not unaware of the need of a prince—Christian or otherwise—to wield power and authority to preserver order and lawfulness in the country; moreover, his text made room for military action abroad, provided the latter was carried out for defensive purposes and as a last resort. At the same time, though not a traditional moralist, Machiavelli was not entirely averse to pronouncing moral judgments—as Bobbio recognizes. Despite all his justifications for political behavior deviating from common morals, he says, "a tyrant remains a tyrant" even for Machiavelli. Although asserting that, in the interest of public safety, considerations of "kind or cruel" must be set aside, he still "denounced Agathocles as a tyrant for 'ill using' his cruel actions."[232] The contrast, however, is more puzzling still for another reason: the theme announced in the book's title, namely, the "praise of meekness." As it happens, Bobbio's praise of this disposition—his "*elogio della mitezza*"—is one of the finest tributes paid to religious and classical virtues in recent political-philosophical literature. In introducing the disposition, Bobbio immediately refers to Jesus's Sermon on the Mount, and especially to the "beatitude" which

---

[231] *Ibid.*, pp. 47-48, 79-80. The reference is to Gerhart Ritter, *The Corrupting Influence of Power* (Tower Bridge, UK: Hadleigh, 1952).
[232] Bobbio, *In Praise of Meekness*, p. 67.

states "Blessed are the meek (*mites*) for they shall inherit the earth." He also points to classical teachings about virtues, noting that meekness is "certainly an ethical virtue" (as distinguished from intellectual or "dianoetic" virtues) and, in fact, belongs among the "cardinal" virtues. In the same context, he refers again to Erasmus's *The Education of a Christian Prince*, commenting that, in that text, we find "the supreme virtues of the ideal prince: clemency, kindness, equity, civility, benevolence, as well as prudence, integrity, sobriety, temperance, vigilance, generosity, and honesty"—qualities which clearly bear an affinity with meekness.[233]

Importantly, meekness for Bobbio is not simply a private feeling or idiosyncracy, but rather a social attitude implying a relation to fellow beings. In this respect, he distinguishes meekness from "mildness" which is more a "personal" attribute or private character trait. By contrast, he writes, meekness is a "social virtue"—in the sense in which Aristotle differentiated personal virtues, such as courage and moderation, from the highest social virtue of justice; it involves "a positive inclination toward others," whereas courage and moderation are "only positive attitudes toward oneself." Although clearly implying an "inward inclination" or inner disposition, meekness in Bobbio's portrayal "radiates only in the presence of the other"; more specifically still, a meek

---

[233] *Ibid.*, pp. 23, 25, 27. Although Bobbio states (p. 27) that he "could not locate meekness" in Erasmus's text, this seems to be more a terminological than a substantive issue.

person is someone "needed by others to help them defeat the evil within themselves."

In this connection, he refers to another Italian philosopher, Carlo Mazzantini—like him a teacher at the University of Turin—whom he singles out for his perceptiveness and "deep philosophical vocation." In discussing meekness, Mazzantini advanced a remarkable thesis or proposition which underscores its social quality: namely, the thesis that meekness is "the only supreme power," a power which consists in "letting the other be himself" (a phrase clearly resonating with Heideggerian "letting be"). "Note," Bobbio elaborates, "how the word 'power' is used to designate a virtue that reminds one of the opposite, that is, powerlessness, but mind you: not resigned powerlessness." As one can see, meekness—again in a quasi-Heideggerian vein—is identified neither with impotence or passive surrender nor with an aggressive will-to-power, but rather, with a kind of "power-free" potency. Here is a citation from Mazzantini, together with Bobbio's comment:

> "A violent person has no power, because by using violence he disempowers those who wish to give of themselves. Whereas power rests in those who possess the will that does not yield to violence, but is expressed through meekness." "To let the other be himself," therefore, is a social

virtue in the intrinsic and original meaning of the term.[234]

To profile further the quality of meekness, Bobbio contrasts it with a number of counter-terms. The opposites of meekness, he writes, are "arrogance, haughtiness, and domination." Arrogance here means an "exaggerated conception of one's merits" which justifies (or pretends to justify) the abuse of power. Haughtiness, in turn, is a "showy arrogance," a way of "flaunting one's supposed virtues" in a blatant and impertinent way. Compared with the preceding terms, domination or aggressiveness is "even worse," because it consists in "the abuse of power, not only feigned but effectively exercised." Aggressive individuals, Bobbio observes, exhibit their domineering nature in manifold ways—"for instance, as if swatting a fly or squashing a worm"; they exercise their power over others through "all kinds of abuse and outrage, or acts of arbitrariness and, when necessary, ruthless domination." To avoid misunderstanding, the text quickly adds that, in opposing such outrage, meekness does not simply coincide with submissiveness or passive compliance. While a submissive person is someone who "abandons the struggle

---

[234] *Ibid.*, pp. 24-25. Bobbio's text does not give a citation for Mazzantini. For the distinction between power and violence see also Hannah Arendt, "On Violence," in *Crisis of the Republic* (New York: Harcourt Brace Jovanovich, 1969), pp. 105-184. For Martin Heidegger's treatment of power see my "Heidegger on *Macht* and *Machenschaft*," *Continental Philosophy Review*, vol. 34 (2001), pp. 247-267.

due to weakness, fear, or resignation," meek persons "do not yield" or submit because they basically repudiate and transgress the rules of the game governing domination. Being non-submissive, meek persons are also calm, serene, and even cheerful—the latter because "they are inwardly convinced that the world to which they aspire is better than the one they are forced to inhabit." To this extent, Bobbio affirms, a meek person can be depicted "as the precursor of a better world" who anticipates that world by "effectively exercising the virtue of meekness" in daily living—as the herald of an "ideal city" where "the kindness in customs becomes universal practice." Such kindness in customs also involves simplicity and charity or compassion—the first serving as the precondition of meekness and the second as its likely consequence.[235]

In light of this affirmation and even celebration of meekness, the reader is bound to be surprised and chagrined by the conclusion Bobbio draws for politics. After glimpsing an exalted vision of social life, what is

---

[235] Bobbio, *In Praise of Meekness*, pp. 27-33. For Bobbio, meekness exceeds or transcends toleration or recognition because of their reliance on mutuality. As he states, in a passage evoking Derrida's and Levinas's praise of unreciprocated gift-giving (p. 32): "A meek person does not ask for or expect any reciprocity. Meekness is an attitude toward others that does not need to be reciprocated for it to be fully actualized. This is also the case with altruism, kindness, generosity, and mercy, all of which are social as well as unilateral values. . . . Meekness, instead, is a gift and has no predetermined or prescribed limits." See in this context Jacques Derrida, *The Gift of Death*, trans. David Wills (Chicago: University of Chicago Press, 1995); Emmanuel Levinas, *Totality and Infinity*, trans. Alphonso Lingis (Pittsburgh, PA: Duquene University Press, 1961).

one to make of his harsh statement: "Meekness is not a political virtue; rather it is the most apolitical of virtues"? As he elaborates further: "In the predominant meaning of politics, that is, the Machiavellian or the updated Schmittian version, meekness is exactly the opposite side of politics." In this connection, Bobbio draws a distinction between two sets of virtues: "strong" or "high-class" virtues, on the one hand, and "weak" or low-class, on the other. Strong or high-class virtues—like courage, daring, and prowess—are "typical of the powerful" and cultivated by those who have the task of "governing, directing, commanding" people and of "creating and maintaining nation-states." By contrast, weak virtues—like simplicity, gentleness, and meekness—are "inherent to private, insignificant or inconspicuous individuals"; they characterize that section of society where "the poor, the humiliated and hurt" are situated, that is, all those people "who will never become rulers, who die without leaving any other trace of their presence on this earth than a cross in a cemetery bearing their name and a date."

As Bobbio adds bluntly, summarizing this point: "In the political or even democratic struggle . . . the meek have no part."[236] What, the reader may ask, is happening here? How can the meek be unyielding and defiant and even possess a supreme, but non-domineering "power" (in Mazzantini's sense)—and yet play no role in political life?

---

[236] Bobbio, *In Praise of Meekness*, pp. 25-26, 28. The text repeatedly criticizes Carl Schmitt's "friend-enemy" concept; see especially pp. 73-74.

How can they exhibit a "social virtue" and even herald or anticipate an "ideal city"—if that city can never be a *polis*, or if its public significance is absent or indefinitely postponed? After all, are "insignificant" common people not precisely called to be the "rulers" in a democracy understood as people's rule? Is Bobbio here not leading us back into the dilemma of liberal democracy and liberal "neutrality" mentioned at the outset: that is, into the gulf between ethical standards and political indifference (or worse: immorality), into the schizophrenia of private versus public conduct?

DEMOCRATIC ORTHOPRAXIS AND KARMAYOGA

These questions are clearly at the heart of contemporary political life, especially life in a liberal-democratic regime. As previously indicated—and as Bobbio would rightly insist—the solution cannot be found in a simple fusion or synthesis, that is, in the merger of ethics and politics or of morality and public legality. In a liberal democracy wedded to individual freedom, ethical standards can no longer be erected into a public dogma or official creed—at least not beyond certain limited constitutional safeguards. To this extent, liberal democracy remains heir to the central principles of Western modernity: freedom of conscience, freedom of faith, non-coincidence of religion and politics ("church" and "state"), morality and legality. Moreover, it would be extremely odd and even counter-productive if some of the discussed virtues—like meekness or gentleness—would be erected into political ideologies, into instruments of public domination and (conceivably) oppression. The very nature of these virtues seems to run counter and undermine any such attempt. From this angle, Bobbio's concluding observations appear in a new and more favorable light—but only if politics is identified with sheer power politics or the pursuit of unfettered self-interest (in a "Machiavellian" or "Schmittian" vein).

But why grant the latter a monopoly in the political domain? Could one not conceive of a politics where Bobbio's preferred virtues—and the virtues/beatitudes of Jesus and the ancients—would function not as oppressive masters but as vigilant servants and custodians of public conscience? In this case, these virtues would not simply be "apolitical," but remain politically relevant as counter-weights to oppressive tendencies, as guideposts of an ongoing democratic struggle: that is, as guideposts of a critical *orthopraxis*.

Curiously, Bobbio himself provides clues pointing in this direction. Tucked away in a footnote of his text, we find a reference to another fellow Italian, Aldo Capitini, who is described as a "defiant philosopher" and "liberal-socialist thinker" whose opposition to political domination—especially fascist domination—was both morally and religiously inspired. He contended, the note states, that there was a need "to go beyond the contrast between capitalism and communism," and "to use non-violence and non-cooperation as the basis" for this struggle; in this respect, "he was deeply influenced by Gandhi's thought and actions."[237] Despite its brevity and

---

[237] *Ibid.*, p. 35, note 4.

obscure location, one can hardly fail to recognize the direct import of this reference. By all accounts, Gandhi was one of the foremost practitioners of those "weak" virtues highlighted by Bobbio: gentleness, meekness, kindness, compassion. At the same time, he was a champion of those "insignificant or inconspicuous individuals," of all "the poor, humiliated and hurt" people shunted aside and trampled upon by the powerful. Neither his engagement for the poor nor his cultivation of "weak" virtues, however, kept Gandhi away from politics or from involvement in political struggle. Like the "meek" described by Bobbio, he was non-submissive and unyielding, as well as calm and frequently cheerful; but he was particularly unyielding when dealing with abusive and oppressive political power. In his struggle for India's independence, Gandhi did not shrink from inserting himself in the thick of politics—but a politics of a different kind, carried on in a different register, at odds with, and in defiance of, sheer power politics. As he stated at one point:

> Politics pervades all our activities; [and] I am not talking of retirement from politics in this broad sense. . . . But power politics should be kept out [of our proceedings]. We are taking that step not out of cowardice, but for the sake of self-purification. That is the way of non-violence. I know that in this country all constructive activities are part of politics; in my view this

is true politics. [But] non-violence can have nothing to do with the politics of power.[238]

In his entire life-work, Gandhi provided crucial lessons for modern liberal democracy: the lesson of being involved in politics without being corrupted by power-lust and self-seeking; and the lesson of how to cultivate moral and religious virtues without erecting them into public dogmas or official creeds. Apart from being a moralist in the footsteps of Ruskin and Tolstoy, Gandhi was also a deeply religious person in a broadly ecumenical sense but with special attachment to his native Vaishnava tradition. In the language of that tradition, he was above all a *karmayogin*, that is, one committed to purified action or *orthopraxis*. In this capacity, his entire life-conduct exemplified the great teachings of the *Bhagavad Gita*, especially these lines: "Set your heart on work (*karma*), but never on its reward. . . . Do your work in the peace of *yoga*, free from selfish desires, unmoved by success or failure." And these: "Offer to me all your works and rest your mind on the Supreme. Free from vain hopes and selfish thoughts, and with inner peace, conduct your struggle or fight." Deep religious commitments of this kind, however, never prompted Gandhi to sponsor an "established" religion or a religious "establishment" in India. Throughout his life he opposed the idea of an independent India governed by "Hindus" alone (an idea

---

[238] Speech in Malikanda, February 21, 1940; in Raghavan Iyer, ed., *The Moral and Political Writings of Mahatma Gandhi*, vol. I: *Civilization, Politics, and Religion* (Oxford: Clarendon Press, 1986), p. 416.

which today is promulgated as "Hindutva"). The guiding principle here was the distinction between public doctrine and practical conduct, between official dogma and *orthopraxis.* As he stated a few months before his assassination: "If I were a dictator, [organized, official] religion and the state would be separate. I swear by my religion; I will die for it. But . . . the state has nothing to do with that." The situation was different on the level of practical conduct—where religion really is put to the test. If you were to watch my life, he added, "how I live, eat, sit, talk, behave in general—then the sum total of all this is my religion." Such religiosity, for Gandhi, offered hope for the future—a future when religion would no longer be reduced to "a Saturday or a Sunday affair" but "lived every moment of one's life": "Such religion, when it comes, will rule the world" (though not in the manner of power politics).[239]

Even more than in his own life-time, Gandhi's exemplary conduct provides a beacon for our troubled period—a time when Gandhian-style virtues are almost entirely eclipsed by selfish interests and power plays (now under the auspices of neo-liberalism and the struggle for planetary control). Under the aegis of globalized markets, democratic politics is almost everywhere surrendered to the dictates of economic advantage—dictates which usually privilege the rich over the poor,

---

[239] Iyer, ed., *The Moral and Political Writings of Mahatma Gandhi*, vol. I, p. 395. The verses are from *Bhagavad Gita*, Book 2, lines 47-48, and Book 3, line 30. See *The Bhagavad Gita*, trans. Juan Mascaró (New York: Penguin Books, 1962), pp. 52, 58-59.

the affluent and arrogant over the "humiliated and hurt." At the same time, under the impact of ethnic cleansing, terrorist acts and campaigns against terrorism, politics is steadily being assimilated to warfare—with the result that the age-old longing for cosmopolitan peace is perverted into global militarism or militarization (now extending itself into outer space).[240]

In this situation, Gandhi's approach—his option not for an exit from politics, but for another kind of politics grounded in nonviolence (*ahimsa*) and ethical action (*karmayoga* and *satyagraha*)—retains more than ever its instructive value. So does Bobbio's embrace of meekness and related traditional virtues. As Bobbio makes quite clear, his choice should be seen as "a reaction to the violent society in which we are forced to live." This reaction, he adds, is not the result of a naïve belief that human history "has always been idyllic"; rather, it derives from the unprecedented magnitude of possible violence, from the accumulation of weapons of mass destruction which can "destroy the earth many times over." This destructive potential, moreover, is not restricted to superpowers (or the only remaining superpower), but through a kind of contagion is steadily disseminated around the globe: "What terrifies me is those dreaded megatons combined with the persisting will to power," a

[240] While the maintenance of lawfulness and order is a regular task of government—a part of its "police function"—the label "war on terrorism" unduly militarizes this function with detrimental effects on politics and the rule of law. See in this regard Richard Falk, *The Great Terror War* (New York: Olive Branch Press, 2003).

will which spreads from great powers to smaller states and even to private agents—such as "the lone assassin, the small terrorist group, or someone who throws a bomb into a crowd, or in a bank, a crowded train . . . where it can cause the death of the largest possible number of innocent peoples."[241]

Probably the most significant lesson of Gandhi's life-work has to do with the quality of politics in a modern liberal democracy. As indicated, Gandhi's conduct combined open-minded fairness with religious faith, liberal tolerance and commitment to freedom with ethical *orthopraxis*. To this extent, his conduct exemplified the qualities extolled by Erasmus in his instructions to a Christian prince: wisdom, justice, kindness, and zeal for the public good. These instructions, in turn, harken back to the teachings of the "divine" Plato who commended a "quiet and mild nature" in princes (while relegating people with "excitable" tempers to a military career).

As stated before, these teachings are particularly important in a liberal democracy where ordinary people are the rulers—and hence are expected to display the qualities or virtues of rulership championed by Erasmus and the ancients. These virtues cannot be legislated or dogmatically imposed, but only be cultivated in a slow learning process, aided by good example, which gentles and transforms behavior. Such a learning process is at the heart of the future "ideal city" envisaged by Bobbio in his "praise of meekness"—a city where "kindness in customs

---

[241] Bobbio, *In Praise of Meekness*, pp. 34-35.

becomes universal practice."[242] Given the immensity of possible destruction in our time, this future deserves to be cherished and fondly anticipated. To return to a point made earlier: unjust, vicious or violent rulers place the welfare and even survival of populations at risk; by contrast, just and kind rulers are a boon and a blessing to people. In the words of Erasmus: on the good qualities of rulers "depends the felicity of the country"—we might add today: the felicity and survival of our world.

University of Notre Dame

---

[242] *Ibid.*, p. 33. Somewhat provocatively (but entirely correctly) Bobbio ascribes to this city a "feminine virtue," adding (p. 34): "I am aware that, by saying that meekness has always seemed desirable to me precisely because of its femininity, I am disappointing all those women who stood up against centuries-old male domination. [But] I believe the practice of kindness is bound to prevail when the city of women is realized." In this connection, one may recall not only the ending of Goethe's *Faust*, but also the assignment of certain feminine qualities to Gandhi by Ashis Nandi who writes that "Gandhi's androgyny sought to give back to femininity a part of the traditional sacredness and magic associated with it." See "From Outside the Imperium," in Nandy, *Traditions, Tyranny, and Utopias: Essays in the Politics of Awareness* (Delhi: Oxford University Press, 1987), p. 144.

Chapter XV

Religious Democracy: Some Proposals

Fred R. Dallmyr

> Islam demands loyalty to God, not to thrones.
>
> Mohammad Iqbal

The question I want to raise is this: How can democracy be religious? How can we bring religion into democracy, and democracy into religion? In his Political and Social Essays, the French philosopher Paul Ricoeur addresses forthrightly the situation of the religious believer in the modern world, especially in modern secular society. Quoting from scripture (Matthew 5, 13), he insists that believers are meant to be "the salt of the earth"—a phrase militating against both world domination and world denial, that is, against the dual temptation of either controlling or rejecting worldly society. As he writes poignantly, "the salt is made for salting, the light for illuminating," and religion exists "for the sake of those outside itself," that is, for the world that faith inhabits. In Ricoeur's view, religion—including (especially) Christianity—has been for too long enamored or in collusion with political power and domination, a collusion that some recent theologians have aptly labeled "Christendom" and that has exerted a "demoralizing effect" on believers and non-believers alike, driving them to "cynicism, amoralism, and despair." However, the situation is perhaps not entirely bleak. When it emerges from this collusion, he adds, religion "will be able to give light once more to all men—no longer as a power, but as a prophetic message."[243]

As one of the great world religions, Islam faces the same challenges. Like Christianity, Islam has been sorely tempted by the lure of worldly power and public dominion; this at least is the impression given by a large number of its adherents, especially by many so-called Islamic governments and Islamist movements (often labeled "fundamentalist" in Western media). As in the case of Christianity, this lure or collusion is baffling and disconcerting—given the strong commitment of Islam to equality and its opposition to any kind of idolatry, that is, to the substitution of any worldly images or power structures for the rule of the one transcendent God (*tawhid*). How can Muslim believers be expected to submit or surrender themselves to any worldly potentates, no matter how pious or clerically sanctioned, if their faith is defined as surrender ("*islam*") to nothing else but the eternal "light" of truth? How can they be asked to abandon their religious freedom (in the face of the divine) for the sake of contingent political loyalties to rulers who often lack even a semblance of public or collective legitimation? As in the case of traditional Christendom, Islam's collusion with public power has often exerted (in Ricoeur's words) a "demoralizing effect" on believers and

---

[243] Paul Ricoeur, *Political and Social Essays*, ed. David Stewart and Joseph Bien (Athens: Ohio University Press, 1974), pp. 105, 123.

non-believers alike, driving many of them to "cynicism, amoralism, and despair." In this situation, it is high time for Muslims and all friends of Islam to take stock of the prevailing predicament. Concisely put: it is time, not to abandon Islam in favor of some doctrinaire secularism or laïcism, but to reinvigorate the "salt" of Islamic faith so that it can become a beacon of light both for Muslims and the world around them. Differently phrased: it is time to recuperate the meaning of Islam as a summons to freedom, justice, and service to the God who, throughout the *Qur'an*, is called "all-merciful and compassionate" (*rahman-i-raheem*).

To me it seems that contemporary Islam is in a state of agony, with the fortunes of recovery hanging in the balance. The point here is not to impugn the motives of political Islam or political Islamists. What is at issue is rather the wisdom and sensibility of politicized religion, seeing that the yoking together of power and religion inevitably exacts a heavy toll both on the sobriety of political judgment and on the integrity of religious faith.

To speak in general terms, religion and politics are neither synonyms nor necessarily antithetical. On a theoretical level, one can distinguish a limited number of ideal-typical constellations involving the two terms. On the one hand, there is the paradigm of complete separation or isolation (an extreme version of the Augustinian formula of "two cities"). In this paradigm, religious faith withdraws (or is forced to withdraw) into inner privacy while politics maintains a radical indifference or agnosticism vis-à-vis scriptural teachings or spiritual meanings. As can readily be seen, both sides pay a heavy price for this mutual segregation: faith by forfeiting any relevance or influence in worldly affairs, and politics by tendentially shriveling into an empty power game. In the historical development of religion and politics, this segregationist paradigm has been relatively infrequent (leaving aside the phenomenon of monastic retreat). Much more common has been another paradigm or constellation: that of fusion or amalgamation—which may be accomplished in two ways or along two roads: either religion strives to colonize and subjugate worldly politics, thereby erecting itself into a public power, or else politics colonizes religious faith by expanding itself into a totalizing, quasi-religious panacea or ideology. History shows that the former strategy has been the preferred option of most religions in the past.

Turning to Islam: some kind of fusion has tended to prevail in the past. With minor variations, public power in Islamic society during the early centuries was wielded either by semi-divine leaders (the "righteous caliphs") or else by a combination of dynastic imperial rulers (presumably descendants of the Prophet) and a battery of clerical jurists or jurisconsults (*fuqaha*). In his account of political authority in early Islam, Ira Lapidus distinguishes between two models or (what he calls) two "golden ages": namely, an "integral" or holistic model and a more "differentiated" or symbiotic structure. In the first model, he writes, Islamic society "was integrated in all dimensions, political, social, and moral, under the aegis of Islam." The prototype of this model was the unification of Arabia under the guidance of the Prophet and his immediate successors. In the second, more differentiated model, imperial Islamic government—from the Umayyads and Abbasids to the Ottomans—was erected on the diversified structures of traditional Middle Eastern societies, thus yielding a complex, symbiotic amalgam. In this case, the original caliphate was transformed "from the charismatic succession to the religious authority of the Prophet" into a far-flung imperial regime governed both by religious norms (*shari'a*) and more adaptive political laws, or rather by a mixture of imperial-political authority and clerical jurisprudence (resembling the medieval theory of "two swords").[244]

According to Lapidus, contemporary Islamic traditionalists or "revivalists" harken back—though often unsuccessfully—to the two models of Islam's "golden ages." To this extent, Islamic revivalism or political Islamism necessarily is at odds with basic features of modern life—given that, in its core, "modernity" (at least in its Western form) aims at the differentiation, disaggregation and radical diffusion of the unified, holistic worldviews and political structures of an earlier age. Being an integral part of modernity and its way of life, modern democracy inevitably falls under the same verdict of traditionalists: namely, as testifying to the modern abandonment of faith in favor of an "un-godly"

---

[244] Ira M. Lapidus, "The Golden Age: The Political Concepts of Islam," *The Annals of the American Academy of Political and Social Science* vol. 524 (November 1992), pp. 14-16. On the important role of jurists or legal scholars (*fuqaha*) in traditional Islam compare also Tamara Sonn, "Element of Government in Classical Islam," *Muslim Democrat* vol. 2 (November 2000), pp. 4-6 (published by the Center for the Study of Islam and Democracy, Washington, DC).

secularism or nihilism. Here we have the crux of the problem of the relation between Islam and modern democracy: how can holism and differentiation be reconciled? Are Islam and democracy compatible, or are they basically incompatible? There are two ways to assert their incompatibility: either one claims that democracy negates or destroys Islam, or one asserts that Islam negates democracy.

Traditional Islamists basically make the first claim: that democracy (and modernity in general) undermines faith. Their strategy is to present the transition from tradition to modernity (and postmodernity) under the simplistic image of reversal or antithesis. According to this strategy, modernity (or modernization) means a lapse from faith into non-faith, from religious devotion into agnostic rationalism, and from the holistic unity of "truth" into a radical relativism (denying "truth"). In a similar vein, the argument is sometimes advanced that, while earlier ages were founded on "virtue," modernity is founded on freedom and non-virtue (as if virtue without freedom were somehow plausible or even desirable). In the most provocative formulation, Islamists assert that modernity has replaced the reign of God (*hakimyya*) with the reign of "man" or humanity—a replacement equalling a lapse into paganism and the state of pre-Islamic "ignorance" (*jahiliyya*).

In the present context, the latter formulation is particularly significant. Under political auspices, the charge implies a reversal of public supremacy—namely, the alleged replacement of God's sovereignty with the sovereignty of the people (the latter equated with democracy). In large measure, this charge is at the heart of the anti-democratic sentiments espoused by many revivalists and/or "fundamentalists." In discussing the "political discourse" of contemporary Islamist movements, Youssef Choueiri highlights this point as central to that discourse. Referring especially to the writings of Sayyid Qutb and al-Maududi, Choueiri underscores the holistic religious quality of "God's sovereignty," writing that the phrase affirms God's authority "in the daily life of His creatures and servants," revealing that "the universe is judged to be one single organic unity, both in its formation and movement: The unity of the universe mirrors the absolute oneness of God." Judged by the standard of this unity, modern humanity—including modern democracy—exists in a state of disarray and incoherence, that is, in "a second *jahiliyya*, more sinister in its implications than the *jahiliyya* of pre-Islamic days." Pushing this point still further, radical Islamists tend to view the entire course of Western history as "a connected series of *jahiliyyas*: Hellenism, the Roman Empire, the Middle Ages, the Renaissance, the Enlightenment, and the French Revolution" (and its democratic offshoots). As an antidote to modernity and modern democracy, Islamist thinkers typically propose a return to "God's sovereignty," that is, to a semi- or quasi-theocracy (which usually means some form of clerical authority or elitism). Thus, Qutb supported the idea of a "Muslim vanguard" (patterned on various revolutionary vanguards of the twentieth century). In turn, al-Maududi called for an "international revolutionary party" ready to wage Islamic *jihad*.[245] In all these formulations, Islam (and religion in general) "trumps" democracy.

It becomes urgent here to look at the presumed transfer of sovereignty and its underlying premises. Is such a transfer plausible or persuasive (even on strictly religious grounds)? The idea of sovereignty implies the rule of absolute will or will power untrammeled by any rational constraints or intelligible standards of justice. To ascribe such sovereignty to God means to construe God as a willful and arbitrary despot—which is hardly a pious recommendation. Several of the great Islamic philosophers (of the classical period) had already objected to this construal, complaining that it transforms God into a tyrant similar to such tyrants as Genghis Khan or Tamerlane.[246] Whatever the status of God's sovereignty may be, however, modern democracy represents by no means a simple reversal in the sense of installing the people as sovereign despots. On the contrary, whatever else modern democracy means, it certainly means a

---

[245] Youssef Choueiri, "The Political Discourse of Contemporary Islamist Movements," in Abdel Salam Sidahmed and Anoushiravan Ehteshami, eds., *Islamic Fundamentalism* (Boulder, CO: Westview Press, 1996), pp. 22-23, 28-30. Regarding Qutb, see also the discussion in Roxanne L. Euben, *Enemy in the Mirror: Islamic Fundamentalism and the Limits of Modern Rationalism* (Princeton, NJ: Princeton University Press, 1999), pp. 49-92.

[246] As Oliver Leaman writes, Averroes (Ibn Rushd) criticized fideist theologians for "only being prepared to accept a concept of God which is remarkably similar to that of a very powerful human being, God with a status rather similar to that of Superman." See Leaman, *Averroes and His Philosophy* (Oxford: Clarendon Press, 1988), p. 14.

dispersal of power and a constant circulation of power holders. Several leading democratic theorists, including Hannah Arendt, have gone so far as to urge the removal of "sovereignty" from the vocabulary of political discourse, in order to make broader room for grassroots participation. What emerges here is a conception of democracy not as a fixed power but as an open-ended and experimental process—open-ended precisely also toward the discourse of religion.[247]

As indicated before, there is a second way to insist on the incompatibility of Islam and democracy. Whereas the first formulation says: Islam and democracy are incompatible, hence democracy has to be jettisoned, the second formulation draws the conclusion that, for the sake of democracy, Islam has to be jettisoned—or at least be pushed into a completely inner realm of belief. This retreat into an inner realm is called "privatization," and is exemplified by the effort of Western Enlightenment to "privatize" Christianity. This strategy tends to be privileged by radical secularists and agnostics, but (curiously) also by some forms of mysticism or illuminationism. An example is the Algerian-American Lahouari Addi who wrote an essay titled "Islamicist Utopia and Democracy." For Addi, Islamist "utopia" is another term for public or politicized Islam—a model

---

[247] For the critique of "sovereignty" see Hannah Arendt, "What is Freedom?" in *Between Past and Future* (New York: Penguin Books, 1980), pp. 164-165; also Jean Bethke Elshtain, *New Wine and Old Bottles: International Politics and Ethical Discourse* (Notre Dame, IN: University of Notre Dame Press, 1998), especially pp. 6-25.

which is precisely incompatible with modern democracy. Public Islam, in Addi's view, is a relic of the past, of an obsolete "medievalism." As he writes: "It is necessary to show how political modernity is incompatible with the public character of religion and how modernity is built on the 'depoliticization' (that is privatization) of religion."[248]

In fairness, I should add that Addi does not completely banish religion from social life. He admits that Islam can continue to have a "moral authority" in culture and civil society (though not in politics or the state). If this path is pursued, he is moderately hopeful that Islam and democracy may be able to coexist and hence to become compatible. In his words: "Such a creation of modernity by way of Arab-Islamic culture is theoretically possible, for there is no reason—everything else kept the same—why democracy should be inherently Western and absolutism [or despotism] inherently Muslim."[249] In arguing in this manner, Addi joins a number of recent and contemporary Muslim intellectuals who have suggested or advocated a new understanding of political rule, and also a new view of the relation between religion and worldly politics, or between the sacred and the secular. Among these intellectuals one might mention the Moroccan Muhammad al-Jabri, the Egyptian Hassan

---

[248] Lahouari Addi, "Islamicist Utopia and Democracy," *The Annals of the American Academy of Political and Social Science,* vol. 524 (November 1992) pp. 122, 124.
[249] Addi, *Islamicist Utopia and Democracy*, p. 126.

Hanafi, the Tunisian expatriate Abdelwahab Meddeb, the Iranian Abdolkarim Soroush, and others.

From the angle of political theory or philosophy, one of the crucial demands today is the shift of attention from the "state" or central governmental structures to the domain of "civil society" seen as an arena of free human initiatives. This shift of focus is a prominent ingredient in recent Western political thought which, in this respect, has derived significant lessons from Eastern European experiences (particularly the atrophy of society under totalitarian state bureaucracies). The shift brings into view a possible co-existence or symbiosis of religion and democracy without fusion or identification. Such a symbiosis would be able *both* to re-energize democracy by elevating its moral and spiritual fiber (its commitment to the public good) and to enliven and purify religion by rescuing it from conformism and the embroilment in public power. By renouncing domination or "religious despotism," religion is capable of regaining its basic spiritual quality and thereby to serve (in Ricoeur's words) as the "salt of the earth" or the salt of democracy.[250]

In order to perform this role, religious discourse has to broaden its range and accommodate a more general humanistic vocabulary: especially the vocabulary of human rights, individual freedoms, and social justice. In our time, engagement or confrontation with these issues

---

[250] Soroush, *Reason, Freedom, and Democracy in Islam*, trans. and ed. Mahmud Sadri and Ahmad Sadri (New York: Oxford University Press, 2000), pp. 151-152.

is a requisite for the relevance and viability of religion (Islamic or otherwise). Discussion of human rights, one might say, belongs today to the domain of philosophical theology (*kalam*) and philosophy in general. Although not directly nurtured by religious motives (at least in the modern era), human rights discourse is today religiously unavoidable, and a religious faith oblivious to human rights—as well as to human freedom and justice—is no longer tenable in the modern world. The tendency of many religious people to accentuate duties or obligations over rights should not be construed in a binary sense, but rather as a supplement or corrective to narrowly secular "rights talk." In a positive vein, religious discourse enriched by human rights vocabulary counteracts the pretense of "inalienable" *a priori* rights, sometimes termed "divine rights," of public or clerical elites. In a "religious democracy"—no less so than in a secular regime—rulers (including religious rulers) cannot be self-appointed but need to be approved through democratic methods accepted by all.

By inserting religious faith into an open-ended democratic discourse, religious democracy makes a contribution to a major conundrum that has beleaguered Islam as well as other religions throughout the course of their historical development: the dilemma of the relation between reason and faith. Religious democracy cannot resolve this dilemma through fiat: either through fusion or radical separation. Rather, what such a regime brings into view is a difficult and tensional relationship, an ongoing mutual enrichment and contestation where both sides resist self-enclosure. Religious scholars cannot afford to be oblivious to extrareligious reasoning, especially to such key categories of public discourse as social justice, public interest, and human rights. Self-encapsulation in a religious or theological idiom can only lead here to circularity and doctrinaire rigidity—which is detrimental to both reason and faith. On the other hand, religious or spiritual vocabulary can serve as an antidote to sluggish, conformist and consumerist tendencies in modern public life—an antidote highlighted by the role of prophets whose mission has always been that of accelerating human spiritual evolution by bringing the path of humanity closer to God, augmenting justice, and eradicating tyranny. Once reason and faith are correlated in this manner, an enviable symbiosis is achieved. As one writer puts it: "Heaven and earth are reconciled and the severity of the paradox of religiosity and rationality is reduced."[251]

By way of conclusion, allow me to venture a proposal with specific reference to the Islamic Republic of Iran. I make this proposal as a friend of Iran, speaking from a distance and without any special authority. As I understand the constitutional structure of Iran, there are presently two tiers of institutions which operate in tension and possible conflict with each other: a "democratic" component consisting of an elected Parliament (Majlis) and an elected President; and a more or less "theocratic" component consisting of the "Council of Guardians" or "Trusteeship of Jurists" (*velayat-i-faqih*) whose members are un-elected religious authorities. The

---

[251] *Ibid.*, p. 154.

radical difference between these two components is liable to pull the country in opposite directions, with potential harm to its welfare and stability.

As an antidote to this structural conflict, I want to suggest a way of building a bridge and reconciling the two components: namely by transforming the "Council of Guardians" into an upper chamber after the model of the British House of Lords. Britain is recognized as a leading example of modern Western democracy; and yet, its House of Lords is not an elected body and includes, next to hereditary peers, leading figures of the Anglican Church. If this model were adopted in Iran, the Council as an upper chamber could be given equal legislative powers with the Majlis; or else it could be given a merely delaying and advisory power (as is the case in the House of Lords today). Whichever power would be allocated, the Council reconstituted as an upper chamber would greatly contribute to the visibility and transparency of the governmental process. The restructuring would help to reconcile the presently opposed components of the constitution, and would thereby strengthen the legitimacy of the entire government. This, in turn, would lead to a more open and peaceful development of the country—something which both Iranians and friends of Iran can only welcome and applaud.

University of Notre Dame

Epilogue

Dialogue between Religions and Cultures

George F. McLean

There can be little doubt that as we enter into newly global times we find the world sinking rapidly into mutual fear and conflict. Some would propose to solve this by a kind of spiritual lobotomy or negative mode of tolerance that leads via relativism to a flaccid indifference.

If however, religion is the key to having life and that more fully – as is the very essence of religion – then abandoning faith commitments or employing them against one another is not a reasonable proposal. Rather it becomes the most urgent task of our day to search deeply into how our universal faiths relate to the diversity of the cultures they inspire and hence to their mutual encounters in global times.

But were religion and culture to be two alien or even antithetic realities then we might be doomed to failure and hence to conflict. Our task would be simply one of conflict resolution or attenuation by external manipulation. The argument of this paper is the contrary, namely (a) that the history of thought indicates that originally religion and culture were one and not distinguished, but (b) that in the West the emphasis on objectivity from the time of Socrates and Plato directed the mind away from culture and in modern times has made it difficult to appreciate religion as well. In response

(c) the important new appreciation of human intentionality and subjectivity opens new paths to understanding both culture and religion as it were from within and as mutually important.

THE FOUNDATIONAL UNITY OF RELIGION AND CULTURE

The religious dimension of life, if taken as an absolute point of reference, has been foundational for all cultures, as far back as we can trace human life. This can be charted by following the evolution of the modes of understanding by the human intellect. In its earliest form human understanding proceeded in terms of the external senses. Hence social organization was structured in relation to some one reality available to the senses. Whether animate or inanimate this one was not itself subject to use as were all other things, but rather was treated with the greatest reverence as the key to the meaning of the whole and of each of its parts. This has come to be called a totem. To dishonor or abuse it in any way – to break a taboo – was the ultimate crime and unless corrected considered to be destructive not only of the individual but of the social welfare of the whole.[252]

With the progress of human consciousness to an ability to think also in terms of the internal senses or imagination, human thought became able to unfold the inherent sense of the one totem as key to all into a

---

[252] G.F. McLean, *Ways to God* (Washington, D.C.: The Council for Research in Values and Philosophy, 1999), chap. 1.

pattern of gods. These were identified either as, or with, the parts of nature and were understood in a hierarchy culminating in a highest god who simply or in a community of gods consciously directed and judged all of life. All of reality was understood in these terms and expressed in a florid pattern of myths, through the patterns of which can be traced the cultural interaction between peoples. Late in this stage of thought Hesiod wrote his *Theogony* or genesis of the gods to attempt to trace this pattern of the gods[253] and thereby the structure of reality.

In continuity with this background the history of philosophy in the West began once the ability was developed to think not only in terms of what can be sensed by the external senses (totem) or imaged by the internal sense (myth), but what could be directly known by the intellect properly in its own term. What that turned out to be is particularly indicative for our issue of religion and culture. First, totemic thought had centered the mind in a absolute one, while mythic thought structured its vision in terms of a family of gods whereby the structure of the universe was articulated in relation to that one. Now philosophy proper was opened by Thales and, as metaphysics, especially by Parmenides in his *Poem* he argued rigorously that reality would be unintelligible if there was no difference between being and nonbeing. This required that it be ultimately one, without

---

[253] *Ibid.*, chap. 2

beginning and unchanging, all of which would engage non-being in the very nature of being itself.[254]

Thus far we have seen human thought founded in one absolute reality whether totem, highest god or being itself, in terms of which all of life is shaped, normed and inspired. This is so much the case that for example when any vision arose which could seem to threaten this key to social life (as Socrates in Greece or Christianity later in Rome) it was seen as needing to be eliminated for the welfare of the community as a whole.

FROM OBJECTIVITY TO SUBJECTIVITY

Indeed it is first here that Western thought took a decisive turn. Seeing its own need for norms and orientation it proceeded to make the virtues, which Socrates sought, into stable things – like stars in the firmament – according to which people could guide their lives. Thus Plato gave them the ontological status of things, ideas existing at another level of reality or in another world beyond that of humans. They were unable to be shaped by human history, but able to provide stable guidance as norms of the human good. People were then challenged to live in time but in accord with this principle of unity, truth and goodness.

It was essential that human life be directed by and according to this principle seen precisely as higher than and not subject to humankind. Indeed, the transcendence of this absolute reality over and above humans was so

---

[254] *Ibid.*, chap. 3.

essential that the Greeks could not understand how this principle could know anything less than itself. It was as it were turned away from humankind as a reality over against or it ob-ject.

To a degree this would change with Christianity and its sense of divine love and providence for humankind, and indeed for all creation. As Augustine would observe: we did not first love God; God first loved us. Nevertheless the transcendence of God reinforced the attention to the objective character of knowledge. God was understood as creator and saviour, with man created in His image, serving as His vice regent. The Aristotelian emphasis in Christian theology pointed to God beyond man; the Augustinian pointed to God within or the immanence of God. But whether to God or neighbor the direction of thought and concern was to the other or objective, rather than to the human subject.

There remained, however, something inconvenient for human pride, for man was ever subject to the objectively higher one, which could never be exhaustively understood or controlled. Hence, in the reformation and Rennaisance which initiated the modern period an effort was made to reduce the field of concern to objects which could be grasped clearly and distinctly; all else was removed from consideration. Not God and infinite truth, but human reason would be the measure of all. Our world became not what man could do with and in the infinite truth and love of the creator, i.e. the world of nature inhabited by man, but what he could construct in terms which to him would have the clarity and certainty of science. This was not the living world of nature and human beings, but the artificial world of robots and mechanics, the economic world of profit through competition or exploitation, and the political world of power mutually applied. Reality, rather than being opened toward infinity, was assiduously shrunk to objects which humans could control.

By mid 20th century, in the face of suppression by the great ideologies of fascism, Marxism and colonialism the existentialists rightly called out for a recognition of human freedom. I believe that Sartre missed the mark in saying that if God existed man could not be free. Man is free in infinite and transcending love; only when restricted to limited human mind is there no room for freedom.

SUBJECTIVITY AND A NEW AWARENESS OF CULTURE AND RELIGION

The Recovery of Subjectivity

But if there is more to human consciousness and hence to philosophy, in analogy to the replacement of a tooth in childhood the more important phenomenon is not the old tooth that is falling out, but the strength of the new tooth that is replacing it. A few philosophers did point to this other dimensions of human awareness. Shortly after Descartes Pascal's assertion "Que la raison a des raisons, que la raison ne comprend pas" would remain famous if unheeded, as would Vico's prediction that the new reason would give birth to a generation of brutes - intellectual brutes, but brutes nonetheless. Later Kiekegard would follow Hegel with a similar warning.

None of these voices would have strong impact while the race was on to "conquer" the world by a supposed omni-sufficient scientific reason.

But as human problems mounted and were multiplied into world wars by technological achievements the adequacy of reason to handle the deepest problems of human dignity and purpose came under sustained questioning. More attention began to be given to additional dimensions of human capabilities.

There has been a strikingly parallel development in philosophy. At the beginning of this century, it had appeared that the rationalist project of stating all in clear and distinct objective terms was close to completion. This was to be achieved in either the empirical terms of the positivist tradition of sense knowledge or in the formal and essentialist terms of the Kantian intellectual tradition. Whitehead wrote that at the turn of the century, when with Bertrand Russell he went to the First World Congress of Philosophy in Paris, it seemed that, except for some details of application, the work of physics had been essentially completed. To the contrary, however, it was the very attempt to finalize scientific knowledge with its most evolved concepts which made manifest the radical insufficiency of the objectivist approach and led to renewed appreciation of the importance of subjectivity.

Wittgenstein began by writing his *Tractatus Logico-Philosophicus*[255] on the Lockean supposition that significant knowledge consisted in constructing a mental map corresponding point to point to the external world as

---

[255] *Ibid.*, pp. 167-175.

perceived by sense experience. In such a project the spiritual element of understanding, i.e., the grasp of the relations between the points on this mental map and the external world was relegated to the margin as simply "unutterable". Later experience in teaching children, however, led Wittgenstein to the conclusion that this empirical mapping was simply not what was going on in human knowledge. In his *Blue and Brown Books*[256] and his subsequent *Philosophical Investigations*[257] Wittgenstein shifted human consciousness or intentionality, which previously had been relegated to the periphery, to the very the center of concern. The focus of his philosophy was no longer the positivist, supposedly objective, replication of the external world, but the human construction of language and of worlds of meaning.[258]

A similar process was underway in the Kantian camp. There Husserl's attempt to bracket all elements, in order to isolate pure essences for scientific knowledge, forced attention to the limitations of a pure essentialism and opened the way for his understudy, Martin Heidegger, to rediscover the existential and historical dimensions of reality in his *Being and Time*.[259] The religious implications of this new sensitivity would be articulated by Karl Rahner in his work, *Spirit in the World*, and by the

---

[256] Tr. C.K. Ogden (London: Methuen, 1981).
[257] (New York: Harper and Row).
[258] Tr. G.E.M. Anscombe (Oxford: Blackwell, 1958).
[259] Brian Wicker, *Culture and Theology* (London: Sheed and Ward, 1966), pp. 68-88.

Second Vatican Council in its Constitution, *The Church in the World*.[260]

For Heidegger the meaning of being and of life was unveiled and emerged - the two processes were identical - in conscious human life (*dasein*) lived through time and therefore through history. Thus human consciousness became the new focus of attention. The uncovering, unveiling or bringing into the light (the etymology of the term "phe-nomen-ology") of the unfolding patterns and interrelations of subjectivity would open a new era of human awareness. Epistemology and metaphysics would develop - and merge - in the very work of tracking the nature and direction of this process.

Thus, for Heidegger's successor, Hans-Georg Gadamer,[261] the task becomes uncovering how human persons, emerging as family, neighborhood and people, by exercising their creative freedom weave their cultural tradition. This is not history as a mere compilation of whatever humankind does or makes, but culture as the fabric of the human consciousness and symbols by which a human group discovers and weaves a pattern of relations which is life giving, a way of cultivating the soul, and thereby unveals being in its time and place.

With this new interior insight into the working of human consciousness it is as if a whole new world opens before us as we become self aware of the free inclinations and decisions by which we open new horizons, and of the

---

[260] (New York: Harper and Row, 1962).

[261] *Documents of Vatican II*, ed. W. Abbott (New York: New Century, 1974).

preferences and commitments by which we give shape to the realm or ambit of our life in its relations and engagements. In these terms the reality of cultures and their diversity can be seen, and also the significance of their basic relatedness in terms of their religious foundations. What had been lived intuitively if intensely in totem and myth now becomes the delicate and deliberate center of human responsibility.

CULTURE

This search to realize the good had been manifest objectively as the object of desire, namely, as that which is sought when absent and which completes life or renders it "per-fect", understood in its etymological sense as completed or realized through and through. Hence, once achieved, it is no longer desired or sought, but enjoyed.

In this manner, things as good, that is, as actually realizing some degree of perfection and able to contribute to the well-being of others, are the bases of an interlocking set of relations. As these relations are based upon both the actual perfection things possess and the potential perfection to which they are thereby directed, the good both attracts when it has not yet been attained and constitutes one's fulfillment upon its achievement. Hence, goods are not arbitrary or simply a matter of wishful thinking; they are rather the full objective development of things and all that contributes thereto.

However, if this be taken not exteriorly or objectively about what fulfills, but interiorly in terms of the realization of being itself it is reflected in the manner in which each thing, even a stone, retains the being or reality it has and resists reduction to non-being or nothing. (The most we can do is to change or transform it into something else; we cannot annihilate it.) For a plant or tree, given the right conditions, this growing to full stature and fruition. For an animal it means protecting its life -- fiercely, if necessary -- and seeking out the substinence needed for its strength.

But in the light of this new awareness of human subjectivity being as affirmation, or as the definitive stance against non-being central to the work of Parmenides, the first Greek metaphysician, can now be understood also as the drama of free self-determination, and hence of the development of persons and of cultures.

As human this is the work not only of the chemical or biological lows, but of the human intellect working with the active imagination to conceive, evaluate and decide. In this work values and virtues come to the fore and with them the shaping of a culture and a tradition.

Values. The moral good is a more narrow field, for it concerns only one's free and responsible actions. This has the objective reality of the ontological good noted above, for it concerns real actions which stand in distinctive relation to one's own perfection and to that of others - and, indeed, to the physical universe and to God as well. Hence, many possible patterns of actions could be objectively right because they promote the good of those involved, while others, precisely as inconsistent with the real good of persons or things, are objectively disordered or misordered. This constitutes the objective basis for what is ethically good or bad.

Nevertheless, because the realm of objective relations is almost numberless, whereas our actions are single, it is necessary not only to choose in general between the good and the bad, but in each case to choose which of the often innumerable possibilities one will render concrete.

However broad or limited the options, as responsible and moral an act is essentially dependent upon its being willed by a subject. Therefore, in order to follow the emergence of the field of concrete moral action, it is not sufficient to examine only the objective aspect, namely, the nature of the things involved. In addition, one must consider the action in relation to the subject, namely, to the person who, in the context of his/her society and culture, appreciates and values the good of this action, chooses it over its alternatives, and eventually wills its actualization.

The term 'value' here is of special note. It was derived from the economic sphere where it meant the amount of a commodity sufficient to attain a certain worth. This is reflected also in the term 'axiology' whose root means "weighing as much" or "worth as much." It requires an objective content -- the good must truly "weigh in" and make a real difference; but the term 'value' expresses this good especially as related to wills which actually acknowledge it as a good and as desirable.[262] Thus, different individuals or groups of persons and at different periods have distinct sets of values. A people or community is sensitive to, and prizes, a distinct set of goods or, more likely, it establishes a distinctive ranking in the degree to which it prizes various goods. By so doing, it delineates among limitless objective goods a certain pattern of values which in a more stable fashion mirrors the corporate free choices of that people. For some peoples the highest good may be harmony while other considerations are ordered to this; for other peoples competition may be primary and other considerations such as courage are interpreted and ordered quite differently.

This constitutes the basic topology of a culture; as repeatedly reaffirmed through time, it builds a tradition or heritage about which we shall speak below. It constitutes, as well, the prime pattern and gradation of goods or values which persons experience from their earliest years and in terms of which they interpret their developing relations. Young persons peer out at the world through lenses formed, as it were, by their family and culture and configured according to the pattern of choices made by that community throughout its history - often in its most trying circumstances. Like a pair of glasses values do not create the object; but focus attention upon certain goods rather than upon others.

Virtues. Martin Heidegger describes a process by which the self emerges as a person in the field of moral

---

[262] *Truth and Method* (New York: Crossroads, 1975).

action. It consists in transcending oneself or breaking beyond mere self-concern and projecting outward as a being whose very nature is to share with others for whom one cares and about whom one is concerned. In this process, one identifies new purposes or goals for the sake of which action is to be undertaken. In relation to these goals, certain combinations of possibilities, with their natures and norms, take on particular importance and begin thereby to enter into the makeup of one's world of meaning.[263] Freedom then becomes more than mere spontaneity, more than choice, and more even than self-determination in the sense of determining oneself to act. It shapes -- the phenomenologist would say even that it constitutes -- one's world as the ambit of human decisions and dynamic action.

This process of deliberate choice and decision transcends the somatic and psychic dynamisms. Whereas the somatic dimension is extensively reactive, the psychic dynamisms of affectivity or appetite are fundamentally oriented to the good and positively attracted by a set of values. These, in turn, evoke an active response from the emotions in the context of responsible freedom. But it is in terms of responsibility that one encounters the properly moral and social dimension of life. For, in order to live with others, one must be able to know, to choose and finally to realize what is truly conducive to one's good and to that of others. Thus, persons and groups must be able to judge the true value of what is to be

---

[263] Ivor Leclerc, "The Metaphysics of the Good," *Review of Metaphysics*, 35 (1981), 3-5.

chosen, that is, its objective worth, both in itself and in relation to others. This is moral truth: the judgment regarding whether the act makes the person and society good in the sense of bringing authentic individual and social fulfillment, or the contrary.

When this is exercised or lived, patterns of action develop which are habitual in the sense of being repeated. These are the modes of activity with which we are familiar; in their exercise, along with the coordinated natural dynamisms they require, we are practiced; and with practice comes facility and spontaneity. Such patterns constitute the basic, continuing and pervasive shaping influence of our life. For this reason, they have been considered classically to be the basic indicators of what our life as a whole will add up to, or, as is often said, "amount to". Since Socrates, the technical term for these especially developed capabilities has been 'virtues' or special strengths.

Cultural Tradition. In their concrete circumstances and histories peoples working together with both intellect and imagination set a pattern of values and virtues through which they exercise their freedom and develop their pattern of social life. This is called a "culture". On the one hand, the term is derived from the Latin word for tilling or cultivating the land. Cicero and other Latin authors used it for the cultivation of the soul or mind (*cultura animi*), for just as good land, when left without cultivation, will produce only disordered vegetation of little value, so the human spirit will not achieve its proper results unless trained or educated.[264] This sense of culture corresponds most closely to the Greek term for education (*paideia*) as the development of character, taste and judgment, and to the German term "formation" (*Bildung*).

Here, the focus is upon the creative capacity of the spirit of a people and their ability to work as artists, not only in the restricted sense of producing purely aesthetic objects, but in the more involved sense of shaping all dimensions of life, material and spiritual, economic and political into a fulfilling pattern. The result is a whole life, characterized by unity and truth, goodness and beauty, and, thereby, sharing deeply in meaning and value. The capacity for this cannot be taught, although it may be enhanced by education; more recent phenomenological and hermeneutic inquiries suggest that, at its base, culture is a renewal, a reliving of origins in an attitude of profound appreciation.[265] This points one beyond self and other, beyond identity and diversity, in order to comprehend both.

On the other hand, "culture" can be traced to the term *civis* (citizen, civil society and civilization).[266] This reflects the need for a person to belong to a social group

---

[264] V. Mathieu, "Cultura" in *Enciclopedia Filosofica* (Firenze: Sansoni, 1967), II, 207-210; and Raymond Williams, "Culture and Civilization," *Encyclopedia of Philosophy* (New York: Macmillan, 1967), II, 273-276, and *Culture and Society* (London, 1958).
[265] V. Mathieu, *ibid.*
[266] V. Mathieu, "Civilta," *ibid.*, I, 1437-1439.

or community in order for the human spirit to produce its proper results. By bringing to the person the resources of the tradition, the *tradita* or past wisdom produced by the human spirit, the community facilitates comprehension. By enriching the mind with examples of values which have been identified in the past, it teaches and inspires one to produce something analogous. For G.F. Klemm, this more objective sense of culture is composite in character.[267] E.B. Tyler defined this classically for the social sciences as "that complex whole which includes knowledge, belief, art, morals, law, customs and any other capabilities and habits required by man as a member of society."[268]

In contrast, Clifford Geertz focused on the meaning of all this for a people and on how a people's intentional action went about shaping its world. Thus to an experimental science in search of laws he contrasts the analysis of culture as an interpretative science in search of meaning.[269] What is sought is the import of artifacts and actions, that is, whether "it is, ridicule or challenge, irony or anger, snobbery or pride, that, in their occurrence and through their agency, is getting said."[270] This requires attention to "the imaginative universe within which their acts are signs."[271] In this light, Geertz defines culture

---

[267] G.F. Klemm, *Allgemein Culturgeschicht der Menschheit* (Leipzig, 1843-1852), x.
[268] E.B. Tylor, *Primitive Culture* (London, 1871), VII, p. 7.
[269] Clifford Geertz, *The Interpretation of Cultures* (London: Hutchinson, 1973), p. 5.
[270] *Ibid.*, p. 10.
[271] *Ibid.*, p. 13.

rather as "an historically transmitted pattern of meanings embodied in symbols, a system of intended conceptions expressed in symbolic forms by means of which men communicate, perpetuate and develop their knowledge about and attitudes toward life."[272]

The development of values and virtues and their integration as a culture of any depth or richness takes time, and hence depends upon the experience and creativity of many generations. The culture which is handed on, or *tradita,* comes to be called a cultural tradition; as such it reflects the cumulative achievement of a people in discovering, mirroring and transmitting the deepest meanings of life. This is tradition in its synchronic sense as a body of wisdom.

The cumulative process of transmitting, adjusting and applying the values of a culture through time is not only heritage or what is received, but new creation as this is passed on in new ways. Attending to tradition, taken in this active sense, allows us not only to uncover the permanent and universal truths which Socrates sought, but to perceive the importance of values we receive from the tradition and to mobilize our own life project actively toward the future.

The Genesis of Tradition in Community. Because tradition has sometimes been interpreted as a threat to personal and social freedom, it is important to note that a cultural tradition is generated by the free and responsible life of the members of a concerned community and enables

---

[272] *Ibid.*, p. 85.

succeeding generations to realize their life with freedom and creativity.

Through the various steps of one's development, as one's circle of community expands through neighborhood, school, work and recreation, one comes to learn and to share personally and passionately an interpretation of reality and a pattern of value responses. The phenomenologist sees this life as the new source for wisdom. Hence, rather than turning away from daily life in order to contemplate abstract and disembodied ideas, the place to discover meaning is in life as lived in the family and in the progressively wider social circles into which one enters.

If it were merely a matter of community, however, all might be limited to the present, with no place for tradition as that which is "passed on" from one generation to the next. In fact, the process of trial and error, of continual correction and addition in relation to a people's evolving sense of human dignity and purpose, constitutes a type of learning and testing laboratory for successive generations. In this laboratory of history, the strengths of various insights and behavior patterns can be identified and reinforced, while deficiencies are progressively corrected or eliminated. Horizontally, we learn from experience what promotes and what destroys life and, accordingly, make pragmatic adjustments.

But even this language remains too abstract, too limited to method or technique, too unidimensional. While tradition can be described in general and at a distance in terms of feed-back mechanisms and might seem merely to concern how to cope in daily life, what is being spoken about are free acts that are expressive of passionate human commitment and personal sacrifice in responding to concrete danger, building and rebuilding family alliances and constructing and defending one's nation. Moreover, this wisdom is not a matter of mere tactical adjustments to temporary concerns; it concerns rather the meaning we are able to envision for life and which we desire to achieve through all such adjustments over a period of generations, i.e., what is truly worth striving for and the pattern of social interaction in which this can richly be lived. The result of this extended process of learning and commitment constitutes our awareness of the bases for the decisions of which history is constituted.

This points us beyond the horizontal plane of the various ages of history and directs our attention vertically to its ground and, hence, to the bases of the values which humankind in its varied circumstances seeks to realize.[273] It is here that one searches for the absolute ground of meaning and value of which Iqbal wrote and which we will examine with Paul Tillich as a way of appreciating religion. Without that all is ultimately relative to only an interlocking network of consumption, then of dissatisfaction and finally of anomie and ennui.

The impact of the convergence of cumulative experience and reflection is heightened by its gradual elaboration in ritual and music, and its imaginative configuration in such great epics as the *Iliad* or *Odyssey*. All conspire to constitute a culture which, like a giant

[273] Gadamer, pp. 245-53.

telecommunications dish, shapes, intensifies and extends the range and penetration of our personal sensitivity, free decision and mutual concern.

Tradition, then, is not, as is history, simply everything that ever happened, whether good or bad. It is rather what appears significant for human life: it is what has been seen through time and human experience to be deeply true and necessary for human life. It contains the values to which our forebears first freely gave their passionate commitment in specific historical circumstances and then constantly reviewed, rectified and progressively passed on generation after generation. The content of a tradition, expressed in works of literature and all the many facets of a culture, emerges progressively as something upon which personal character and civil society can be built. It constitutes a rich source from which multiple themes can be drawn, provided it be accepted and embraced, affirmed and cultivated.

Hence, it is not because of personal inertia on our part or arbitrary will on the part of our forbears that our culture provides a model and exemplar. On the contrary, the importance of tradition derives from both the cooperative character of the learning by which wisdom is drawn from experience and the cumulative free acts of commitment and sacrifice which have defined, defended and passed on through time the corporate life of the community.[274]

---

[274] *Ibid.* Gadamer emphasizes knowledge as the basis of tradition in contrast to those who would see it pejoratively as the result of arbitrary will. It is important to add to knowledge the free acts

Ultimately, tradition bridges from the totemic age, through philosophy to civil society today. It bears the divine gifts of life, meaning and love, uncovered in facing the challenges of civil life through the ages. It provides both the way back to their origin in the *arché* as the personal, free and responsible exercise of existence and even of its divine source, and the way forward to their divine goal, the way, that is, to their *Alpha* and their *Omega.*

RELIGION

In one sense we have been speaking in horizons that are increasingly restricted to the human: from objective dimensions which in modern terms come to be restricted to sciences totally constructed by, and at the disposition of, man to human subjectivity which could become reduplicatively self referential in terms of human whims and desires.

Yet another path is also opened by human subjectivity and it is precisely one which leads to the other term of our theme, namely, religion. Mohamed Iqbal points to this in his *Reconstruction of the Sciences of Religion* when he distinguishes between religion and the philosophy of his day when awareness of subjectivity was

---

which, e.g., give birth to a nation and shape the attitudes and values of successive generations. As an example one might cite the continuing impact had by the Magna Carta through the Declaration of Independence upon life in North America, or of the Declaration of the Rights of Man in the national life of so many countries.

only beginning to emerge. He saw philosophy as more objective, abstract and coldly rational, whereas he located religion in the realm of human subjectivity as alive and relational.

> The aspiration of religion soars higher than that of philosophy. Philosophy is an intellectual view of things; and as such, does not care to go beyond a concept which can reduce all the rich variety of experience to a system. It sees reality from a distance as it were. Religion seeks a closer contact with Reality. The one is theory; the other is living experience, association, intimacy. In order to achieve this intimacy thought must rise higher than itself, and find its fulfillment in an attitude of mind which religion describes as prayer – one of the last words on the lips of the Prophet of Islam.[275]

Metaphysics is displaced by psychology, and religious life develops the ambition to come into direct contact with the ultimate reality. It is here that religioin becomes a matter of personal assimilation of life and power; and the individual achieves a free personality, not by releasing himself from the fetters of the law, but by discovering the

---

[275] Iqbal, *Reconstruction of Religions*, ed. M. Saeed Sheikh (Lahore, Pakistan: Iqbal Academy and Institute of Islamic Culture, 1984), p. 143.

ultimate source of the law within the depths of his own consciousness.[276]

This does not remove religion from rationality but enables rationality to expand to the unique and ultimately personal savoring of being and truth of which al-Ghazali speaks in his *Deliverance from Error and Mystical Union with the Almighty*.[277]

For Parmenides it had been a highly rational exercise of abstract reasoning which identified the basis of being as one, eternal and unchanging. For Aristotle at the culmination of his metaphysics this was life divine, contemplation on contemplation itself (*noesis noeseos*), but unable from so exhalted a position to know our world of multiple beings with their tragedies and triumph.

All this is reversed when we review these issues with the new sensibility to subjectivity and in ways that bring us directly to culture. For if, as we have seen, cultures are most radically the values and virtues of a people then we must ask what is the basis of valuing by a people. Using an early form of phenomenology Paul Tillich sees this not only as their external or objective interests but their inner concerns, indeed their ultimate concern in terms of which all has meaning.

---

[276] *Ibid.*, pp. 48-49.

[277] *Deliverence from Error and Mystical Union with the Almighty*, English trans. Muhammad Abulaylah; introduction and notes G.F. McLean (Washington, D.C.: The Council for Research in Values and Philosophy, 2001).

This appears in the thought of Paul Tillich in both the thesis and the antithesis of his dialectic. In the former he speaks of God not only as absolute being but phenomenologically as man's "ultimate concern". This approach notes that we are never indifferent to things, simply recording the situation as does a light or sound meter. Rather, we judge the situation and react according as it reflects or falls away from what it should be. This fact makes manifest essence or logos in its normative sense. It is the way things should be, the norm of their perfection. Our response to essence is the heart of our efforts to protect and promote life; it is in this that we are basically and passionately engaged. Hence, by looking into our heart and identifying basic interests and concerns — our ultimate concern — we discover the most basic reality at this stage of the dialectic.

In these terms, Tillich expresses the positive side of the dialectical relationship of the essences of finite beings to the divine. He shows how these essences can contain, without exhausting, the power of being, for God remains this power. As exclusively positive, these might be said to express only the first elements of creation, that they remain, as it were, in a state of dreaming innocence within the divine life from which they must awaken to actualize and realize themselves.[278] Creation is fulfilled in the self-realization by which limited beings leave the ground of being to "stand upon" it. Whatever be said of the negative or antithetic step about this moment of

---

[278] Paul Tillich, *Systematic Theology I* (Chicago: University of Chicago Press, 1951), 238, 255.

separation, the element of essence is never completely lost, for "if it were lost, mind as well as reality would have been destroyed in the very moment of their coming into existence."[279] It is the retention of this positive element of essence that provides the radical foundation for participation by limited beings in the divine and their capacity for pointing to the infinite power of being and depth of reason. Such participation in the divine being and some awareness thereof is an absolute prerequisite for any religion.

After the tragic stage of the antithesis or the contradiction of the human exercise of freedom, Tillich returns to the ultimate concern as experienced in true ecstasy. There one receives ultimate power by the presence of the ultimate which breaks through the contradictions of existence where and when it will. It is God who determines the circumstances and the degree in which he will be participated. The effect of this work and its sign is love, for, when the contradictions of the state of existence are overcome so that they are no longer the ultimate horizon, reunion and social healing, cooperation and creativity become possible.

Tillich calls the cognitive aspect of ecstasy inspiration. In what concerns the divine, he replaces the word knowledge by awareness. This is not concerned with new objects, which would invade reason with a strange body of knowledge that could not be assimilated, and, hence, would destroy its rational structure. Rather, that which is

---

[279] *Ibid.*, p. 83; Cf. "A Reinterpretation of the Doctrine of Incarnation," *Church Quarterly Review*, CXLVII (1949), 141.

opened to man is a new dimension of being participated in by all while still retaining its transcendence.

It matters little that the contemporary situation of skepticism and meaninglessness has removed all possibility of content for this act. What is important is that we have been grasped by that which answers the ultimate question of our very being, our unconditional and ultimate concern. This indeed, is Tillich's phenomenological description of God. "Only certain is the ultimacy as ultimacy."[280] The ultimate concern provides the place at which the faith by which there is belief (*fides qua creditur*) and the faith that is believed (*fides quae creditur*) are identified.

It is here that the difference between subject and object disappears. The source of our faith is present as both subject and object in a way that is beyond both of them. The absence of this dichotomy is the reason why, as noted, Tillich refuses to speak of knowledge here and uses instead the term 'awareness'. He compares it to the mystic's notion of the knowledge God has of Himself, the truth itself of St. Augustine.[281] It is absolutely certain, but the identity of subject and object means that it is also absolutely personal. Consequently, this experience of the ultimate cannot be directly received from others:[282] Revelation is something which we ourselves must live.

---

[280] *Dynamics of Faith*, Vol. X of *World Perspectives*, ed. Ruth Nanda Anshen (New York: Harper & Brothers, 1957), 17.

[281] *Ibid.*, pp. 8-11.

[282] "The Problem of Theological Method," *Journal of Religion*, XXVII (1947), 22-23.

What does this mean for our issue of a dialogue between religion and culture; for recognizing the vast and rich diversity of cultures and the uniqueness of the divine? Tillich distinguishes the point of immediate awareness from its breadth of content. The point of awareness is expressed in what Tillich refers to as the ontological principle: "Man is immediately aware of something unconditional which is the *prius* of the interaction and separation of both subject and object, both theoretically and practically."[283] He has no doubt about the certainty of this point, although nonsymbolically he can say only that this is being itself. However, in revelation he has experienced not only its reality but its relation to him.[284] He expresses the combination of these in the metaphorical terms of ground and abyss of being, of the power of being, and of ultimate and unconditional concern.

Generally, this point is experienced in a special situation and in a special form; the ultimate concern is made concrete in some one thing. It may, for instance, be the nation, a god or the God of the Bible. This concrete content of our act of belief differs from ultimacy as ultimacy which is not immediately evident. Since it remains within the subject-object dichotomy, its acceptance as ultimate requires an act of courage and venturing faith. The certainty we have about the breadth

---

[283] "The Two Types of Philosophy of Religion," *Union Seminary Quarterly Review*, I (1946), 10.
[284] *Systematic Theology*, I, p. 109.

of concrete content is then only conditional.[285] Should time reveal this content to be finite, our faith will still have been an authentic contact with the unconditional itself, only the concrete expression will have been deficient.[286] (Here it is important to keep in mind Buber's caution with regard to the thought of Max Scheler. Is it enough to change the object; is indeed the act of concern the same if the object is different? Or is a concern that is essentially relational in an I-thou rather than an I-it manner not differentiated in quality by its object?)

Tillich sees two correlated elements in one's act of faith. One is that of certainty concerning one's own being as related to something ultimate and unconditional. The other is that of risk, of surrendering to a concern which is not really ultimate and may be destructive if taken as if it were. The risk arises necessarily in the state of existence where both reason and objects are not only finite, but separated from their ground. This places an element of doubt in faith which is neither of the methodological variety found in the scientist, nor of the transitory type often had by the skeptic. Rather, the doubt of faith is existential, an awareness of the lasting element of insecurity. Nevertheless, this doubt can be accepted and overcome in spite of itself by an act of courage which affirms the reality of God. Faith remains the one state of ultimate concern, but, as such, it subsumes both certainty concerning the unconditional and existential doubt.[287]

---

285 "The Problem of the Theological Method," *loc. cit.*, pp. 22-23.
286 *Dynamics of Faith*, p. 18.
287 *Ibid.*

Can a system with such uncertainty concerning concrete realities still be called a realism? Tillich believes that it can, but only if it is specified as a belief-full or self-transcending realism. In this, the really real — the ground and power of everything real — is grasped in and through a concrete historical situation or culture. Hence, the value of the present moment which has become transparent for its ground is, paradoxically, both all and nothing. In itself it is not infinite and "the more it is seen in the light of the ultimate power, the more it appears as questionable and void of lasting significance."[288] The appearance of self-subsistence gradually melts away. But, by this very fact, the ground and power of the present reality become evident. The concrete situation becomes *theonomous* and the infinite depth and eternal significance of the present is revealed in an *ecstatic* experience.

It would be a mistake, however, to think of this as something other-worldly, strange or uncomfortable. It is *ec-static* in the sense of going beyond the usual surface observations and calculations of our initial impressions and scientific calculations, but what it reveals is the profundity of our unity with colleagues, neighbors and, indeed, with all humankind. Rather, then, than generating a sense of estrangement, its sign is the way in which it enables one to see others as friends and to live comfortably with them. As ethnic and cultural differences emerge, along with the freedom of each people to be themselves, this work of the Spirit which is

---

[288] *The Protestant Era*, p. 18.

characteristic of Tillich's dialectic comes to be seen in its radical importance for social life.

DIALOGUE BETWEEN RELIGION AND CULTURE

We have now come to the point of relationship between religion and culture and precisely in ecstasy or the point of Ghazali and Iqbal which was omitted by James.[289] Religion then is not another realm of human experience alongside others, but rather the source from which we come, the foundation on which we live, and the goal which we seek through all our values and virtues – and hence cultures.

Some would want to distinguish between beliefs which they would see, on the one hand, as many, related to earlier levels of experience and expressed in the various theologies and, on the other hand, faith which is the deeper level of experience, the ultimate concern which is literally inexpressible or unutterable. It is the former which specifies and distinguishes the multiple cultures and the latter as that in which all human life – indeed all reality whatsoever – is grounded.

---

[289] Prof. G. Aavani, Director of the the Iranian Institute of Philosophy has noted that while William James begins his *Characters of Religious Experience* with a quote from al-Ghazali. The translation he had before him omitted the crucial passage in which Ghazali speaks of this in terms of the ultimately personaly experience of lasting or pavoring the divine.

Such a distinction is not without merit in that it takes account of the diversity and multiplicity of cultures and religions. Unfortunately, what we distinguish we too often separate and then proceed to conceive separately from the other. As a result the concrete or specific beliefs of a people lose their depth of meaning and become only cultural artifacts similar to their dances or songs. As seen by the sociologist or anthropologist these religious acts lose their properly religious significance.

Hence, if we can distinguish beliefs from faith we must not separate the two, but understand rather that beliefs are the ways in which faith is lived in time and place. In this relationship it is faith which holds the primacy and gives to beliefs (or culture) their sacred and salvific character.

In this light then the term dogma should be rethought. In the modern rationalist context anything based on a faith that went beyond reason was rejected as beyond the realm of assured truth, and hence as blind, arbitrary and willful. In post modern terms, however, with its implicit critique of rationalism, it is rather the restriction of the intellect to that which is clear and distinct (or universal and necessary) which has come to be seen as willful, blind and arbitrary.

What then is the proper relation between the one faith and the multiple sets of beliefs and the cultures and civilizations they inspire. Properly controlled insight can be garnered from the extensive work done on the system of analogy, which Cornelio Fabro rightly termed the language of participation. This was developed by Plato to express the way in which the many reflected (he used the term "mimesis" or "imaged") the one, and the many good realities which shared in and expressed the absolute idea of the good. Each in itself and each of its beliefs is sacred and salvific.

There is similarity in difference between multiple religions as each properly realizes its religious life in its own way. This is termed an analogy of proper proportionality. That is the existence of A is realized according to the essence of A in a manner not identical or equal, but proportionate to the way the existence of B is realized in a manner proportionate to the essence of B (existence of A: essence of A : : existence of B : essence of B). In this manner the religion of Islam as lived according to (:) the nature of Islam is not identical, but proportionate (::) to the way the Christian religion is lived according to (:) its own nature as Christian. Neither is in any part the same as the other; neither can be replaced by the other. The similarity lies rather in each realizing itself as fully as possible.

Here, however, we are talking not about mere human cultures, but about religions which are first of all the creative and salvific work of God. This requires as well what is technically termed analogy of attribution according as each of the many is denominated precisely in terms of its relation to the One (the way food and scalpel are termed healthy as supporting the health that is found only in the living body). Each is properly religious by an analogy of attribution according as which each explicitly expresses that man is from and toward the one God.

For our purposes I would like to suggest that this means not only that the many cultures religions and beliefs receive a truly sacred character from the faith that inspires them, but that each expresses that faith in the absolute or the absolute itself in a unique and wonderful manner. If this be so then the insight of Nicolas of Cusa takes on new importance for our global times. For in meeting other cultures founded in their religions one encounters not only something holy like my own, but a manifestation of the divine that my own culture, shaped as it has been by its own distinctive beliefs (or experience), has not been able to express. If, however, my goal is to express God as fully as possible then the other religion is not alien and contradictory, but a sister which complements may commitment to God. Hence in their very difference religions need each other, as all tend toward the one absolute and absolutely loving source and goal. This is the deeper significance of the dialogue of religion and culture.